June 06

th
fm

and affection.

Cauf

The Joan Palevsky Imprint in Classical Literature

In honor of beloved Virgil—

"O degli altri poeti onore e lume . . ."

—Dante, *Inferno*

THUCYDIDES' WAR NARRATIVE

Carolyn J.
Dewald · THUCYDIDES'
WAR NARRATIVE

A Structural Study

University of California Press

Berkeley Los Angeles London

University of California Press, one of the most
distinguished university presses in the United States,
enriches lives around the world by advancing
scholarship in the humanities, social sciences, and
natural sciences. Its activities are supported by the
UC Press Foundation and by philanthropic
contributions from individuals and institutions.
For more information, visit www.ucpress.edu.

University of California Press
Berkeley and Los Angeles, California

University of California Press, Ltd.
London, England

Library of Congress Cataloging-in-Publication Data

Dewald, Carolyn.
    Thucydides' war narrative : a structural study /
Carolyn J. Dewald.
        p.   cm.
    Includes bibliographical references and index.
    ISBN 0–520–24127–4 (cloth : alk. paper)
    1. Thucydides. History of the Peloponnesian War.
    2. Greece—History—Peloponnesian War, 431–
404 B.C.—Historiography   I. Title.

DF229.T6D48   2005
938'.05—dc22   2004014199

Manufactured in the United States of America
13   12   11   10   09   08   07   06   05
10   9   8   7   6   5   4   3   2   1

This book is printed on Natures Book, which contains
50% post-consumer waste and meets the minimum
requirements of ANSI/NISO Z39.48–1992 (R 1997)
(Permanence of Paper).

For Bradley Tyler Jones

CONTENTS

TABLES

PREFACE

This book is divided into two parts. Part 1 (chapters 1 through 4) considers the narrative structure of Thucydides' *History of the Peloponnesian War*, ii.1–v.24. This portion of the *History*, commonly called the Archidamian War, tells the story of the first ten years of the twenty-seven-year war. I argue that the structure Thucydides uses to narrate the Archidamian War is paratactic in nature. The term "parataxis," originally used of a military battle line, was adopted by literary critics and linguists to describe some distinctive features of early Greek prose. It is sometimes glossed in English from Aristotle's description in the *Rhetoric* (1409a24) as the "strung-along style." In a work written in the paratactic style, discrete segments of either poetry or prose follow each other in sequence. The image often used for this kind of narrative arrangement is that of beads on a string—the string, or thematic unity of the whole, often remaining tacit or implicit in the way the sequence of segments unrolls.

In my discussion of Thucydides' paratactic organization of the narrative of ii.1–v.24, I call the narrative segments that form its "beads," or building blocks, units of action. To analyze how Thucydides uses these units of action, I use a particular terminology, most of which is explained in chapter 1. In chapter 2 the introductory sentences of the Archidamian units of action are examined in detail. Most of the lists of examples, and the tables quantifying the overall statistics about these introductory sentences, have been relegated to appendix B, which can be read separately as an account of everything one ever wanted to know about the formular first sentences Thucydides uses in his narrative of the first ten years of the war. In other chapters, the tables that support the argument are included in the body of the chapter.

Of the two other appendices, appendix A sets out the units of action themselves (although in vi.8–viii.109 they are called scenes, and represent a much less clear-cut phenomenon). Appendix C consists of a table that compares expressions of time used in the introductory sentences of the earlier years of the war with those used in the years of the Peace (years 11–16), the Sicilian expedition (years 17–19), and the Aegean War (years 20–21).

In the second, shorter part of the book, I discuss the transformation that takes place in Thucydides' prose as the original, journal-entry paratactic style is modified in the direction of increasing narrative integration. Again to use a Greco-Roman rhetorical terminology, what we see is an increasing use of hypotaxis, or a prose that integrates and subordinates many narrative strands into a larger unified and complex whole. In chapter 5, narrating v.25–vi.7 or the years of the Peace, I show that the units of action of the earlier years are still being used, but in very severely modified ways. In chapter 6 I argue that a new, hypotactic style is in evidence in both the narrative of the Sicilian expedition and the narrative of the later war, which I have here called the Aegean War. (Others have described it as the Ionian War, and an important sub-branch of it as the Decelean War.) The discussion of narrative segments is much less technical in these books, because the important point is the one made by Professor Sherlock Holmes, about the dog that didn't bark in the night. Chapter 6 concerns what it means for our reading of Thucydides that the unit of action so in evidence in the early years of the war has now been abandoned.

I have tried to make this study accessible both to Thucydidean scholars and to interested students of early Greek historiography and prose. All of the Greek has been translated into English; Steven Lattimore has generously allowed me to use his very careful, literal translation of Thucydides' *History*. He has also allowed me to modify it slightly when it is required by the Greek word order; the result is almost always an English version less elegant than his own. In the very rare cases of difference in interpretation of the Greek, words I have inserted into his translation have been placed in brackets. The spelling of proper names follows conventional English use (as found, say, in R. Warner's Penguin translation), rather than the more systematically Hellenized version Lattimore adopts.

Many more people should be thanked than can properly be acknowledged here, since this work has been more than a quarter century in its gestation. The underpinnings of its scholarship are owed to Helen North and Martin Ostwald, since this study of Thucydides' narrative style is the outgrowth of work undertaken under their tutelage many years ago on early prose, both as history and as rhetoric. Ronald Stroud oversaw the initial doctoral dissertation; the task of convincing an acute and skeptical epigrapher that what I was seeing in Thucydides was a real, quantifiable phenomenon forced a degree of rigor into the project it would not otherwise have had. Robert and Barbara Rodgers turned the work into a manuscript. Kendrick Pritchett, Raphael Sealey, Jonathan Dewald, Lionel Pearson, Anthony Raubitschek, and Michael Jameson all gave substantial attention to my efforts to find a language for analyzing something as complicated as Thucydides' prose, and Robert Connor first encouraged me, many years ago, to try to publish it.

Over the years, Helene Foley, Donald Lateiner, Florence Mini, Elisabeth Smadja, Deborah Boedeker, Albert Henrichs, Rosaria Munson, Kurt Raaflaub, Seth Schein, and Susan Stevens have listened patiently and responded generously to my efforts to find a language for describing something as potentially impressionistic as narrative style. Colleagues and students at the University of Southern California and Bard College have helped in many ways. Discussions and close reading with Alex Watts-Tobin have sharpened my sense of Thucydides' military interests, and I have profited from his 2000 University of Southern California dissertation, *Generals and Particulars in Thucydides*. I would like to thank Dean Donal Manahan and the Zumberge Scholarship Fund of USC for making possible the transformation of a typed manuscript into computerized form, and I thank Richard Buxton, Nathalie Sado, and especially Philip Purchase for undertaking the bulk of this laborious work. Marjorie Becker, Tom Habinek, Heather James, and Greg Thalmann at USC clarified my thinking about the way prose works in history, as have Nancy Leonard, Bill Mullen, and Jamie Romm at Bard College.

Those friends and scholars who have helped me understand and articulate the more global themes advanced in the introduction of this work are thanked at its end. Greg Crane, Simon Hornblower, John Marincola, Lisa Kallet, Chris Pelling, Tim Rood, Philip Stadter, and Dan Tompkins have more recently provided much-needed encouragement as well as the model of their own historiographic scholarship on Thucydides. Lisa Kallet in particular gave her own time most generously, helping me see what from my earlier formulations would continue to be most useful in the context of our current reading of Thucydides. The year I spent at Vassar College as the Blegen Professor made it possible to write the introduction and to rethink the project as a book with some relevance to the present, and I owe great thanks to the entire Classics Department, and to Rachel Kitzinger and Mary Decker in particular. Alan Shapiro of The Johns Hopkins University and Dr. Vinzenz Brinkmann of the Staatliche Antikensammlungen und Glyptothek of Munich made the jacket illustration possible. Emma Dewald, Kira Grennan, Alex Jones, Christine Kanakis, Jeff Rustin, and especially Marian Rogers were of great help in the final stages of preparation for publication. Lauren Boehm and Averill Leslie helped prepare the index, and Cindy Fulton guided the manuscript through the whole process. I am grateful to them all.

Finally, two debts cannot really be acknowledged adequately. It is a great sadness to me that I cannot put this book into the hands of Judith Ginsburg, the friend and Tacitus scholar most engaged in its initial articulation. And the dedication acknowledges my father, the person who first interested me in history and the Greek historians.

· Introduction

It was no accident that I chose to think about Thucydides in the early 1970s at Berkeley. I had first encountered the *History of the Peloponnesian War* as an undergraduate, studying with Martin Ostwald at Swarthmore College, and I continued to study Thucydides under the direction of Ronald Stroud, Kendrick Pritchett, and Raphael Sealey at the University of California. For many students of the ancient world at that time, Thucydides' voice was crucial in articulating a certain difficult kind of reflection on the nature of communities at war. Thucydides iii.82–83, for instance, has never had a clearer resonance than it did for many of us then. Like a number of university communities, Berkeley was deeply embroiled in the politics of the Vietnam War. Thoughtful citizens of all political persuasions went head to head debating national politics on the local level and often found their discourse both represented and grotesquely misrepresented on the evening news, with enormous consequences for local, state, and national politics. A significant number of the men in my entering graduate class had been drafted into military service before the academic year began, and others left graduate studies throughout the late 1960s and early 1970s.

As a woman I was not going to be drafted, but like many of my peers, male and female, I found it difficult to engage effectively with the often violent ambiguities of the present. I read and reread Thucydides' text with attention, because the precision of Thucydides' authorial voice seemed to promise a clarity and intellectual integrity lacking in contemporary political discourse. Even if in my own context I could not lucidly reflect on the kinds of things he observed about political processes and the shapes they took in the violence of war, I could think about how Thucydides himself used language to organize his thinking into a coherent narrative of events. I read the *History* repeatedly in a variety of venues and for a variety of reasons. I began my dissertation, *Taxis: The Organization of Thucydides' History, Books ii–viii,* in 1972 and finished it in 1975.

All this is by way of observing that the work published here, over a quarter of a century later, originally took shape as a decidedly formalist piece of research. It was written under the influence of Henry Immerwahr's structural study of Herodotean narrative, and, in Thucydidean scholarship, it drew on A. W. Gomme's magisterial commentary, which was in the process of being finished by A. Andrewes and K. J. Dover.[1] Crucial in forming my project's basic assumptions about Thucydides were Jacqueline de Romilly's *Histoire et raison chez Thucydide* (1956), still to my mind one of the best books written on Thucydides, and Hans-Peter Stahl's groundbreaking *Thukydides: Die Stellung des Menschen im geschichtlichen Prozess* (1966).

In some respects this study is dated by the conditions of its inception and remains a product of its original time and place. It lacks, for instance, the theoretical underpinnings of narratology that would have provided a simpler (or at least a more systematic) language for many of my conclusions. On the other hand, some of the recent narratological studies on Thucydides have resonated with my original project's stylometric concerns, and it is my hope that the publication in 2005 of a stylometric study on Thucydides will prove a useful addition to the current scholarly conversation. Although the argument remains substantially the same as it was in 1975, it has been reorganized in the interest of economy and clarity, and the footnotes have been simplified. Thucydides' book i was omitted from the earlier study and has not been a major focus of attention in this version either, although I have added some pages to a new conclusion suggesting possible points of connection. Book i was formed on narrative principles quite different from those used to organize books ii through viii; it was composed as a series of discrete and largely analytical introductory essays that do not have as their primary objective telling the ongoing narrative of the war.[2]

THUCYDIDEAN NARRATIVE STYLE

To introduce this study, which is essentially now more than a quarter century old, I want to begin with the general state of Thucydidean scholarship and some of the larger presuppositions about historiography that prevailed when I started to think about the narrative structures of Thucydides' *History* in the early 1970s, and then go on to consider some of the major changes that have taken place in the last twenty-five or thirty years. Thucydides was already beginning to write his *History* as Herodotus, his older coeval and the coinventor of history as a narrative genre, was bringing his own narrative to a close. A close look at these early texts, and Thucydides' text in particular, suggests some important ways in which issues of style and narrative structure are central to the larger theoretical issue of history's ability meaningfully to represent the past. The "linguistic turn" taken by historiography in the last quarter of a century has developed new ways of looking at historical narrative. Here I want to reflect on how our reading of Thucydides has changed in consequence, and also to explore how issues of narrative structure, put in a more contemporary critical context, suggest some insights into history's distinctive capacities as a narrative genre that were much harder to articulate a generation ago.

To begin with a curious fact about the *History*'s style: the narrative of the first ten years of the war (ii.1–v.24: the Archidamian War) is formed on principles quite different from those shaping the narrative of the years that follow (v.26–viii.109: the years of the Peace, the war in Sicily, the Aegean War). The paratactic organization underlying the year-by-year narrative (of which Thucydides himself was justifiably proud) also controls the individual narrative structures of the Archidamian years far more pervasively than is generally recognized.[3] In fact, the Archidamian narrative is composed as a sequential series of 119 discrete units of action, systematically arranged (as Thucydides himself said) by summers and winters. Each new narrative unit announces its subject, the action undertaken, the place, and (in almost 90 percent of the units) a rough indication of time. The units fall into five different structural types that I call simple picture units, list units, developed picture units, extended narrative units, and complex, *a-b-a* structures. These five patterns allow Thucydides to shape each new piece of narrative idiosyncratically; in each year, a sequence of units of different types provides an orderly, roughly chronological account of the year's activities.[4]

As the *History* continues past 421 into the troubled years of the so-called Peace of Nicias (v.25–vi.7), although the division into years is continued, the internal organization of each year's narrative undergoes substantial transformation. The paratactic structure created by the earlier units of action is not quite abandoned, but the units themselves are used in quite a different way; book v tends to alternate extremely abrupt simple picture units with long extended narrative units that seem structurally flat in comparison with those of the first ten-year narrative stretch.[5] Moreover, the extremely short simple picture units no longer convey material that is apparently less important but nonetheless necessary for continuing the ongoing sequence. They bristle instead with details that we would like to know more about, suggesting an atmosphere fraught with unarticulated political and military complexities. Transitions between units become harder to see. While a time formula introduces twenty-two of the twenty-four short units of the Archidamian narrative, in the years of the Peace, the ratio is seven to twenty-one; the longer units no longer focus individually on a single topic. In general, the isolation of the year, as well as the relatively static and self-contained focus of the individual unit, is superseded in v.25–vi.7 by other considerations. The impression is one of intense activity, related approximately in the order that it occurs, with relatively little attempt to distinguish between events that produce large results and those that eventually come to nothing. Here Thucydides seems to be interested not so much in results as in processes, highlighting the kinds of activity that give the years of the Peace their special, swiftly moving character.[6]

Most interesting of all is the fact that the rest of book vi and books vii–viii, comprising the last five years of the *History*, abandon the previous narrative structure altogether. Neither in the Sicilian books nor in book viii does Thucydides organize his account as a sequence of discrete units of action. The formular first sentence is discarded, and the individual units, or scenes as we should perhaps call them at this point, can no longer be clearly distinguished from each other, since each new focus represents some facet of an ongoing and complex topic: the war in Sicily in books vi and vii, the Aegean and Decelean wars in book viii. Diverse elements are often considered, and make sense, together as complementary aspects of a larger ongoing, multifaceted account.

These changes in structure mean that in books vi through viii the *History* is no longer a paratactic progression of independent units but has become instead a hypotactically organized sequence in which no individual scene stands as separate and self-sufficient. And although book viii is obviously unfinished, in the complexity and sophistication of its narrative structures it resembles the Sicilian narrative, not book v or the Archidamian narrative. It is a truncated, interrupted but single ongoing narrative, focused on the Aegean and the intricate lines of power that thread and rethread themselves across it, linking Athens, Sparta, Syracuse, the Ionians, the Hellespontines, and the Persians Tissaphernes and Pharnabazus into one giant and complicated picture.

Although these results from my analysis of Thucydides' narrative seemed reasonably clear as they emerged, in 1975 they raised as many questions as they answered. The most important question then in my mind had to do with Thucydides' development as a historian: what do we learn about his own underlying understanding of his project, or of his role as an author/researcher, by looking at changes found within the *History*'s narrative structures? One obvious answer in the mid-1970s concerned the venerable "thukydideische Frage," the arguments about the chronology of various putative strata of Thucydides' work.[7] Since the decades after the First World War, when Schwartz, Schadewaldt, Pohlenz, and others took up the issue first articulated by Ullrich in the 1840s, vast amounts of scholarly energy had been spent trying to isolate early and late layers of Thucydidean composition. The assumption was that if these could be definitely ascertained, one could also in consequence trace the changes in Thucydides' own thoughts and his development as a historian through the twenty-seven long years of the Peloponnesian War.

By the 1970s, this project had been virtually abandoned, as it had become clear to almost everyone that it was doomed to circularity; no two scholars could agree on the criteria that would mark a given passage as early or late.[8] It was nonetheless still seductive as a set of issues to which my stylistic data could be applied, because in v.26 Thucydides himself implicitly signals possible changes in his research and writing procedures by stating that his exile had permitted him to talk to combatants on both sides. It was easy to think of the various distinctive changes I had recorded in Thucydides' narrative as suggesting an early completion, if not publication, of a history of the Archidamian War, with a later, quite different narrative structure used for writing the later books.

Even in the mid-1970s, however, it seemed clear to me that to apply my observations about narrative structure in this fashion, as an aspect of the composition question, was also to misinterpret what they meant. Viewed as a purely practical matter, the formally marked, paratactic arrangement of narrative units for the first ten years of the war suggests how easily Thucydides, at any point in the long process of writing, might have returned to any given unit of the earlier text and revised it individually. Some of the units in the early years of the Archidamian narrative could have remained virtually the same throughout the writing process, although other neighboring units were revised, either totally or in part, in the light of much later events.[9]

Even the change at the beginning of the Sicilian narrative from an essentially paratactic to an essentially hypotactic structure does not necessarily reflect a sudden break and change in Thucydides' thought processes or writing habits occurring some time after 415. It could easily have been the result (to advance one hypothesis among many) of his use of something like a journal started at the war's beginning and kept steadily throughout. It is possible that once the Sicilian expedition began to unroll to its disastrous conclusion, Thucydides' narrative version of particular events increasingly took the form of an ongoing single account with a momentum of its own, because by this point Thucydides thought that he had himself come to a much more global understanding of the shape and significance of the course of the war. He was no longer based in Athens, seeing individual Athenian expeditions go out and return, participating in some, collecting reports of others in the Assembly and elsewhere (v.26.5). By the time of the Sicilian expedition, he had followed the war's development long enough, and had applied himself so intensively to the task of understanding and recording it, that perhaps he now saw and could begin to write up his narrative's various threads as intertwined aspects of a single ongoing process. Perhaps he thought the complexities of the multiple interactions among different theaters of war now required new and different narrative techniques of him as a writer—even as he continued at the same time individually to rethink and rewrite some of the earlier, much more discrete narrative units. Whether this particular reconstruction of the transformation of his writing habits seems as plausible to other readers of Thucydides as it does to me, the fundamental point remains, that it is dangerous to argue anything about the date of composition from a particular kind of observed break in style, particularly in a work whose narrative habits include radical discontinuity of structure.[10]

This leads to a central feature of my study that is considerably easier to understand now than it was when I first began to argue it: Thucydides' habit, throughout the different parts of the *History*, of boldly juxtaposing narrative materials of very different sorts. The sudden disjunctures and apparent inconcinnities that result from his initial choice of discontinuous narrative structures repeatedly require us as readers to do much of the work of connecting up the interpretive or even causal links between one stage of the account and the next, both in the early narrative units and among the various parts of a single continuous narrative later on. Sometimes one unit is juxtaposed with another in a way that establishes a patently ironic connection; one thinks immediately of the funeral oration's relation to the plague, or the relation of Melos at the end of book v to Sicily at the beginning of book vi. Within an individual complex unit, Thucydides often inserts a speech inside a narrative of events but requires us as readers to construct connections between what was said, what was decided, and then what happened as a result of the speeches and actions.[11]

Although Thucydides' use of radical disjuncture seemed somewhat puzzling and controversial when I first confronted it in the 1970s, by now it has become part of a mainstream reading of the *History*, and recent trends in critical theory have provided a more precise language for its analysis. Robert Connor's study in 1984, as well as the two volumes of Simon Hornblower's *Commentary* published so far, shows the fruitful use to which reception theory and narratology have been put in Thucydidean studies: both Connor and Hornblower take disjunctive aspects of the text as communicative choices rather than as signs of incompleteness or error. Many other recent studies showing careful attention to the distribution of details in the narrative have also significantly changed how Thucydides is read. In general, close readings that pay attention to disjunctures in the text are often less securely globalizing in their pronouncements than those found in earlier Thucydidean scholarship. What they give us instead is a narrative replete with language full of meanings constituted as much by dissonances and interpretive silences as they are by explicit passages of first-person authorial judgment or clear exercises of authorial opinion. This "postmodern Thucydides" is not authoritatively telling us his conclusions; he is rather using his narrative to develop a dialogue with his readers about the difficulties of comprehension, communication, and intelligent, effective action within a complicated and lengthy war.[12]

To find meaning in Thucydides' history requires careful attention to various elements of style and language, such as repetition, juxtaposition, focalization, and correspondences between speeches and narrative. The Thucydides-in-the-text of contemporary scholarship is acutely aware of his audience. His language leads that audience through the narrated processes of the war. Either, as Connor argues, he makes them participate moment to moment in the doubts, triumphs, and dismayed astonishment of the actors in events, or, in the more narratological terms used recently by Tim Rood, he involves them deeply in the kinds of evaluative thinking and expectations of the participants—expectations that subsequent events often confound or at least complicate.

THUCYDIDES AND THE HISTORICAL ENTERPRISE

These kinds of changes in the literary-critical methods available for analyzing prose have made it easier in one respect to see Thucydides' text as a narrative enterprise of considerable subtlety and complexity. In historiography, however, other changes in the same quarter of a century have also tended to isolate Thucydides' text as an intellectual achievement, not so much under attack as apparently now irrelevant to some of the larger interpretive concerns of contemporary historians and philosophers of history.

In the mid-1970s, Thucydides' place in our collective, western imagination remained substantially intact; he was generally still seen as the first social scientist and in many respects the first real historian, in his drive to establish "wie es eigentlich gewesen ist" for the Peloponnesian War. Thucydides was not the first Greek to be interested in the utility of an accurate grasp of *Realien*. But he was the first we know of to make it foundational for the task of narrating—that is, both telling and assessing the meaning of—events in Greek public, civic life.[13] Early in book i, just after the essay on very early Greek history that we call the Archaeology, chapters 20–22 explicitly emphasize the efforts Thucydides had made in order to obtain as accurate a report as possible of both the *erga*, deeds, that had been done and the *logoi*, (public) speeches, that had been delivered in the war. The passage concludes with several sentences that are worth quoting:

> Finding out the facts (*ta erga tōn prachthentōn*, i.22.1) involved great effort, because eye-witnesses did not report the same specific events in the same way, but according to individual partisanship or ability to remember. And the results, by avoiding [a tendency to storytelling and literary polish], will perhaps seem the less enjoyable for listening. Yet if they are judged useful by any who wish to look at [what is clear] about both past events and those that at some future time, in accordance with human nature, will recur in similar or comparable ways, that will suffice. It is a possession for all time, not a competition piece to be heard for the moment, that has been composed.[14]

> ἐπιπόνως δὲ ηὑρίσκετο, διότι οἱ παρόντες τοῖς ἔργοις ἑκάστοις οὐ ταὐτὰ περὶ τῶν αὐτῶν ἔλεγον, ἀλλ᾽ ὡς ἑκατέρων τις εὐνοίας ἢ μνήμης ἔχοι. καὶ ἐς μὲν ἀκρόασιν ἴσως τὸ μὴ μυθῶδες αὐτῶν ἀτερπέστερον φανεῖται· ὅσοι δὲ βουλήσονται τῶν τε γενομένων τὸ σαφὲς σκοπεῖν καὶ τῶν μελλόντων ποτὲ αὖθις κατὰ τὸ ἀνθρώπινον τοιούτων καὶ παραπλησίων ἔσεσθαι, ὠφέλιμα κρίνειν αὐτὰ ἀρκούντως ἕξει. κτῆμά τε ἐς αἰεὶ μᾶλλον ἢ ἀγώνισμα ἐς τὸ παραχρῆμα ἀκούειν ξύγκειται. (i.22. 3–4)

That is to say, both past events and analogous future ones would become more comprehensible if one studied the exact details of this terrible war, and Thucydides uses i.22 to advance the proposition that reading his nonfiction text would prove worth the effort for those interested in obtaining such comprehension.[15]

Two elements in this Thucydidean cluster of ideas were still generally thought central to the task of writing history in 1975, at least among classical historians: first, that a reasonably accurate narrative representation of a complicated set of real-life events is possible; and second, the closely allied notion that valuable knowledge will result from this process, since human nature exhibits observable regularities that will endure over wide gaps of time and space. It was generally assumed that the accurate narration of a particular set of events in the past would not be of mere antiquarian interest but could also implicitly contain information about how certain kinds of events tend to happen and how people behave when they do. As Thucydides himself seemed to imply, such information about precisely described events in the past, made available to human beings in other times and places, might help those readers better to understand their own times as well as the past. Even the aspects of radical discontinuity and ironic juxtaposition so prevalent in Thucydides' narrative structures were read as part of his allegiance to accuracy as the first professional historian, since they could be read as stemming from Thucydides' habit of saying only what he thought he knew, and carefully distinguishing (hard) fact from (fallible) explanation.[16] The structural idiosyncrasies of individual sections of narrative revealed him struggling in each case to express precisely what was going on, and not bound by the conventions of *to muthōdes*, the aspects of the narrative plot found in poetry or prose performed for an audience that give it an artistic shape and make it appealing (i.22.4).[17] All this seemed to confirm that it was still useful on the whole to describe Thucydides as a "scientific" historian.[18]

The idea of scientific history itself, however, was about to become much more problematic in the historiography of the late 1970s. Both in practice and in its theoretical aims, the scientific model of objective research had certainly shaped the way history had evolved over the course of the last several centuries. History as a modern field of study had been formed under the aegis of the heroic, Promethean science of the seventeenth century, culminating in Newton's *Principia*—not that the struggle to define history according to a scientific model had been an easy one. Over the course of the nineteenth century, victory was achieved in that part of the "Enlightenment project" that respected objective research in the humanities and social sciences as well as in the physical sciences, in large part as a result of the huge gains in prosperity and overall physical welfare in the western world brought about by nineteenth-century science.[19] Whatever the particulars of this development, the implicit scientism of the concept of objective research remained a vigorously articulated and effectively unquestioned ideal for history as a discipline for more than a hundred years.[20]

Already in the 1960s this state of things had started to change. The impeccability of science and the scientific method was called into question by T. Kuhn's *Structure of a Scientific Revolution* (1962). Kuhn was a historian of science who argued that science itself should be understood sociologically, as a group enterprise exhibiting many of the same kinds of dynamics that prevail in the interactions of other kinds of apparently less disciplined interpretive communities.[21] Kuhn's research was only part of a larger and more complicated picture, however, that also included the social activism emerging from American universities in the 1960s and 1970s, and the growing intellectual presence of poststructuralism as a theoretical model. [22] A massive epistemological crisis ensued in the humanities and social sciences, in which the possibility of objectivity in the study of language, culture, or history was increasingly seen as chimerical. The new set of intellectual positions that resulted is often referred to as the interpretive or hermeneutic turn, with a rough division being made between those issues of more relevance to the social sciences (called the cultural turn) and those more germane to language and the interpretive models of the humanities (the linguistic turn).[23] One of the most striking features of the interpretive turn as a whole, however, was that the dividing line that had traditionally separated the study of language and literature from the study of human cultures and social dynamics was itself evaporating. Texts and contexts became highly relevant to both fields, and arenas of sometimes violent contestation in both.

This hermeneutic or interpretive crisis did not so much call into question Thucydides' fierce allegiance to the task of getting it right, as it rather questioned the possibility of anyone "getting it right" at all—that is, calling into question the whole idea of the model of history for which Thucydides had traditionally been a crucial exemplar. In history, the cultural turn had a huge effect, as social scientists within many different disciplines emphasized their newly enhanced awareness of the interconnectedness of all the different parts of a given culture, including the mores and assumptions of its social scientists. What became clear was how idiosyncratically different societies understood and described both themselves and others.[24] Scholars became more sensitized to their own roles in a larger interpretive system and their own cultural preconceptions; the corollary was that if as observers they were themselves part of the system they observed, their own research was hardly objective or value-free. "Ideology" became a term in common critical use, signifying those aspects of a culture's beliefs that, although highly culture-specific, seemed self-evidently true and grounded in reality to members of that culture.[25] Historians, both ancient and modern, were seen to be not only students of culture and ideology but also sophisticated purveyors/reproducers themselves of the ideologies of their own class, gender, and time.

Michel Foucault was probably the most prominent prophet of this new vision, at least for the English-speaking world. Foucault's early work had been published in the 1960s and was becoming widely known in the United States in the late 1970s. Foucault stressed the ways in which all the densely interlocking symbolic systems of a given culture at a given time were part of a larger *epistēmē* that could only be understood on its own terms, from the inside, as it were. Thus although we may think that as scholars we are the heirs of the Enlightenment and the scientism of the seventeenth century, in that world Newton was also a serious alchemist, and our many-times-removed great-grandmothers seriously went out to pick a flower whose seeds looked like eyeballs, in order to heal an eye infection.[26] According to Foucault, we cannot really understand the science or the religious controversies of the early modern and Enlightenment eras, or their politics or poetry, as mirror images of our own practices, any more than we can grasp their medicine or sexual mores, because all of these are embedded in an *epistēmē,* an interlocking network of symbols and symbolic meanings profoundly different from our own. Thus there is no such thing as a discipline of "history" that can be understood as existing independent of the workings of time. As a historian, Thucydides cannot be thought to address us directly as someone having a set of familiar goals and procedures to which we as historians also self-evidently adhere. Whatever discipline shaped his sense of his project, it now seemed to be rooted in a world to which we no longer have real access.[27]

Foucault and other practitioners of the cultural turn recognized that language itself was a potent shaping device of culture and ideology. This idea lay behind the allied phenomenon of the linguistic turn.[28] In general, what was emphasized in the postmodernism and poststructuralism of the 1970s and the 1980s was the denial of functionalism and even rationality as quintessential underlying organizing values for human intellectual activity. In language study, doubts were raised about the autonomy and lucidity of the "subject," or individual thinker, and a corresponding emphasis was placed on the arbitrary constructedness of language. Seriously now called into question was the possibility of using language as a tool either to uncover or to represent an underlying reality.[29]

Because Thucydides was sometimes seen as a historian whose basic credo was expressed in the sentences from i.22 quoted above, for much of this period in the larger intellectual culture of the west he went out of style, appearing (in contradistinction to his almost-peer, Herodotus) a profoundly old-fashioned author. While Herodotus looked full of the play of a metanarrative language in a way that was provocatively sympathetic to many of the stances of contemporary criticism and assumptions mentioned above,[30] to many readers the language and intellectual assumptions of Thucydides seemed stiff and resistant, uncongenial to the Foucauldian *epistēmē* that had begun to dominate much of the humanities and social sciences. His obsessive use of neologisms and dense precision of language in the service of narrative exactitude appeared solipsistic or even dishonest to many students of culture and literature, a power play designed to intimidate us as readers into submission. The narrative authority that Thucydides exerts in his *History* seemed to require from the reader an allegiance to Thucydides' own stated assumption that through his careful language and investigation of facts he could understand and authoritatively explain the Peloponnesian War.[31]

During this period, Thucydides was by no means neglected. Many classical historians and historiographers continued to work as they always had, carefully studying the language of Thucydides' text and the congruence between what he gives as data in the *History* and the data that could be gleaned from elsewhere about the last third of the fifth century B.C.E.[32] The interpretive turn, however, also led many to a study of Thucydides that took issues of language and culture much more fully into account. As Connor notes, the period of the Vietnam War introduced among classical scholars a much heightened appreciation of the degree of engagement and intensity in Thucydides' text; it also brought our awareness back to the emotional impact that his text had been famous for in the ancient world.[33] With the demise of the notion of history as the unproblematic representation of the past, and a greater sense of the mutual constructedness of culture and language, a more subtle and sociologically defined Thucydides was emerging in the scholarly literature.

Important work had already been done by the "new unitarians"—scholars teasing out a more complicated authorial intentionality and more nuanced set of social and political issues than we had seen before in Thucydides' text. Adam Parry and Colin Macleod were influential forerunners here, whose work remains immensely suggestive in its sense of the kinds of themes and arguments that interested Thucydides. Already in the early 1970s Virginia Hunter had presented a portrait of Thucydides as an ideologically committed author, using the argumentative and narrative tools emerging in the First Sophistic tendentiously to shape his account. Ernst Badian's version of Thucydides' willingness to manipulate both language and data was more extreme than Hunter's, but for both Hunter and Badian, Thucydides appeared a most deliberate author, shaping his argument to achieve somewhat dishonest ideological ends of his own. Other scholars also were in the process of reexamining the kinds of meaning implicit in the text of Thucydides, stripped as much as possible of pious preconceptions about the fifth-century gentleman who wrote it in the first place. As Nicole Loraux observed, it was now clear that in order to understand Thucydides at all, we must begin by acknowledging that he is "not a colleague."[34]

Developments in the cultural history of the ancient world also changed our views of Thucydides and his project. As members of the Vernant school and other anthropologically or sociologically oriented scholars have given us a much fuller picture of classical Athens, they have also made it clearer how much of the material of his own culture Thucydides deliberately excluded, in order to tell the story of the

Peloponnesian War in his *History*.[35] Thucydides' narrative focus on the military and political course of this particular twenty-seven-year war omitted much that would have been of considerable interest to us in understanding more deeply the culture of his own *epistēmē* and the war as well: information about religion and religious issues, economics, the politics of cities other than Athens, and even important but largely elided parts of Athenian culture—for instance, the role played by nonciti-zen participants, the role of women or families in the war, and some of the specific irrationalities of Athenian politics to which Aristophanes alludes in his comedies. In the early twenty-first century it is no longer a startling thought that what Thucy-dides gives us is the Peloponnesian War as defined by the ideology of a particular class of aristocratic and wealthy Athenian males—the same class from which Plato would later launch his own more far-reaching indictment and restatement of "the ancient simplicity." [36]

Work on fifth-century Athens as an oral culture and on Thucydides' own aware-ness of writing as a relatively new technology also changed our understanding of what Thucydides thought he was doing in producing his *ktēma es aiei*, or "posses-sion for all time." Lowell Edmunds, Nicole Loraux, and Catherine Darbo-Peschan-ski among others have addressed the fact that Thucydides was the first extant his-torian to set his signature on his project as an author. He self-consciously assumes ownership of its dense and difficult prose and presents himself in the text as the au-thor not just of the narrative but of the war itself, fashioning it both for audiences of his own time and for those of the future interested in the issues it raises.[37] He differs from his predecessor Herodotus in emphasizing that the *logos* is his own cre-ation and the result of his own investigatory efforts and authorial judgment.[38]

These are some of the positive effects of the changed interpretive conditions of the last quarter century on Thucydidean scholarship. When we consider the rele-vance of Thucydides' narrative structures as an aspect of his work as a historian, however, the interpretive turn and in particular the linguistic turn had consequences more complicated than this brief and partial survey indicates. In the 1970s and 1980s, deconstruction per se did not unsettle most ancient historians and historiographers; as Peter Novick observes, many historians felt little need to take seriously writings that carefully argued the pointlessness of careful and objective scholarship.[39] Much more serious in their implications for the writing of history were the varieties of postmodernist narrative theories developed by the philosopher Louis Mink and the historiographer Hayden White, among others.[40]

White's genius lay (and still lies) in journalistic synthesis; for several decades now he has written articles disseminating the results of many new cultural and language-based theories among his fellow historians and historiographers. His own concern from the beginning was presentist and ethical; at base he saw narrative history as a part of rhetoric—as it had been in fact in the ancient world.[41] Although many have accused him of doing so, he did not question the idea of a real past or the idea that the data from the past could be taken into account by the conscientious historian. He did insist that what gave a work of history meaning, making it a coherent and convincing account both to its author and to its readers, was its constructed (literally, fictive) nature as a piece of literature shaped by its historian-author in terms relevant to the concerns of the present. A respect for data or adherence to some disciplinary notion of accuracy did not per se result in a superior capacity truthfully to represent the reality of the past.[42] For White in his magnum opus, *Metahistory*, a work of narrative history was fashioned either as a romance, a tragedy, a comedy, or a satire, using the governing tropes of metaphor, metonymy, synecdoche, or irony. Although other historiographers did not necessarily follow White in his use of Northrop Frye's theories of emplotment through the categories of four governing tropes, like him, many of them also began to view the narrative structures of a history as, precisely, the sign of its literary constructedness—one of the most important elements that deprive it of the possibility of being a serious, accurate representation of past events.[43] As Louis Mink succinctly put it, "So we have a . . . dilemma about the historical narrative: as historical it claims to represent, through its form, part of the real complexity of the past, but as narrative it is a product of imaginative construction, which cannot defend its claim to truth by any accepted procedure of argument or authentication."[44]

Alun Munslow has usefully outlined several different kinds of response made by historians and historiographers to criticism that questions the ability of a narrative structure actually to represent the past.[45] My own position in his schema (shaped, no doubt, by my participation in the *epistēmē* of the last quarter century) is as a chastened reconstructionist, since I still believe that we can learn a great deal both about the mind-set of Thucydides as a historian and about the war he narrates by attending closely to the intersection of form and content in the text that he has given us.[46] In what follows, I want briefly to argue that the structure of a historical narrative— in particular, the structure of Thucydides' narrative—is not, in Mink's terms, by definition a sign of its separation from the truth of the past, but is rather one of the most important vehicles by which the working historian both understands the past and tries to convey something of its particular realities to others. My arguments here have been shaped by those of Mink himself and by A. MacIntyre, A. Norman, D. Carr, N. Carroll, G. Spiegel, C. Roberts, and the joint work of Joyce Appleby,

Lynn Hunt, and Margaret Jacob, but my chief concern in thinking through this issue has remained the text of Thucydides. At the very beginning of the genre of history writing, the narrative structure of Thucydides' text challenges us with its claims to an authority the genre is rarely given in our current *epistēmē*.

Briefly summarized, my argument here will be that Thucydides' *History* is organized to tell its story in a way that allows both the decisions and actions of people in the past and the historian's own understanding of them to emerge, in tandem with one another, as coherent and credible for the reading audience. The narrative constructs the rules, as it were, both articulating how the events under narration happened and performatively showing why we should trust this version as a credible account of them. The narrative is the vehicle through which a complex, three-pronged act of dialogic connection unfolds, linking the historian, the people whose decisions and actions originally came together to create events, and the *History*'s past, present, and future audiences.

Although the argument I make here is about Thucydides' narrative, it can also be made to apply more broadly to the genre of writing he began; in the diachronically organized details of its unrolling narrative structure, a historical narrative sends out claims that distinguish it from other kinds of "fictive" account. The way Thucydides structures his narrative does not prove, as was sometimes earlier thought, that the historian is telling us "how it really was" (wie eigentlich gewesen); the narrative does, however, set up a tacit contract with its readers that gives priority to the representation of the quiddity of past realities. That is, although a historical narrative often leaves us, the readers, to decide on the meaning of the unrolling sequence of events narrated, it claims to be trustworthy in its presentation of the material from the past out of which we are to construct our readerly judgments. In constructing the text, the historian as narrator presents himself as using the same kinds of thinking— thinking I elsewhere call secular, pragmatic, prudential—as do the most competent, intelligent actors within the account.[47] I will argue below that the historical narrative of Thucydides is, to adopt Mikhail Bakhtin's useful term, profoundly dialogic in its effects, since the emphasis it puts on the decisions and actions of the actors within the account also links their rational behavior, as people whose actions are under narration, to the corresponding rationality of the narrating historian. Both the thinking of the historian and the thinking that leads to action by the actors in events are conveyed simultaneously to the reader, through the way the narrative structure is organized.

To explore some of these issues briefly, I am going to start in a roundabout fashion, following the example of many of the historiographers listed above. What makes a narrative about the past make sense, that is, seem believable to us as readers? The most obvious answer is, the same things that make any narrative of human actions in the world look coherent. Human beings make sense of their lives by looking back, thinking about what happened either to them or others, and telling stories that embody their conclusions. The kind of thinking they do—including at least the attribution of causality, the ascription of motive, the weighing of the relative importance of different elements in a situation and their arrangement into a coherent and connected sequence—must by definition be a commonsensical one, if they expect it to interest anyone but themselves. This was well articulated by Aristotle, discussing in the *Rhetoric* what it means to deliver a convincing account of something; he saw that although *to prepon* and *to eikos,* the appropriate and the reasonable/probable, may not be definable by any standard of absolute truth, when applied as a working rule of thumb to narratives about people of our own time and place, we "know it when we see it."[48] Therefore the most crucial task of any speaker (or writer of speeches) who wished to be credible was to fashion a discourse that employed the same kinds of commonsensical thinking its audience habitually used. Without the attributes of *to prepon* and *to eikos,* no discourse, however fact-filled, carries conviction.[49]

For Aristotle's purposes, considering speeches fashioned for the law court or political assembly, credibility was more important than accuracy per se.[50] But in the context of Thucydides' war narrative, the situation is somewhat different, because the goals the text sets out for itself are different. If we leave aside the idea of absolute truth (something in any case unattainable in history),[51] but retain Aristotle's idea of the innate persuasiveness of a *common* sense, it makes sense that the historian arranges his history's narrative structure not only to look plausible to his reading public, but also to demonstrate in practice the efforts that he has made accurately to convey the particularities of what happened to whom, in a given sequence of past events. So the arrangement of the narrative structure itself contains a very particular form of Aristotle's plausibility: by arranging his narrative to reveal how the thoughts and actions of people in the past made sense as they struggled with the contingencies that confronted them, the historian also testifies to his own possession of the same kind of practical attention to reality as that possessed by the most competent actors within the narrative.

Thucydides was the first historian to make this process transparent. He both encodes into his narrative the fact that intelligent observation of the relevant circumstances confronting them is more likely to bring success for the actors who act upon it, and at the same time he comments pointedly on his own authorial efforts to engage a comparable kind of attentiveness to the facts confronting him—these are, in his case, the details out of which he must construct his narrative.[52] Pericles includes in his list of Athenian excellences that "we ourselves either ratify or even propound successful policies, finding harm not in the effect of speeches on action but in failing to get instruction by speech before proceeding to what must be done" (ii.40). Because the Athenians understand both naval warfare and local conditions, they are brilliantly successful when they encounter the fledgling Peloponnesian navy in the Crisaean Gulf early in the war (ii.83–92). Because he does not understand the art of generalship, Cleon loses the most valuable troops Athens has, as well as his own life, in his humiliating defeat at Amphipolis (v.10). In large part because Nicias puts more reliance on soothsayers and whispered rumors from Syracuse than on the data in front of his nose and the judgment of his fellow generals, the Athenian fleet meets defeat in the harbor at Syracuse (vii.49, 50). And because Thucydides himself in these and many other places carefully fashioned his narrative to trace what people both did and said during the Peloponnesian War, the record he gives us of their speech and action is (he claims, in i.22) a serious and useful one for his readers.

This means that a curious correspondence, or even a metanarrative parallelism, informs the way actors in events, Thucydides the historian, and finally we his readers process an awareness of relevant data; the narrative structure of the *History* provides the link that creates and sustains this parallelism. Our attention as readers is correspondingly twofold. We take Thucydides' *History* seriously precisely because it seems responsibly to try to depict the real undertakings of real people, and to show what happened, as a result of their decisions and actions. But we are simultaneously, in the act of reading, also paying attention to how Thucydides the historian engages with his material. The way he chooses events to narrate, arranges them in sequence, and portrays the causal connections among them—all these narrative habits of the author help us form a judgment about his alertness to the complex particulars he narrates, and the degree of our trust in him as a working historian.

So to return to the issues raised by Hayden White and Louis Mink: if a historical narrative is by definition constructed to reveal the historian's ongoing negotiation of how the historical actors in the narrative coped with the plethora of events and facts they faced in making decisions, it follows that the narrative structure of that history is also a highly idiosyncratic affair. It cannot be emplotted globally and tropically; both the historian's own alertness and that of the actors in the account are being negotiated, event by event, as the narrative continues. The historian may be (indeed, is, in this instance) a great prose artist as a writer. The narrative structure, however, is what testifies to an overriding interest as an author in confronting and making clear to readers a real attentiveness to the course of events that (the historian thinks) really happened.

Gabrielle Spiegel acutely observes that the epistemology of historical narrative is at base a question of ethics.[53] Even in our own post-postmodern world, it continues to be the case that by assiduous attention to detail, and the integration of each small detail into the larger ongoing narrative, a historian uses the narrative structure to signal to the reader that this account is to be trusted, because it makes appropriate use of the extant traces of the past human thoughts and actions that undergird its construction. The narrative structure of a history plays a significant role in determining whether or not we, as readers, trust the historian who fashioned it. This is not an original observation—in volumes of instruction for the young historian, an alert, ongoing attentiveness to data is often called the historian's tact, common sense, sense of the actual, empathy, and so on.[54] But its force as an ideal has in the past been compromised by being assimilated into a naïve realism that believes that we can in an unreflective way "just state the facts." The poststructuralists are right to emphasize the intimate connection between ideology and the systematic constructedness of language that forms the foundation of our attempts to make the world make sense; as a number of contemporary historiographers have argued, at least in our current *epistēmē* alertness to *this* fact on the part of the historian makes better, because more trustworthy, history.[55]

But what does the historian's "responsible alertness to the decisions and actions of people from the past" mean in a post-postmodern world, where the extant traces of such decisions and actions are no longer viewed as facts that lie around inertly on the ground, for the historian to pick up and catalogue neatly in the museum of history? Here an extension of Mikhail Bakhtin's ideas on language and social reality seems particularly helpful. Dialogue (also sometimes called dialogism) was a concept central to Bakhtin's notion of prosaics: the study of literary forms that are not poetic in origin but rather based more closely on the speech patterns of ordinary communicative discourse between human beings—what we, like Molière's M. Jourdain, practice every day without knowing it.[56] Bakhtin formulated the idea of dialogue and the dialogic to undercut what he saw as the Russian formalist tendency to an "aesthetic totalitarianism." He felt that in aesthetics, the standard structuralist distinction between *parole* and *langue* profoundly misrepresented the realities of language, since it often turned *parole*, the actual act of communication between two or more particular people, into an evanescent, temporary manifestation of the underlying structural reality of *langue*.[57] Gary Morson and Caryl Emerson use an analogy that efficiently captures the quality of Bakhtin's objections to the primacy of abstract and analytic patterns: it would be as though someone analyzing clothing insisted that the only way to understand it was to investigate the composition of cloth—the chemical arrangement of the thread, the dyes, the process of weaving— omitting altogether the intensely social, communicative intent, that "clothes are designed to be worn," and that they are worn by individual people, for specific reasons and on specific occasions.[58]

Bakhtin thought that linguistic structures were of course important, but that they take shape and have their reality in specific and idiosyncratic acts of communication. In making language (and, by extension, poetics) a matter of abstract rules, the scholarly observer misses the whole point and energy of the process. Language lives, and it takes its meaning from the fact that it emerges anew each time it is used, as an act of communication linking two or more people. It is meaningful not as an abstract grid but as a living reality, part of the present in which it arises. This is why for Bakhtin it is always not "language," but "languages," since each person's working vocabulary reflects a wide diversity of different beliefs, experiences, implicit values; for this set of ideas, Bakhtin uses the Russian term *raznogolosie,* translated into English as "heteroglossia."[59] A work of narrative art that attempts to represent the reality of the social fabric—that is, the efforts that people make trying to bridge the gaps between their multiple private languages—must take the encoding of this sense of multiple discourses in dialogue into its overarching and ongoing whole as one of its primary tasks. Bakhtin himself usually calls this process dialogic polyphony (*dialogicheskaia polifoniia/dialogicheskoe mnogogolosie*).[60]

It has always puzzled me that Bakhtin, a classicist by training, apparently did not extend his theories about the way multiple voices interact in a text to the narratives of the first historians, Herodotus and Thucydides, and their representations of the thoughts and actions of the individuals in their historical narratives, but instead wrote about Dostoevsky as an almost-sociologist, and his precursors among the ancient authors—Homer, the dramatists, and the Greek and Roman novelists. Recently, however, a colleague who knew Bakhtin well and worked with him in the 1970s supplied an answer that should have been obvious: Bakhtin could not write on history or historians, since he lived in a society in which the only history was by definition Marxist. Writing on historiography in mid-twentieth-century Russia was dangerous to begin with, and certainly not permissible in terms of the radical and idiosyncratic communicative freedom and ethical responsibility that dialogic polyphony as a theory entailed.[61]

Although Bakhtin himself did not do so, we can use his theory of dialogic polyphony to help us think through the implications of how the ongoing narrative structure of Thucydides' *History* sets up a three-pronged connection among the actors in events, the historian narrating their decisions and actions, and the understanding of the history's later readership, as I have sketched it out above. If we use Bakhtin's language, we can say that, as a historian, Thucydides uses the narrative structure to convey what he saw as the meaningful interactions of the community of actors inside the narrative with one another. Writing as a historian rather than a novelist, he orders the narrative so as to disclose to the reader the specifics of each particular causal chain of events from the past he is trying to represent, and also to make comprehensible the complexities that went into shaping the decisions and actions of the human beings involved. The same narrative simultaneously communicates to the reader the quality of his own authorial intelligence, since the structure itself has been built out of hundreds of authorial decisions about what to narrate and how to narrate it. The process of narration *performs* the judgment of the historian, as it mediates between the reported consciousness of the actors in events and the judgment of the historian's own community of readers, present and future; thus it represents the historian's own working sense of dialogic polyphony in action.

In this way the narrative structure of Thucydides' *History* is fashioned out of Thucydides' determination to convey to us, his readers, that what is narrated is not one story, or a story told from one standpoint, but an account that seriously tries to take account of the multiple consciousness of many different actors who in real time reacted to each other, with many different aims and opinions and ways of proceeding.[62] Thus his own dialogic depiction of reality is doubly performative: it depicts a multiply voiced consciousness, a composite formed by, but not limited to, the sum of the voices of all of the actors within it. Not limited, because the historian's own observant, critical voice is also at work within the narrative, negotiating the different viewpoints at play in the narrative and also the interests of the community that constitutes the audiences for whom that narrative must make sense. It is the author/ historian's overarching narrative that brings all these concerns together in a single context.

This description of how a postmodern theoretical context now informs my own reading of Thucydides suggests the limitations but also some of the healthier instincts of my earlier readings of this text. I did not read Thucydides in the late 1960s and early 1970s with such concentration simply because I found the Peloponnesian War fascinating. Rather, Thucydides the narrator and historian was a model suggesting what a certain kind of engagement in historical understanding might mean. The narrative structures out of which Thucydides built his *History of the Peloponnesian War* speak to his own overriding, ferocious determination to keep looking at the complex particulars of how real people dealt with the circumstances of their lives—and to continue doing so even when what he saw was almost intolerable. He did not try to simplify or overinterpret what he saw; his narrator's voice is the one that weaves together and mediates the many other points of view that have gone into creating the polyphonic text. Moreover, his construction of a polyphonic, dialogic narrative allowed him to use even inconcinnities and disjunctures to reveal something of the complexities of thought, word, and deed demonstrated by the multiple characters within the *History* in interaction with one another. Thus he can depict a Nicias who speaks wisely but is one of the most grotesque failures in action of the whole war—and expressly admire him (vii.86.5); he can depict a fear-driven Phrynichus, personally obsessed with his hatred of Alcibiades—and give him one of the most detached and intelligent pieces of judgment in the whole *History* (viii.48.4–7). Thucydides admires and celebrates imperial Athens—and also clear-sightedly narrates the stupidities and misjudgments that would eventually defeat it. In terms of structure, he can change his most basic narrative habit and abandon his earlier use of narrative parataxis when it is no longer adequate to the task of registering the interconnecting complexity of developing events late in the Peloponnesian War. As he weaves together as accurately as he can the multiple voices and interpretive threads that make up the twenty-seven-year war, his own authorial voice continues attentively to negotiate the many other human voices we encounter in the *History*.

> One does not have to argue the reality
> of history; necessity does that for us.
>
> Fredric Jameson[63]

Postmodernism has shown us the constructedness and ideological power of narrative. We no longer believe that a historical narrative attains the Truth of the Past (something we would not recognize even if it were somehow given us). And yet one of the most important markers of Thucydides' narrative as a history rather than a novel or a piece of propaganda is the tangible effort the narrative structure makes to trace the dialogic linkages connecting real human decisions and actions in the past to the understanding of audiences in the present and future, using in the process all the available contemporary intellectual tools at the historian's narrative disposal. What I take away from Thucydides' *History* as a reason to trust its ability to account meaningfully for the events it narrates is finally this: Thucydides has fashioned a narrative structure that embodies his efforts to come to terms with the ineluctable "reality of history" to which Fredric Jameson alludes. It makes us trust that he is trying to tell a true but complicated story, in its responsible dialogism, in its ethical adherence to the principle of *akribeia*, exactitude, and in the way that the structure of the narrative embodies the complexities of this adherence.[64]

PART ONE

CHAPTER ONE

An Overview of the
Archidamian Narrative
Structure (ii.1–v.24)

Thucydides structures the first book of his *History* to provide a relatively complicated overview of long-term and short-term causes for the Second Peloponnesian
War, the war that he himself lived through and that engulfed the whole Greek world
between 431 and 404 B.C.E. The narrative of the war proper starts at the beginning
of what we call book ii, where Thucydides also sets out the basic narrative strategy
he intends to follow:

> And now, from this point, begins the war between the Athenians and the
> Peloponnesians and the allies on both sides, during which they no longer
> communicated with one another without heralds and, once they started,
> fought continuously. This has been written in the order that events occurred,
> divided into summers and winters.

> ἄρχεται δὲ ὁ πόλεμος ἐνθένδε ἤδη Ἀθηναίων καὶ Πελοποννησίων καὶ
> τῶν ἑκατέροις ξυμμάχων, ἐν ᾧ οὔτε ἐπεμείγνυντο ἔτι ἀκηρυκτεὶ παρ᾿
> ἀλλήλους καταστάντες τε ξυνεχῶς ἐπολέμουν· γέγραπται δὲ ἑξῆς ὡς
> ἕκαστα ἐγίγνετο κατὰ θέρος καὶ χειμῶνα. (ii.1)

The first ten years of the war, books ii–v.24, are often given a name of their own:
the Archidamian War, after the Spartan king who led the first invasion of Attica in
431. Thucydides' account of the Archidamian War is quite distinctive in the systematic way that the text is organized to carry out the claim of ii.1. If we look closely

at its narrative construction, we see that in ii.1–v.24 Thucydides has written a series of independent, discrete short narratives that follow one upon another "in the order that events occurred, divided into summers and winters" (ἐξῆς ὡς ἕκαστα ἐγίγνετο κατὰ θέρος καὶ χειμῶνα, ii.1). Thucydides marks the structural integrity and topical distinctiveness of the individual narrative units by beginning each new unit with a formular introductory sentence that includes the following items: a new personal subject, an active verb, an indication of place, and a marker of time.[1]

This chapter will give a general overview of how the units of action that comprise the narrative of ii.1–v.24 work, sketching both the nature and importance of their distinctive introductory sentences and also the structural patterns of the units themselves. Chapter 2 will consider the formular nature of the introductory sentences in more detail, chapter 3 will consider more closely how the narrative material inside the units is organized, and chapter 4 will consider how the Archidamian units are organized into larger thematic patterns that help us understand significant aspects of the war as a process. The basic assumption pervading this study is that form and function are interrelated. By examining the formal construction of the narrative attentively, we can see some of what Thucydides wanted his narration of the first ten years of the war to communicate. To begin with a brief overview of how the units work in sequence, separate but resonating with each other, this chapter will look briefly at the organization of the first year of the war, and then at the very schematic narrative of year six.

The narration of the first event of the war proper, the invasion of Plataea by the Thebans in the summer of 431 B.C.E., has an especially elaborate introductory sentence. It starts with an extensive identification of time, listing the number of years that have elapsed in the thirty-year truce between Athenians and Peloponnesians, the length of time during which Chrysis had been priestess of Hera at Argos, the relevant ephorate at Sparta, and the eponymous archonship at Athens, as well as the phrase that Thucydides will use thereafter regularly, "at the beginning of spring" (ἦρι ἀρχομένῳ). Then come the subject of the sentence ("just over three hundred Thebans," Θηβαίων ἄνδρες ὀλίγῳ πλείους τριακοσίων), an active verb ("entered," ἐσῆλθον), and finally the place ("into Plataea," ἐς Πλάταιαν). With this sentence Thucydides serves notice that the Peloponnesian War has formally begun.

The Plataean narrative that begins year one takes up about five Oxford pages, and it is followed by a number of diverse narratives concerning other activities at other places: preparations on both the Lacedaemonian and the Athenian sides for war; the lining up of allies; an Athenian naval expedition to the Peloponnese; another to Locris and Euboea; the expulsion of the Aeginetans; an eclipse; proceedings in Thrace; more movements of the Athenian fleet; Athenian and Corinthian involvement in Acarnania; and finally, a public funeral at Athens.[2] There are seventeen discrete segments of narrative in all, each narrated as a separate entry in Thucydides' account of the first year's summer or winter, and each marked with its own distinctively introductory first sentence.

As the narrative continues, the succession of small and discrete narrative units of action begins to suggest larger ongoing thematic patterns, as various people, places, or topics appear and reappear, forming discontinuous sequences over several years' worth of narrative, and also appearing in new combinations of contiguity with one another. For instance, in the rest of the narrative of year one, after the completion of the first highly dramatic narrative of the nighttime takeover of an unsuspecting city at peace, Thucydides drops the topic of Plataea and introduces a series of other events that happened that same summer, carefully introducing each new account that narrates some new aspect of the summer's activities. A formular sentence firmly sets out each new unit's actors, the activity undertaken, an indication of time, and an indication of place. After the Theban attack in year one, the fate of Plataea fades as a principal focus; it recurs, however, in the accounts of years three, four, and five. The final narrative of the Plataea story occurs in year five. It begins: "And around the same time in this summer, the Plataeans . . . came to terms with the Peloponnesians in the following way" (ὑπὸ δὲ τοὺς αὐτοὺς χρόνους τοῦ θέρους τούτου καὶ οἱ Πλαταιῆς . . . ξυνέβησαν τοῖς Πελοποννησίοις τοιῷδε τρόπῳ, iii.52). The narrative unit ends bleakly and quite formally: "This was how matters ended for Plataea, in the ninety-third year after it became the ally of Athens" (καὶ τὰ μὲν κατὰ Πλάταιαν ἔτει τρίτῳ καὶ ἐνενηκοστῷ ἐπειδὴ Ἀθηναίων ξύμμαχοι ἐγένοντο οὕτως ἐτελεύτησεν, iii.68).

As we shall see at greater length in chapter 2, the regularity of the introductory sentences that mark one unit off from another throughout the Archidamian narrative is very striking; they distinctively define each new change of subject. The account of year six, iii.89–116, demonstrates the general format particularly clearly. It is not one of the more exciting in the Archidamian narrative; in fact, arguably it forms a prosaic breather, sandwiched in between the very dramatic accounts of Mytilene, Plataea, and Corcyra in year five and Pylos and Corcyra in year seven. But its organization is quite schematic and shows the underlying narrative principles that organize the whole of books ii–v.24. Thirteen narrative units occur in sequence, each set off at its start from the preceding narrative by a complete change of subject matter and by a distinctive introductory sentence of the sort just described. The first sentence of each unit is listed below, in order of occurrence in the text.

iii.89.1: In the following summer, the Peloponnesians and their allies went as far as the isthmus intending to invade Attica . . . [topic of unit: aborted invasion because of earthquakes]

τοῦ δ' ἐπιγιγνομένου θέρους Πελοποννήσιοι καὶ οἱ ξύμμαχοι μέχρι μὲν τοῦ Ἰσθμοῦ ἦλθον ὡς ἐς τὴν Ἀττικὴν ἐσβαλοῦντες . . .

iii.89.2–5: During this period when earthquakes were prevalent, the sea at Orobiae on Euboea retreated from what was then the coastline, and forming a wave it returned over much of the city . . . [topic of unit: inundations]

καὶ περὶ τούτους τοὺς χρόνους, τῶν σεισμῶν κατεχόντων, τῆς Εὐβοίας ἐν Ὀροβίαις ἡ θάλασσα ἐπανελθοῦσα ἀπὸ τῆς τότε οὔσης γῆς καὶ κυματωθεῖσα ἐπῆλθε τῆς πόλεως μέρος τι . . .

iii.90: During the same summer there was various fighting in Sicily, according to individual situations, both by the Siceliots themselves . . . and by the Athenians along with their allies . . . [topic of unit: Athenian exploits in Sicily]

τοῦ δ' αὐτοῦ θέρους ἐπολέμουν μὲν καὶ ἄλλοι, ὡς ἑκάστοις ξυνέβαινεν, . . . καὶ αὐτοὶ οἱ Σικελιῶται . . . καὶ οἱ Ἀθηναῖοι ξὺν ξυμμάχοις . . .

iii.91: In the same summer, the Athenians sent thirty ships around the Peloponnese under the command of Demosthenes . . . and Procles . . . and sixty ships . . . against Melos. . . . Nicias . . . was their commander . . . [topic of unit: various exploits of Athenian fleet]

τοῦ δ' αὐτοῦ θέρους οἱ Ἀθηναῖοι τριάκοντα μὲν ναῦς ἔστειλαν περὶ Πελοπόννησον, ὧν ἐστρατήγει Δημοσθένης . . . καὶ Προκλῆς . . . ἑξήκοντα δὲ ἐς Μῆλον. . . . ἐστρατήγει δὲ αὐτῶν Νικίας . . .

iii.92–93: Around the same time, the Lacedaemonians founded Heraclea . . . [topic of unit: motive for founding and initial stages]

ὑπὸ δὲ τὸν χρόνον τοῦτον Λακεδαιμόνιοι Ἡράκλειαν . . . καθίσταντο . . .

iii.94–98: In this same summer, around the time the Athenians were occupied at Melos, the Athenians . . . ambushed and killed some guards at Ellomenus in

Leucadian territory and then moved against Leucas with a bigger expedition
. . . [topic of unit: Demosthenes in Aetolia]

τοῦ δ' αὐτοῦ θέρους, καὶ περὶ τὸν αὐτὸν χρόνον ὃν ἐν τῇ Μήλῳ οἱ Ἀθηναῖοι
κατείχοντο . . . ἐν Ἑλλομενῷ τῆς Λευκαδίας φρουρούς τινας λοχήσαντες
διέφθειραν, ἔπειτα ὕστερον ἐπὶ Λευκάδα μείζονι στόλῳ ἦλθον . . .

iii.99: Around the same time, the Athenians off Sicily sailed to Locris and . . .
defeated the Locrians . . . [topic of unit: Athenians in Sicily again]

κατὰ δὲ τοὺς αὐτοὺς χρόνους καὶ οἱ περὶ Σικελίαν Ἀθηναῖοι πλεύσαντες
ἐς τὴν Λοκρίδα . . . Λοκρῶν ἐκράτησαν . . .

iii.100–102: During this same summer, the Aetolians . . . won support for their
request to send an expedition against Naupactus . . . [topic of unit: response to
Athenian aggression in Aetolia]

τοῦ δ' αὐτοῦ θέρους Αἰτωλοὶ . . . πείθουσιν ὥστε σφίσι πέμψαι στρατιὰν
ἐπὶ Ναύπακτον . . .

iii.103: In the following winter, the Athenians in Sicily, along with their
Hellenic allies . . . came up to Inessa . . . [and] made an attack . . . [topic
of unit: Athenians in Sicily again]

οἱ δ' ἐν τῇ Σικελίᾳ Ἀθηναῖοι τοῦ ἐπιγιγνομένου χειμῶνος ἐπελθόντες
μετὰ τῶν Ἑλλήνων ξυμμάχων . . . ἐπ' Ἴνησσαν . . . προσέβαλον . . .

iii.104: In the same winter, the Athenians purified Delos . . . [topic of unit:
background, procedures of purification]

τοῦ δ' αὐτοῦ χειμῶνος καὶ Δῆλον ἐκάθηραν Ἀθηναῖοι . . .

iii.105–114: In the same winter, the Ambraciots . . . took the field against
Amphilochian Argos . . . [topic of unit: Demosthenes in Ambracia again]

τοῦ δ' αὐτοῦ χειμῶνος Ἀμπρακιῶται . . . ἐκστρατεύονται ἐπὶ Ἄργος τὸ
Ἀμφιλοχικὸν . . .

iii.115: In the same winter the Athenians in Sicily made a landing . . . in the
territory of Himera . . . [topic of unit: Athenians in Sicily again]

οἱ δ' ἐν τῇ Σικελίᾳ Ἀθηναῖοι τοῦ αὐτοῦ χειμῶνος ἐς . . . τὴν Ἱμεραίαν
ἀπόβασιν ἐποιήσαντο . . .

iii.116: At the very beginning of this spring, the fire streamed out of Aetna . . .
[topic of unit: eruption of Aetna]

ἐρρύη δὲ περὶ αὐτὸ τὸ ἔαρ τοῦτο ὁ ῥύαξ τοῦ πυρὸς ἐκ τῆς Αἴτνης . . .

The year ends in that same paragraph (iii.116), with a formulation that Thucydides often uses to conclude the account of a year: "These were the events of this winter, and the sixth year ended of this war that Thucydides recorded" (ταῦτα μὲν κατὰ τὸν χειμῶνα τοῦτον ἐγένετο, καὶ ἕκτον ἔτος τῷ πολέμῳ ἐτελεύτα τῷδε ὃν Θουκυδίδης ξυνέγραψεν).

The scene of action in year six ranges from Sicily to Melos and Delos, Heraclea, and Acarnania. The geographical spread of the units is equaled by the variety of the subjects treated and the various ways in which they are presented. In thirteen units of action there occur two accounts of natural events, an antiquarian excursus, a succinct overview of the foundation of a city, four extended descriptions of campaigns in which Demosthenes takes part, four balder accounts of campaigns in Sicily and the Aegean, and two statements, a sentence each in length, about the Peloponnesian march on Attica and the Athenian campaign in Sicily.

For all its variety of subject matter, year six is not chaotic in arrangement. The units narrating Demosthenes' campaigns take up twelve of the seventeen Oxford pages devoted to year six. He is mentioned at the beginning of the unit about Melos in iii.91, is followed to Leucas in 94, reappears in 102, and his winter activities are brought triumphantly to a conclusion in 105–114. Sicily is another recurring focus in year six. It is introduced in iii.90, briefly referred to in 99, introduces the narrative of the winter of the year in 103, and provides the last military event of the year in 115. Aetna's eruption, the topic of the last unit of all, is also of course Sicilian in setting, but the thematic link is perhaps stronger with the other natural events of the year, the inundations in iii.89.2–5, and the earthquakes that cause the Peloponnesians to turn back at the Isthmus in iii.89.1, the first unit of the year.

Natural phenomena certainly hold an abiding interest for Thucydides, and he tends (as in ii.102–103, iii.87, iii.88, or iv.52) to place units of such material at either the beginning or the end of a season. In year six, a special attempt seems to have been made both to introduce and to end the year with natural events. As Gomme notes ad loc., the earthquakes of iii.89 form part of the seismic disturbances mentioned for the previous winter (iii.87);[3] they could easily have been included there, just as the account of Heraclea in iii.92–93 anticipates events of later years to round out the narrative of the foundation. However, in the text as actually written, the earthquakes that caused the Peloponnesian army to turn back at the beginning of spring are narrated separately from those of the earlier winter, perhaps because Thucydides wished in year six to continue the pattern established in years two, four, and five (and alluded to at the beginning of year three), by beginning or ending a season with such material, or because he wished natural phenomena to form a frame for year six, providing a distinctive beginning and conclusion for the year. The arrangement he chose performs both functions.

Even those events of year six that are introduced abruptly and apparently without context are given sufficient attention in other years to assure that their appearance in year six is not isolated and mysterious. For instance, the antiquarian material in iii.104 is new to the reader, and different in tone from the other units in the year, but it is not completely surprising. Thucydides' interest in such material is already familiar, from the Archaeology in i.2–19, and from ii.29, ii.68, and ii.102. In the rather abrupt narratives in year six concerning events in Sicily and Melos, on the other hand, topics emerge that later become important for the *History* as a whole. Without drawing particular attention to themselves, they allow the reader (especially, perhaps, the rereader) a glimpse into the initial thematic threads of what will later become grippingly significant events. It is important to see that much of this is Thucydides' choice, as narrator: Sicily would in any historian's hand presumably be important and might be mentioned early, but the appearance of Melos in the narrative of year six points toward the distinctively Thucydidean treatment of that small island at the end of book v.[4]

A brief look at the narrative units of action that comprise year six shows something of the kind of units that Thucydides uses throughout his narrative of the first ten years of the war. The thirteen units of year six fall into five separate patterns, as described below; following the description of each pattern is the name I will use for this kind of unit in the more extended consideration of the different unit types in chapter 3.

1. Three units (iii.89.1, iii.99, and iii.116) each focus on a single event: the abortive Peloponnesian invasion of Attica, the Athenian fleet sailing to Locris, and the eruption of Aetna respectively, in what amounts to a bald declarative statement seven lines long or less. Thucydides is in effect making an entry in a journal of events or diary (= *simple picture unit*).[5]

2. Two units extend the description of a single event, to focus more extensively on at least one aspect of it. The unit iii.89.2–5 surveys at some length the reach of the floods, and iii.92–93 considers the focal event, the founding of Heraclea,

from several angles: the Spartan reasons for founding it, but also the fears of the Athenians and the neighbors of the Heracleans. Jacqueline de Romilly calls this kind of description characteristic Thucydidean behavior: an event is "rotated on its axis," so that the point of view splits, to provide the maximum number of angles from which to view what is happening (= *developed picture unit*).[6]

3. A third structural pattern is formed by iii.90, iii.91, iii.103, and iii.115. The narrative does not focus on a single event; instead, one set of actors is followed from one activity to another, so that the sequence of activities undertaken forms a listlike series. This structural pattern is almost always used in its simple form to describe a military campaign: iii.91, for instance, concerns an expedition under the command of Nicias that leaves Athens, goes various places briefly and sequentially described, and returns home (= *list unit*).

4. The three accounts of Demosthenes' exploits in year six, iii.94–98, iii.100–102, and iii.105–114, provide a more complicated narrative that contains both some of the features of the simpler account with a single focus and some resembling those found in the listlike narrative of an expedition. In these units, the scene shifts from place to place and therefore resembles the description of military expeditions like those of iii.91. But one set of actors is not always followed; instead, the linear motion of the list is added to the shifts among various actors that we also see in more complicated single-focus picture units like iii.92–93. All three units of this fourth structural type include shifts in focus from Demosthenes to his enemies and back again. They are complicated as well by a substantial increase in narrative detail—terrain, motives of all the actors, and even mythology (iii.96.1) (= *extended narrative unit*).

5. The final kind of narrative organization found in the units of year six is the most intricately constructed; one example occurs in year six, iii.104. Here, the structure of the unit consists of a framing topic that begins and ends the narrative, with a different kind of narrative contained in the middle. In iii.104, an excursus containing antiquarian material about Delos, including parts of the Homeric Hymn to Apollo, forms the center of the unit, but the unit as a whole both begins and ends with a focus on the event that happened in year six. It begins: "In the same winter, the Athenians purified Delos, certainly in accordance with an oracle of some sort" (τοῦ δ᾽αὐτοῦ χειμῶνος καὶ Δῆλον ἐκάθηραν Ἀθηναῖοι κατὰ χρησμὸν δή τινα, iii.104.1); it ends: "but the [earlier] arrangements for games and most of the festival were discontinued because of misfortunes, as is natural, up to this time when the Athenians established contests and equestrian races, something not held previously"

(τὰ δὲ περὶ τοὺς ἀγῶνας καὶ τὰ πλεῖστα κατελύθη ὑπὸ ξυμφορῶν, ὡς εἰκός, πρὶν δὴ οἱ Ἀθηναῖοι τότε τὸν ἀγῶνα ἐποίησαν καὶ ἱπποδρομίας, ὃ πρότερον οὐκ ἦν, iii.104.6). Thus iii.104 makes an *a-b-a* arrangement, with the Athenian establishment of a new festival in year six occupying the beginning and end of the unit, and description of earlier events, less directly related to the war, in the center (= *complex unit*).

These are the five kinds of building blocks out of which Thucydides constructs the whole Archidamian narrative. There is no particular mystery to them as patterns; they represent several reasonable ways of treating the narrative of a discrete event: as a simple and static picture; as a more extended but still unitary description; as a list focusing on the sequential movements of a single actor or group of actors; as a shifting focus from one set of actors to another that also contains a change of setting; and, finally, as an arrangement resembling any one of the above four, but with the addition of an excursus containing material of quite a different sort set in its middle.

The introductory sentences are crucial in allowing a sequence of such distinctively constructed units to arrange themselves into a coherent ongoing narrative. They provide for the reader a reassuring impression of narrative order, because of their formal repetitiveness. That is, despite the wide (and potentially confusing) variety of unit topics and elaborations of narrative structures found in the longer Archidamian units, as each new introductory sentence begins a new unit, its relatively formular nature helps us adjust to the fact that another discrete piece is being added to the ongoing construction of the Archidamian narrative as a whole. Initially each new unit demands to be understood on its own terms as a discrete entry; only in retrospect does it begin to take its place as part of the larger ongoing narrative. Moreover, in the intensity of their idiosyncratic particularity and variety as narrative structures, the individual units present themselves as the work of an author also struggling to understand the precise nature of immediate events rather than prematurely forcing them into a larger interpretive pattern. As readers of the *History* as a whole, we know how the Peloponnesian War will end and the kinds of error in judgment that will lead to Athens's defeat. Already in the relatively neutral year six the significant topics of Melos and Sicily emerge, as well as intimations of Athenian claims to the leadership of Ionia, in the antiquarian excursus on Delos—themes that books v through viii will explore more fully and bleakly. But in year six Thucydides does not try to anticipate later events or point a moral in the initial narratives of these long-term themes. He rather narrates the precise nature of events unfolding in this particular year, in all their quiddity.

So the units of action provide the building blocks of Thucydides' Archidamian narrative—the individual panels, as it were, in an ongoing frieze of considerable variety—and they also point toward the overall structural complexity of the narrative as a whole. Thucydides' ability to see patterns and combinations of patterns in events allows him to use a variety of units, themselves shaped quite differently from one another, to form larger narrative clusters that also resonate with one another in a number of different ways. As the narrative of the war continues, change will occur both in the way the units of action themselves are constructed and in the kinds of combinations they make with other units. This process begins in the last years of the Archidamian narrative, intensifies in the rest of book v, and undergoes a radical transformation in books vi through viii, as Thucydides moves away from the Archidamian unit of action as a basis for constructing his narrative.

The rest of part 1 of this study examines the Archidamian narrative: the introductory sentences of units of action (chapter 2), the five types of unit that are the building blocks of the Archidamian narrative (chapter 3), and the larger ongoing patterns formed by clusters of units (chapter 4). In both the introductory sentences and the units themselves Thucydides explores a wide variety of occasional stylistic choices but regularly also returns to a few preferred patterns.

CHAPTER TWO

· Introductory Sentences
(ii.1–v.24)

Year six has given us an idea of the building blocks that Thucydides uses to construct the first ten years of his twenty-one-year narrative. Each year is expressly divided into a summer and then a winter narrative. Within each season, discrete narrative units of action follow one another in an orderly sequence; 119 units of action in all make up the narrative of ii.1–v.24.

The beginning of each of these 119 Archidamian narrative units is identified by a formular introductory sentence. In one sense, investigating the nature of these introductory sentences reveals very little about the meaning of the narrative they help construct. It is also true, however, that the formular pattern established by the introductory sentences of the units of action in books ii–v.24 is the strongest indication we have of the methodical and systematic way in which Thucydides undertook to think about the early years of the war he had decided to record "in the order that events occurred, divided into summers and winters" (ὡς ἕκαστα ἐγίγνετο κατὰ θέρος καὶ χειμῶνα, ii.1). The regularity of the introductory sentences suggests that Thucydides may have structured his first efforts at recording the events of the war in a journal-like format, with each new introductory sentence standing as the rubric for another entry. In this chapter we will investigate the nature of these rubrics.[1]

An introductory sentence to a unit of action in the Archidamian narrative normally has four parts: a personal subject, an active verb, an identification of place, and an identification of time. It represents the extension, down into the level of the individual segments of narrative, of the orderly temporal sequence of summers and winters. But the introductory sentences that begin the 119 units of action comprising the narrative of the Archidamian War do more than define and focus each individual unit as part of Thucydides' larger seasonal schema; by their very repetitive and formular nature they also create stylistic continuity. The following figures give some idea of the regularities of their formation.[2]

- 78% (93 sentences) have as their subject people rather than a place or concrete noun. In 10 of the remaining 26 sentences too, a place or concrete noun stands by metonymy for groups of people.
- 93% (111 sentences) have active verbs or verbs in the middle voice whose meaning is fully active.
- 67% (80 sentences) include a prepositional phrase to identify the setting of the unit, either alone or in combination with other expressions of place. In introductory sentences lacking a prepositional phrase of place, either the content of the unit is not limited to one or two specific locations (the eclipse in year six, for instance, or diplomatic negotiations, as in ii.80) or the place is obvious from the subject, as in ii.34: "In this winter, following their traditional custom, the Athenians held burial rites at public expense for the first to die in this war . . . " (ἐν δὲ τῷ αὐτῷ χειμῶνι Ἀθηναῖοι τῷ πατρίῳ νόμῳ χρώμενοι δημοσίᾳ ταφὰς ἐποιήσαντο τῶν ἐν τῷδε τῷ πολέμῳ πρώτων ἀποθανόντων . . .).
- 88% (105 sentences) are introduced by an expression of time, usually either a seasonal formula or a prepositional phrase.
- 69% (82 sentences) have as their first two elements the time phrase and the subject. Fourteen patterns for the first two elements of the introductory sentences are found in Thucydides ii.1–v.24; four of them account for more than 80% of the total number (98 of 119 sentences).

The introductory sentence of the Archidamian unit of action has the specific function of identifying the scene to come by specifying the actors, the initial activity, the place or setting, and the time.[3] In first sentences Thucydides never uses gnomic statements, announces political generalities, or conveys a broad impression then made more substantial and specific in the body of the unit, although sentences of these and many other types are regularly found in the body of the narrative throughout the *History*.[4] Moreover, the tendencies reflected in the above list for introductory sentences are not found with any frequency for other sentences within the body of the Thucydidean unit of action.[5] Only one of the significant regularities found in well over half of the 119 sentences that introduce units of action is also found in arbitrarily selected sentences within the units: verbs are active not only at the heads of units of action, but more generally in Thucydides. Because the other elements common in introductory sentences rarely occur together in other parts of the narrative, it is reasonable to call the pattern a formular one, designed to mark a new unit's beginning.[6]

Because all units begin in a roughly similar way, the reader encounters predictability, continuity, and order at the very moment when substantial change occurs, that is, at the shift in narrative focus that takes place as each new unit commences. Since first sentences of units of action tend repeatedly to present a straightforward summary of the new data in a set of easily identifiable, rather regular locutions, they also do not express or reflect the structural differences found among the units themselves. That is, one cannot tell from the introductory sentence which of the five kinds of unit is being introduced. The first sentence does not tell us how long the forthcoming unit will be, or how complicated a narrative, or whether it will have one focus or a number of different ones.

The figures given in the brief list above suggest a pattern of distribution of formular elements that is broadly applicable in these first books of the *History:* a large variety of occasional usages and an even larger variety of further possibilities are combined with a solid and limited core provided by the most frequent formulae. Although Thucydides does not form all introductory sentences according to a rigidly predictable template, he always uses them to achieve the same goal: to provide the reader with new data, but data expressed in familiar patterns that mark that a new unit is beginning.[7] Here we will explore each of the elements that make the introductory sentences distinctive: their subjects, their main verbs, their settings, and their expressions of time.

2.1 SUBJECTS IN INTRODUCTORY SENTENCES (ii.1–v.24)

Six different subject types are found in the introductory sentences of units of action: Athenians, Peloponnesians, other named collective nouns, named individuals, place names, and some concrete nouns ("ships," "army," and so on). Four of the six categories involve names of people, identified either individually or as groups; these four categories account for the subjects of 78% of the 119 first sentences.

The Athenians, as a collective noun, are the subjects of 32 sentences, or 27% of the total. Peloponnesians are the subject of 13 sentences, or 11% of the total. The contrast in frequency between Athenians and Peloponnesians as subjects of first sentences indicates one of the subtler ways in which the *History*, despite a severely impartial narrative voice, betrays its passionately Athenian focus. The emphasis on Athenian activity is understandable enough; Thucydides undoubtedly had more Athenian than Peloponnesian material in the early years of the war. In any case, Athenians and Peloponnesians together provide 38% of the introductory sentences' subjects.[8]

The third subject type includes all named collective nouns that are neither Athenian nor Peloponnesian. These occur as subjects in 23 of the 119 first sentences, or 19% of the total. Most of them represent national groups: Plataeans, Mytileneans, Corcyraeans, and so on. Seven are more exactly limited in scope: Spartiates in iv.8 or Mytilenean and other Lesbian exiles in iv.52.2.

The fourth and final personal group of subjects is composed of individual people mentioned by name. Twenty-five of these occur in books ii.1–v.24; they comprise 21% of the total. Sometimes only one individual is the subject, as in iii.25 or iv.109.1; sometimes a small group is named, as in ii.58 or ii.67. Together, Athenians, Peloponnesians, other collectives, and individuals mentioned by name account for almost 80% of all 119 first sentences.

Two categories of subject are not collective or personal names; often, however, they stand by metonymy for groups of people. Place-names are the subject of 5 units, and 4 of these actually involve cities (groups of people) being besieged or deciding to revolt. The 21 concrete nouns that are subjects of first sentences also include 6 that represent groups of people, like "army" ($\sigma\tau\rho\alpha\tau\acute{o}s$) in ii.18 and "ships" ($\nu\hat{\eta}\epsilon s$) in iii.17, iii.69, and iv.1.[9] The others are mainly either natural phenomena (earthquakes, eclipses, and so on: 8 in all) or assorted common nouns (news in iii.33.2, the temple of Hera in iv.133.2, an armistice or treaty in iv.58 and v.1a: 7 in all). Thus in the two categories of nonpersonal subjects, 10 of the 26 are merely alternate ways of expressing the same emphasis on personal activity found in the large majority of introductory sentences. In all, 103 sentences, or 87% of the 119 that together make up the narrative of the Archidamian War, involve human agents as subjects.

Some changes occur within this overall pattern. The number of subjects who are Athenian or Peloponnesian remains constant in books ii and iii but drops sharply in book iv: Athenians decline from 37% to 12% of the total number of units in the book, Peloponnesians from 14% to 6%. Other collectives and named individuals, on the other hand, become more frequent as the narrative proceeds. Collective subjects who are not Athenian or Peloponnesian rise as subjects in introductory sentences from 11% in book ii to 22% in books iii–v.24, and individuals named as subject, though dropping to 3% of the subjects in introductory sentences in book iii, rise sharply in books iv–v.24. There they comprise the largest subject type, found in 18 units, or 37% of the total.[10]

Thus as the narrative of the Archidamian War continues, Thucydides' focus turns away from the most common subjects, Athenians and Peloponnesians, and toward the use of smaller national groups and individuals to introduce units of action. In one sense this may be considered a natural development: a variety of individual actors are named in the course of units early in the narrative who can be introduced more abruptly as the war continues. Their relationship to the large power blocs, Athenian or Peloponnesian, no longer requires initial explanation. This shift toward individual and limited collective subjects to introduce units parallels what will happen in the structure of the body of the narrative unit of action: late in the narrative Thucydides abandons the general paragraph that is a third of a page in length, tending to rely instead in books iv–v.24 on either an extremely brief account or a much longer extended narrative or complex unit.[11] This trend toward both specificity and complexity in the narrative, at the expense of a paragraph-sized standardized summary, stylistically parallels the greater variety of subjects used in the units' introductory sentences.

2.2 VERBS IN INTRODUCTORY SENTENCES (ii.1–v.24)

Thucydides looks at the activity in the first sentence of units of action in one of three ways. The verb of the first sentence may prepare the reader for the action that follows in the unit, by describing an action that is clearly introductory: an army "sets out" or someone "comes" or "sails." Such "initiatory" verbs do not convey the important movement of the unit but are rather neutral and allow instead a strong focus on the subject and other supporting material. Forty-nine (41%) of the first sentences in ii.1–v.24 have initiatory verbs; many sentences with verbs of this type concern military undertakings.[12]

The second type of verb found in first sentences is deliberative. That is, it portrays the actors planning an activity that is then carried out later in the unit. Thirteen units (11% of the total) have deliberative first sentences; it is the rarest of the three types. Examples include ii.33 ("In the following winter Euarchus the Acarnanian . . . persuaded the Corinthians," τοῦ δ᾿ ἐπιγιγνομένου χειμῶνος Εὔαρχος ὁ Ἀκαρνὰν . . . πείθει Κορινθίους) and ii.70 ("In the same winter, . . . the Potidaeans . . . under all these circumstances . . . made an offer to come to terms . . . ," τοῦ δ᾿ αὐτοῦ χειμῶνος οἱ Ποτειδεᾶται . . . οὕτω δὴ λόγους προσφέρουσι . . .).[13]

The third type of verb found in first sentences is the most frequent. It does not prepare the reader for activity to come, as both initiatory and deliberative verbs do, but abruptly summarizes a major action.[14] Fifty-seven of the 119 introductory sentences (48%) have verbs of this type. The action described in the body of the unit develops details of the activity summarized in the first sentence, but the first verb does not prepare the reader gradually; instead it immediately plunges into the action at hand. Examples include iii.92 ("Around the same time, the Lacedaemonians founded Heraclea," ὑπὸ δὲ τὸν χρόνον τοῦτον Λακεδαιμόνιοι Ἡράκλειαν . . . καθίσταντο) and iii.2 ("Immediately after the Peloponnesian invasion, all the Lesbians except for Methymna revolted from Athens," μετὰ δὲ τὴν ἐσβολὴν τῶν Πελοποννησίων εὐθὺς Λέσβος πλὴν Μηθύμνης ἀπέστη ἀπ' Ἀθηναίων). Verbs of the initiatory and deliberative type are used less often in book iv, dropping from 69% of the units in book ii to 60% in book iii to 35% in books iv–v.24. Verbs of the summary type rise from 31% to 40% to 65% over the course of the same books.[15]

If we consider not only the quality of the verbal action (initiatory, deliberative, summary) but also the distribution of verbs among the six types of subjects for introductory sentences discussed just above, some of these trends make obvious sense. Initiatory verbs in book iv often occur when the subject is an individual. This reflects the changing distribution of subjects; in book iv, military leaders tend to become the subjects of their units, and the formular verbs of military introduction are now in the singular: ἐστράτευσεν in iv.84 and iv.102, στρατεύει in iv.109.1, ἐξέπλευσε in v.2, and προσβάλλει in v.6.[16]

It is intriguing that the collective nouns that represent subjects other than Athenians and Peloponnesians account for more than half of all the verbs of the deliberative type; only one such verb is found in the first sentences whose subjects are either Athenians or Peloponnesians, although iii.8, for instance, could easily have emphasized Peloponnesians as the first subject and supplied them with a verb of deliberation.[17] Perhaps Thucydides thought that a leisurely introduction of motive, which a first verb of deliberation makes possible, was not required for either of the major powers, but useful both to supply background knowledge and to emphasize the role played in the war by the intention and volition of such groups as Ambraciots and Chaonians, Plataeans, Mytileneans, Aetolians, and Megarians.[18] Such in any case is the effect of these deliberative verbs.

Only 21 (18%) of the 119 introductory sentences include the verb as one of the first two elements of the sentence. Thus the verb is not vital in indicating to the reader that a new unit has begun. Its effect on first sentences is rather more subtle. It is almost always active; it generally conveys movement, either initiatory or of the summary type, rather than contemplation or deliberation. Introductory sentences often announce a scene of vigorous activity.

2.3 SETTINGS IN INTRODUCTORY SENTENCES (ii.1–v.24)

In the verbs and subjects that begin units of action in the Archidamian narrative, there is both change and stability: change, as personal subjects become more limited and specific in books iv–v.24, while verbs are more often of the summary type; stability, in that throughout the three and one-quarter books in question, subjects of first sentences remain, predominantly, named groups or individuals, and verbs are active in meaning. People do things in introductory sentences of units of action.

Place and time are the two aspects of first sentences that remain to be considered. The presence of these two elements in a sentence helps identify it as introductory in nature; they are, then, more strictly formular in function than are subject and verb. Place, the geographical setting of the unit, is less essential as a primary marker of all first sentences than the time phrase; only 13 (11%) of the 119 first sentences include place as one of their first two elements, and in 29 first sentences, or 25% of the total, a noun specifically identifying place does not occur.[19] But this also means that in 90, three-quarters of all first sentences in ii.1–v.24, Thucydides carefully specifies where the action of the unit takes place. Mention of place is an important means by which introductory sentences are made specific and formular vehicles for conveying important data about the unit to come.[20]

In 60, or just over one-half of the 119 first sentences in ii.1–v.24, place is identified by a simple prepositional phrase alone. This proportion does not change markedly as the narrative progresses into book v; in each of the books considered, a prepositional phrase identifies setting in about half the first sentences of units of action. In another 20 sentences, place is identified at least twice in the first sentence; one prepositional phrase at least is included.[21] The various combinations of setting often introduce an element of suspense. In ii.83–92, for instance, the first sentence indicates that the fleet from Corinth and the other allies from the Crisaean Gulf are forced to fight the Athenian fleet stationed in Naupactus. Lines of direction leading to their eventual intersection later in the unit have been drawn here; in the first sentence the reader already anticipates their eventual clash. The unit v.3.6 also builds suspense through a concentrated identification of place, though in this case the resolution will not occur in the immediate unit being introduced. In effect, the whole unit concerns the places marking the stages of Cleon's journey and looks forward to Amphipolis. This very short unit makes every stage in Cleon's journey explicit: "After leaving a garrison in Torone, Cleon set out and sailed around Athos going toward Amphipolis" (καὶ ὁ μὲν Κλέων φυλακὴν καταστησάμενος τῆς Τορώνης ἄρας περιέπλει τὸν Ἄθων ὡς ἐπὶ τὴν Ἀμφίπολιν).

The setting of the unit is the subject of 5 sentences.[22] As we have already seen in discussing personal subjects in introductory sentences, in 4 of the 5, place stands by metonymy for the inhabitants; only Atalanta, uninhabited, does not perform this dual function of indicating people as well as setting. Place is the object of the verb in 10 sentences, and it occurs as a dependent dative or genitive in another 4.[23] These variations show again that Thucydides had available a much broader range of expressions than he usually chose to employ in first sentences. Although he can and occasionally does use other locutions, in fully two-thirds of the 119 introductory sentences, place is identified by means of a prepositional phrase.

When a noun identifying setting does not occur in the first sentence, it is either because other elements in the sentence combine to make it clear without needing a noun of place or because the action of the first sentence is not limited to one or two specific locations. Twenty-nine introductory sentences are without an indication of place. In 16 of these sentences, a collective noun (usually the subject of the sentence) and the verb together tacitly indicate where the action takes place. The action is usually civic; examples include ii.59 ("After the second Peloponnesian invasions, the Athenians . . . had undergone a change in their attitude," μετὰ δὲ τὴν δευτέραν ἐσβολὴν τῶν Πελοποννησίων οἱ Ἀθηναῖοι . . . ἠλλοίωντο τὰς γνώμας) and iv.51 ("During this same winter, the Chians pulled down their new wall on orders from the Athenians," τοῦ δ᾽ αὐτῦ χειμῶνος καὶ Χῖοι τὸ τεῖχος περιεῖλον τὸ καινὸν κελευσάντων Ἀθηναίων). In sentences like these, an additional noun of place would be otiose.[24]

The remaining 13 first sentences focus on an activity not easily identified with a specific setting. Two of them, ii.28 and iv.52.1, concern eclipses. The other 11 describe events not limited in their effect to a specific location; they are mostly diplomatic in nature, like ii.80 ("In the same summer, not long after these events, the Ambraciots and Chaonians . . . persuaded the Lacedaemonians to prepare a fleet," τοῦ δ᾽ αὐτοῦ θέρους, οὐ πολλῷ ὕστερον τούτων, Ἀμπρακιῶται καὶ Χάονες . . . πείθουσι Λακεδαιμονίους ναυτικόν . . . παρασκευάσασθαι) and iv.117 ("In the following summer, as soon as it was spring, the Lacedaemonians and the Athenians made an armistice for a year," Λακεδαιμόνιοι δὲ καὶ Ἀθηναῖοι ἅμα ἦρι τοῦ ἐπιγιγνομένου θέρους εὐθὺς ἐκεχειρίαν ἐποιήσαντο ἐνιαύσιον). All but 3 of them occur in years one, nine, and ten, the beginning and the end of this first period of the war. At these points in the narrative, diplomatic arrangements become important, and the fact of agreement begins the unit rather than a specifically local action.[25] In sum, even in the 13 units where place is not concretely a part of the first sentence, the reader is left in little doubt about the changed orientation of the new unit.

Thucydides does not greatly vary his manner of expressing setting in the course of the narrative of the Archidamian War. Setting seems instead to be a common formular aspect of the sentence, presented in a limited variety of ways. It helps indicate to the reader that a new unit has begun, and presents specific data about it.[26]

2.4 TIME IN INTRODUCTORY SENTENCES (ii.1–v.24)

Even more strongly than a noun of place, a time phrase indicates to the reader that a new unit of action has begun.[27] The time phrase ties the individual unit into the larger summer/winter scheme by which the years of the Archidamian narrative are organized. Of the 119 first sentences, 105 (88%) include a phrase of time, and 93 (78%) display it as one of their first two elements. Time words perform several functions in the text: as a striking and repetitive element of style they help the reader follow the structure of the work; as an aspect of the chronology of the *History* they link the units to each other in terms of a temporal and sometimes logical progression. They also represent the practical application in the text of Thucydides' expressed concerns with chronology.[28] We shall return to these broader considerations below.

Several different types of temporal expression are found in first sentences. Four patterns account for 99 (83%) of the 119 sentences; they range from very general formular phrases to quite precise descriptions of temporal and causal connections between two or more units in the same year. They will be briefly discussed here in the order of their increasing complexity.

The first and simplest temporal expression in first sentences is the general seasonal phrase: "in the following summer" (τοῦ δ' ἐπιγιγνομένου θέρους) at the head of the season; "during the same summer" (τοῦ δ' αὐτοῦ θέρους) in the course of one. Thirty-three units are introduced by such general seasonal phrases alone. The effect is almost completely formular; the reader is notified that another unit has begun, but very little is said about time, relative or exact.[29]

The second type of time phrase is not much more specific but does acknowledge some temporal relationship between the preceding unit and the one being introduced. It involves a preposition and a rather neutral phrase of time, like "at this time" (ὑπὸ δὲ τὸν χρόνον τοῦτον) or "after this" (μετὰ δὲ ταῦτα). Fourteen first sentences contain this type of time formula.[30] The general expression of season and the neutral prepositional phrase together account for 47 (40%) of the 119 first sentences.

The third type, which occurs in 23 units (19% of the total), provides a somewhat more exact description of season. It begins with the "in the same summer" formula but adds to it a word limiting the season more exactly (usually either "straightaway," εὐθύς, or the participle "ending," τελευτῶντος), a neutral prepositional phrase like those found alone in the second category just above, or occasional information about the crops or harvest, like "just when the grain was ripening" (ἅμα τῷ σίτῳ ἀκμάζοντι) in iii.1.[31]

The fourth and final major type of temporal expression is the most precise of all. It is not necessarily more exact in specifying the date one could assign on the basis of its information, but it refers to a specific prior event in the season. An example is provided in ii.59: "After the second Peloponnesian invasion, the Athenians . . . had undergone a change in their attitude" (μετὰ δὲ τὴν δευτέραν ἐσβολὴν τῶν Πελοποννησίων οἱ Ἀθηναῖοι . . . ἠλλοίωντο τὰς γνώμας). A more elaborate form that this exact reference to time may take, including a seasonal formula as well as the prepositional phrase, is found in ii.79: "In the same summer and at the same time as the Plataean campaign, the Athenians campaigned against the Chalcidians . . . when the grain was beginning to ripen" (τοῦ δ᾽ αὐτοῦ θέρους καὶ ἅμα τῇ τῶν Πλαταιῶν ἐπιστρατείᾳ Ἀθηναῖοι . . . ἐπεστράτευσαν ἐπὶ Χαλκιδέας . . . ἀκμάζοντος τοῦ σίτου). Twenty-nine introductory sentences (24%) are of this type.[32] In sum, 99 (83%) of the introductory sentences in the narrative of the Archidamian War are introduced with one of these four expressions: a simple statement of season, a neutral prepositional phrase, a more detailed identification of the part of the season, or finally an explicit reference to other events that happen in the same season.

Of the 20 sentences that remain to be considered, 6 contain idiosyncratic time phrases not conforming to one of the four patterns described above, while 14 contain no mention of time at all. Chapter 1 considered ii.2 as an expression of time that is unusually long and detailed, since it provides the official beginning of the Archidamian War. Thucydides there uses a variety of contemporary methods of dating, making the reference as exact as possible for the Greek-speaking world. The other 5 odd statements of time are more abrupt than usual: ἐνθένδε ἤδη, τότε (twice), ἔτι, εὐθύς—these merely hint at a time distinction different from that of the preceding unit.[33]

Fourteen sentences in ii.1–v.24 do not include a phrase of time.[34] The 8 from books ii and iii all refer very clearly to the continuation of a subject discussed two or three units earlier; Thucydides may have felt that they did not require a second temporal introduction in the same season. The absence of the time word suggests that the topic of the unit is already familiar to the reader. One of the 6 units without an introductory time expression from books iv–v.24 is of approximately the same type;[35] one is the anomalous unit v.20.2. In the case of the other 4 units without a time expression from books iv–v.24, a very brief unit has immediately preceded the unit in question, and the time word at the head of the prior unit suffices for both.[36] Chapter 5 will show that this phenomenon becomes more common in the course of book v, the narrative of the years of the Peace.

Expressions of time, like those of place, emphasize the element of pattern and repetition in first sentences. Within the year, expressions of time are not monotonously repetitive, although the same formular phrases, in much the same proportion, occur throughout the narrative; a majority of the years of the Archidamian narrative show a mixture of all four major types of temporal expression. Most time expressions are built on the same two bases: the season and the prepositional phrase. This means that their effect upon the ear is often very similar indeed. For instance, the bare seasonal formula is repeated not only in the 33 sentences where it occurs by itself, but also in all 23 of the more detailed expressions of season, and in 7 of the precisely referential type. Thus 63, or well over half of the 119 introductory sentences, include this phrase.

Finally, the choice of a less or more specific expression of time often seems to have involved considerations that were not chronological. The time phrase is used to help interpret as well as to date the unit of action. Although some time phrases make the general idea of temporal progression more exact, by identifying early or late summer or by indicating that the time elapsed between two sequential events was quite short, many indicate instead a causal link between the unit just beginning and some previous or subsequent event. In iii.89.2, Thucydides tells us in the course of the unit that earthquakes, mentioned in the introductory sentence and linking this unit temporally to the previous one, were in his opinion the cause of the inundations that the unit as a whole describes. Similarly, the phrase in iv.2.1, "around the same time in the spring, before the grain was ripe" (ὑπὸ δὲ τοὺς αὐτοὺς χρόνους τοῦ ἦρος, πρὶν τὸν σῖτον ἐν ἀκμῇ εἶναι), becomes in iv.6, two units later, an important element in the Peloponnesian decision to retreat from Attica directly after Pylos; they were short of food.[37]

Each of the yearly and seasonal divisions is emphasized by a striking formula. The end of one year and the beginning of the next is announced by a subscription, a title of sorts for the year that has just ended, and "in the following summer" (τοῦ δ' ἐπιγιγνομένου θέρους), standing at the head of the first summer unit.[38] The end of summer and beginning of winter is emphasized by the following combination: "and the summer ended" (καὶ τὸ θέρος ἐτελεύτα), at the end of the last summer unit, and "in the following winter" (τοῦ δ' ἐπιγιγνομένου χειμῶνος) or "in the following winter" (ἐν δὲ τῷ ἐπιόντι χειμῶνι), at the head of the first winter unit. Thus each year becomes almost a separate small book, provided with seasonal formulae to indicate its beginning, midpoint, and end: τοῦ δ' ἐπιγιγνομένου θέρους; καὶ τὸ θέρος ἐτελεύτα; τοῦ δ' ἐπιγιγνομένου χειμῶνος; and καὶ ὁ χειμῶν ἐτελεύτα οὗτος. The end of the year is marked by a particularly emphatic extended formula, as in year three: "And thus winter ended, and the third year ended of this war, which Thucydides recorded," καὶ ὁ χειμῶν ἐτελεύτα οὗτος καὶ τρίτον ἔτος τῷ πολέμῳ ἐτελεύτα τῷδε ὃν Θουκυδίδης ξυνέγραψεν, ii.103. These phrases, all of which occur in most of the twenty-one years of the History, support Thucydides' statement in ii.1, v.20, and v.26: the History was indeed written "according to summers and winters" (κατὰ θέρος καὶ χειμῶνα).

The time formulae at the head of the 119 units of action in the Archidamian narrative are the links between the larger structural units in the History, the years and the seasons within the years, and the smallest structures, the units of action. The expression τοῦ δ' ἐπιγιγνομένου θέρους, as we have seen, is not only a member of the class of phrases that indicate yearly divisions. Within the year, it also comes first in the series of time words in first sentences of units of action. It indicates not only the beginning of a new year but the beginning of a new unit of action and itself provides a narrowing of focus from the large seasonal block to the smaller unit of action. The ten-year narrative of the Archidamian War is arranged as a strongly paratactic sequence. Unit follows unit within the season as, on a larger scale, season follows season and year follows year. The small time formulae in the introductory sentences of units of action articulate these divisions and thus establish the connections between the large yearly structures and the smaller individual units of narrative that comprise them.

In summary, we have seen in each of four major foci of the introductory sentence— subject, verb, setting, and time—the tendency on Thucydides' part to display a wide variety of possible alternative modes of expression, and at the same time a heavy emphasis on certain choices used most frequently. The general effect is strikingly regular: time or the subject of the sentence is one of the first two elements in 116 of the 119 sentences; only 8 of the 119 sentences have a passive verb. People appear as subjects in 93%, 76% include a noun of place, and 88% a time phrase. These figures and the others like them in appendix B demonstrate the extent to which introductory sentences are designed formally to mark for the reader's ear the commencement of a new and discrete narrative unit.

Within the general pattern, some change does occur in the course of books ii.1–v.24. While Athenians and Peloponnesians are the most frequent subjects of first sentences in books ii and iii, other collective nouns and personal subjects provide 57% of the subjects in books iv–v.24. Verbs show change also; verbs that summarize the main action of the unit occur in 36% of the introductory sentences of books ii and iii but account for 65% in books iv–v.24. These changes reflect a trend we shall also see below, in looking more closely at the content of units of action: units late in the narrative of the Archidamian War become more specific and idiosyncratic in their structure. They are less often a paragraph long, more often either very short or very long.

The changes in verb and subject are very subtle, however, compared with the general formular pattern established in the narrative by first sentences. Each unit of action in books ii.1–v.24 of the *History* is introduced by a sentence that systematically gives essential data: the new subject, the action, the place, and the time. An austere unity of tone results. The temporal phrases place the units firmly in the general year-to-year framework of the *History;* all four elements together become a formular thread binding the narrative together, as the units succeed each other to constitute seasons, and the seasons together constitute the years that make up the Archidamian narrative as a whole.

CHAPTER THREE

Internal Structure of the
Unit of Action (ii.1–v.24)

Chapter 2 examined the components that make the introductory sentences of Thucydidean units of action formular in nature, distinctively marking one unit of action off from the next. This chapter considers the units themselves, since they are the building blocks out of which Thucydides constructs the Archidamian narrative as a whole. As we already saw briefly in chapter 1, he uses five unit types in all, three fairly short and two much longer, to construct the 119 narrative units of ii.1–v.24.

Units of action as defined in this study do not provide the only way to describe the narrative of the early books of the *History,* but they do articulate some narrative habits that Thucydides relies on quite consistently. If we look closely at the specifics of unit construction here, in chapter 4 we will be able to see more precisely how Thucydides uses a sequence of narrative units of action to construct larger patterns of developing meaning, over the course of the ten-year narrative. Chapters 5 and 6 can then examine the ways that narrative structures begin to change, as Thucydides moves into later periods of the Peloponnesian War.

The 119 Archidamian units of action cluster in two large groups according to length. That is, most narrative segments are either less than twenty-six lines or more than fifty lines long. Only 13 of the 119 units fall somewhere in between (see table 3.1).

Three types of unit are twenty-five lines or less in length. Very short units of narrative, seven lines long or less, always concern a single event described quite simply. Once a unit is a little longer (ordinarily, eight to twenty-five lines long), it either re-

TABLE 3.1 Distribution of Unit Lengths, ii.1–v.24

Number of lines per unit	Number of units	% of total units
1–25	65	55
26–50	13	11
51 or more	41	34

sembles the very short units in structure but is fleshed out with various kinds of descriptive supplementary material, or it takes a different structure altogether. This third type of short unit narrates a sequence of consecutive activities performed by the same actors, as in a military expedition that goes several places and then returns home. Every very short narrative stretch can be identified as belonging to one of these three types: the short, single-focus unit; the more developed unit that still has a single focus; or the unit that has a single subject but several changes of focus. I have called these three shorter types simple picture units, developed picture units, and list units.

The long units, on the other hand, those over fifty lines in length, almost all exhibit a narrative that is a mixture of the separate elements characteristic of the three simpler types: some static description and analysis, as in the units with a single focus; some linear progression of events involving a string of sequential activities, as in the list units. The striking difference between the two types of longer units concerns the presence or absence of an excursus, consisting of material quite different from that of the narrative unit that surrounds it. I have labeled as extended narrative units those longer narratives that provide an unbroken, continuous account. They generally combine features of both the picture unit and the list unit. Because their length permits static description and sequential activity to be combined in many different ways, extended narrative units do not obviously resemble each other structurally. But they can all be distinguished from the other longer narrative unit type, which I call the complex unit. Complex units have one or more excursuses inserted into the surrounding narrative; they resemble iii.104 from year six, discussed above.[1] All units fifty lines or longer, with two exceptions, fall into one of these two categories.[2]

Thus the five types of unit of action Thucydides uses in the Archidamian narrative are defined as follows:

Simple picture unit: a narrative passage seven lines long or less that contains the brief description of a single activity

Developed picture unit: a passage that describes a single activity, like the simple picture unit, but usually eight to twenty-five lines long and including supporting detail of a variety of types

List unit: a passage similar in length to the developed picture unit, following a single set of actors from place to place, without much supporting detail

Extended narrative unit: a passage more than fifty lines long with an internal shift in narrative focus, combining the detail of the developed picture unit with the linear progression of the list unit

Complex unit: also more than fifty lines long, an original picture, list, or extended narrative unit interrupted by an excursus, so that the unit as a whole forms an *a-b-a* pattern with the narrative portion forming a frame around the excursus

The 13 narrative passages from book ii.1–v 24 that are between twenty-five and fifty lines long can readily be assigned (as either longer or shorter examples than usual) to one of the five types already described, on the basis of their own internal arrangement. Three of them are developed picture units; 2, list units; 4, extended narrative units; and 4, complex units.[3]

The investigation of each of the five unit types that follows is intended to answer some of the following questions for the Archidamian narrative: Does Thucydides always use the same structures for describing the same kinds of material? If not, how does he adapt different structures to the requirements of different activities? Does he use the same kind of units in the same proportion throughout the books considered? At the end of the chapter, and more extensively in chapter 4, we shall consider some of the interpretive consequences entailed by Thucydides' choice of narrative structures for the Archidamian narrative.

3.1 SIMPLE PICTURE UNITS (ii.1–v.24)

ii.1, ii.28, ii.32, ii.47.2, ii.66, iii.87.4, iii.89.1, iii.99, iii.116, iv.2.1, iv.7, iv.49, iv.51, iv.52.1, iv.101.5, iv.109.1, iv.133.1, iv.133.4, iv.134.1, v.1a, v.1b, v.3.5, v.3.6, v.12. Total: 24

Picture units of the simplest type are two to seven lines long. More than any other narrative structure in Thucydides, they create the distinctive discontinuous texture of the ongoing account. They are fully formed units; only 2 of the 24 in ii.1–v. 24 lack the time formula that normally introduces a unit of action. One of these (ii.1) introduces the whole narrative of the war, while the other (v.3.6) follows directly upon another unit a single sentence long that does contain a time formula.

More than two-thirds of the 24 simple picture units describe some form of military activity. Seven of them are formular descriptions of an invasion: ii.47.2, ii.66, iii.89.1, iii.99, iv.2.1, iv.7, and iv.49.[4] Five concern activities around and pertaining to fortification: ii.32, iv.51, iv.109.1, iv.133.1, and iv.133.4. Four concern a variety of other military topics: iv.134.1, v.3.5, v.3.6, and v.12. All together, 16 simple units are military in subject.

The 7 remaining simple picture units include 4 descriptions of natural events (ii.28, iii.87.4, iii.116, and iv.52.1), the war's introduction (ii.1), the announcement of the truce (v.1a), and the announcement of Sitalces' death and Seuthes' succession (iv.101.5).

Three of the 24 simple units are actually bare of description, except for the necessary mention of the action itself and where it occurred: iii.87.4, iv.134.1, and v.1a. The other 21 show some development upon these basic elements.

3.1.1 In 14 simple picture units, the action described in the unit is separated into two stages, indicated by two main verbs.[5] The two stages of action related in these units may be unnecessary or at least self-evident. Unit ii.28 not only gives the fact of the eclipse (ὁ ἥλιος ἐξέλιπε) but also notes that the sun reappeared (καὶ πάλιν ἀνεπληρώθη). Unit ii.47 relates the Peloponnesian invasion in two stages: ἐσέβαλον and ἐδῄουν. Unit iv.101.5 mentions as two separate actions that Sitalces died (ἀπέθανε) and that Seuthes succeeded him (Σεύθης δὲ ... ἐβασίλευσεν). The fact that Thucydides chooses so often to represent even these simplest units of action by means of two main verbs gives them their energy; the action even in such a short compass becomes dynamic, because it is caught—even in one sentence—in the process of change.

3.1.2 Sometimes the unit does not contain two verbs but participles relating subordinate aspects of the action and conveying a sense of intensely observed activity, as in iv.51 or iv.133.1. Sometimes the supporting detail in the body of the unit is principally descriptive, making the action at hand more vivid to the reader. In ii.28, ii.32, ii.47.2, ii.66, iii.116, iv.2.1, and iv.7, for instance, details are included that are not necessary for understanding the implications of the action but do make it a great deal more striking. The description of the eclipsing sun in ii.28 includes that it had been midday (μετὰ μεσημβρίαν), that the sun became moon-shaped (γενόμενος μηνοειδής), and that some stars appeared during the eclipse (καὶ ἀστέρων τινῶν ἐκφανέντων). Or, in ii.32, we are told not only that the Athenians fortified Atalanta, but also the location of the island (ἡ ἐπὶ Λοκροῖς τοῖς Ὀπουντίοις νῆσος) and that it had earlier been uninhabited (ἐρήμη πρότερον οὖσα).

Details are not always merely descriptive. Each of the units ii.28 and ii.32 includes more functional information too. In ii.28 there occurs the phrase "at the beginning of the lunar month, which appears to be the one and only time this can happen" (κατὰ σελήνην, ὥσπερ καὶ μόνον δοκεῖ εἶναι γίγνεσθαι δυνατόν), which is a causal explanation, to the extent that Thucydides can give one, for the eclipse. Such causal subordinate material is also part of iv.133.1, iv.134.1, and v.3.5, though in v.3.5 it is expressed merely in the dative "through treachery" (προδοσίᾳ), which can also be read as a dative of means. In iv.134.1 it is expressed by the phrase "because of the armistice" (διὰ τὴν ἐκεχειρίαν), while it is more developed still in iv.133.1: "now that it had been made easier after what had been the flower of their youth had perished in the battle against the Athenians" (παρεσχηκὸς δὲ ῥᾷον ἐπειδὴ καὶ ἐν τῇ πρὸς Ἀθηναίους μάχῃ ὅτι ἦν ἄνθος ἀπωλώλει). Even in these shortest of units, Thucydides has not just described the event but has also accounted for it in some specific way.

3.1.3 Sometimes the supporting detail is neither descriptive nor causal but gives instead the reflections of the actors about the action, as reason or intention. In ii.32 (the fortification of Atalanta), in addition to the description of the place, there occurs "to keep pirates from sailing out of Opous and elsewhere in Locris and causing damage to Euboea" (τοῦ μὴ λῃστὰς ἐκπλέοντας ἐξ Ὀποῦντος καὶ τῆς ἄλλης Λοκρίδος κακουργεῖν τὴν Εὔβοιαν), as the reason why the Athenians decided to fortify Atalanta. Sometimes such material is very briefly expressed, as in the expression of Cleon's goal in sailing around Mount Athos in v.3.6: "going towards Amphipolis" (ὡς ἐπὶ τὴν Ἀμφίπολιν). Units iv.51 and iv.133.1 also convey the thoughts of some of the actors. In the latter unit, Thucydides relates not only the Thebans' real reason for tearing down the Thespians' wall, "since they had always wanted to do this" (βουλόμενοι μὲν καὶ αἰεί), but the pretext too, "on the charge of atticism" (ἐπικαλέσαντες ἀττικισμόν).

These three types of supporting material—descriptive, causal, and motivational—occur more extensively in the longer developed picture units discussed below. But even the units that are only a sentence long contain considerable amounts of analysis. In the course of a sentence, Thucydides both conveys a sense of motion in the main action and includes material that explains how it happened and why it matters.

The simple picture unit is a small narrative of particular intensity. Within the space of a single sentence, or two at most, an entire scene is briefly described. This structure is a potentially disruptive one, since it tends to break the narrative flow very abruptly. The actual grammatical links between simple picture units and those units that precede and follow them are not unusual,[6] but simple picture units seem to be placed carefully within the summer-winter scheme that provides the larger framework for the narrative. Seventeen of the 24 simple picture units occur either at the change of seasons or one unit away from that change; 11 occur clustered around the change of the year, while the other 6 occur around the change within the year from summer to winter.[7] There does not seem to be a particular selection of material involved in placing some simple units at the turn of the season and others in the course of one; military and nonmilitary topics alike are represented in each grouping. But Thucydides often uses simple picture units to emphasize the structural prominence of two points in the year, the change from summer to winter and the change from winter to summer.

3.2 DEVELOPED PICTURE UNITS (ii.1–v.24)

ii.24, ii.27, ii.31, ii.57, ii.58, ii.70, ii.79, ii.93–94, iii.1, iii.17, iii.18, iii.20–24, iii.25, iii.26, iii.27–28, iii.51, iii.69, iii.86, iii.87.1–3, iii.88, iii.89.2–5, iii.92–93, iv.1, iv.6, iv.46–48, iv.50, iv.76–77, iv.123, iv.133.2–3, iv.134.1–2, iv.135, v.13, v.20.2. Total: 33

The simple picture units discussed above express a very circumscribed sphere of action; they are seven lines long or less. The longer, more developed picture units, however, also maintain the focus on a single topic or scene of action. Although in some of these developed units a great deal of material is included, it is again arranged as descriptive, causal, or motivational support for the main subject of the unit, just as in the shorter units discussed above. Because of the variety of supporting material they contain, developed picture units resemble each other superficially much less than simple picture units do.

The longer, developed picture units are distinguishable from the other kinds of long units of action discussed below by the temporal and logical relations among the three elements in the unit: the first sentence, the body of the unit, and the conclusion. In all 33 developed picture units, the first and last sentences focus on a single event in itself not more extensive than those described above in the simple units. They are longer because one or two elements in the body of the unit are chosen by Thucydides for more extended elaboration.

In different developed picture units, different aspects of the action are singled out and emphasized, conveying both the fact of the event at hand and something of its particular significance. I will discuss two of these units. In iii.27–28, the surrender of Mytilene is related in twenty-five lines. The first sentence gives the essential information, that for lack of Peloponnesian support and food the Mytileneans were forced to surrender. Then, in the fourth line, Thucydides goes back in time, in order to account for the surrender (διὰ τάδε). Line 10 of the unit returns to the time of the first sentence. The agreement itself and then the activity in Mytilene after Paches' entry are considered. The causal and motivational material, although important, does not in the unit itself overshadow the description of events in Mytilene.

Another developed picture unit, iii.86, is structured very differently. Here the action of the present is limited to the first and last sentences of the unit. The first sentence gives the essential subject, the fact that the Athenians sent twenty ships to Sicily. The next sentences give the cause for such an action (the Syracusans and the Leontinians were at war), the balance of power in Sicily, the reasons the Leontinians had sent for help from Athens, and the reasons, both real and alleged, why the Athenians had responded. In the very last sentence, the actual subject is again introduced: the ships reach Rhegium and begin to help in the war. Obviously, in this unit the subject of the first sentence, the movement of Athenian ships, is overshadowed in importance by the account of the forces behind it, conditions in Sicily and calculations in Athens that bring the event about. By a selective distribution of details, Thucydides has created a very different emphasis from that found in iii.27–28.

If one plotted the shifts in time in the two units, the outlines would appear as shown in figure 3.1.

Both units describe a single situation: the surrender of the Mytileneans, and the sending of an Athenian fleet to Sicily. But in the unit about Mytilene, Thucydides appears to be concerned not only with the background but also with the details of the actual surrender; in the Sicilian unit, on the other hand, the actual event at hand acts rather as a platform for conveying the real point of the unit, discussion of the political situation that brought it forth.

Developed picture units are composed of two elements: the narrative facts related in the first and last sentences of the unit, and the interpretive material included in the body of the unit. But these categories are not inherent attributes of the events themselves; Thucydides chose them. Unit iii.27–28 could have been narrated chronologically in the order that the events in the unit occurred. The first sentence would then have stated that the Mytileneans were awaiting help from the Peloponnese. By manipulating the temporal sequence within the unit, Thucydides chooses, instead of such a simple narration of an event unfolding from beginning to end, an analytical and selective structure for the picture unit, which first states one core event, and then arranges the rest of the material around it as descriptive, motivational, or

iii.27–28	iii.86
ἀναγκάζονται	Ἀθηναῖοι ἔστειλαν
ὁπλίζει	καθέστασαν
οὔτε ἠκροῶντο	ἦσαν
ποιοῦνται ὁμολογίαν	οὐ ξυνεπολέμησαν
ἡ ξύμβασις ἐγένετο	ἦσαν
καθίζουσιν	πείθουσι πέμψαι
Πάχης κατατίθεται	εἴργοντο
καθίστατο	ἔπεμψαν
	ἐποιοῦντο

were forced	the Athenians sent
gave hoplite armor	were [at war]
would no longer listen	were
joined in making the agreement	did not fight together
these were the terms	were
sat	persuaded
Paches deposited	were blockaded
deployed	sent
	carried on

past→present→future (iii.27–28)	past→present→future (iii.86)

FIGURE 3.1
Temporal outline of iii.27–28 and iii.86

causal elaboration. The distribution of detail within the developed picture unit conveys not only the gist of the unit but a distinctive focus for it as well.

Unlike the shorter simple picture units, picture units eight lines or longer cannot be distinguished according to whether the subject is military or nonmilitary. The interpretive material offered in these longer units almost always ties them to the central theme of the *History*, the progression of the war. Only 3 of the 33 can be considered completely nonmilitary in scope: iii.89.2–5, the description of the inundations in year six; iv.133.2–3, the description of the destruction of the temple of Hera in Argos, and v.20.2, a discussion of Thucydides' chronological method of order-ing the *History*.[8] The other 30 developed picture units concern the war more directly.

The subjects of the 30 units concerned directly with the war are quite varied. Two are completely idiosyncratic. As structures they represent perhaps the simplest form of the relation between introduction, body of the unit, and conclusion found in the developed picture unit. Unit iii.87.1–3 concerns a second outbreak of the plague; the remark "so that nothing afflicted and damaged Athenian strength more than this" (ὥστε Ἀθηναίους γε μὴ εἶναι ὅτι μᾶλλον τούτου ἐπίεσε καὶ ἐκάκωσε τὴν δύναμιν) and the figures that follow tie it to the theme of the war. Unit ii.24 describes a se-ries of Athenian administrative decisions taken after the retreat of the first Pelo-ponnesian invasion. Both these units are descriptions of a situation rather than de-tailed narratives of a particular event; they do not therefore form a dynamically focused account like those discussed just above, iii.27–28 (the siege of Mytilene) and iii.86 (the Athenians in Sicily).[9]

Eleven developed picture units are roughly political in subject; they concern de-cisions made by various governments or private individuals with an eye to affect-ing the course of the war.[10] They do not as a group with a similar subject matter share a more detailed structure of their own. A general distinction can be made in the structure of political picture units between those in which an individual provides the focus (iii.25, iv.46–48, iv.50, and iv.76–77) and those in which a corporate de-cision introduces the unit (iii.20–24, iii.92–93, iv.1, and iv.123).[11] Again this repre-sents a deliberate decision on the part of Thucydides as author. For instance, in iii.25 the initial focus selected is the arrival of Salaethus in Mytilene; the decision of the Mytileneans not to come to terms with Athens is described in the unit as a result of his arrival. In iv.123, on the other hand, Mende the town, not Brasidas the individ-ual, provides the introductory focus, perhaps because Thucydides wished to end the unit with the Athenian sense of outrage at the revolt of Mende. A general intro-ductory statement that revolt occurred establishes a strong structure of action and reaction that would have been less striking if Brasidas had been the subject of the first sentence. A significant part of the interpretive power and impact of the unit comes from a deliberate positioning of its various elements.[12]

Two groups of subjects remain to be considered. The first and larger contains those 13 units that are not merely connected to the theme of the war in a general fashion but describe a specific act of military initiative.[13] They deserve particular attention because, unlike the more political units considered above, they do follow a more detailed structure of their own, under which all descriptive, causal, or mo-tivational material in the unit is organized. This structure applies not only to the 13 developed military picture units, but also to the 7 simple picture units listed above whose subject matter is military invasion.[14]

The progression of action in a unit of military aggression can be outlined as follows (phrases from various units are appended to the outline to serve as examples):

1. Subject and time formula:

τοῦ δὲ θέρους εὐθὺς ἀρχομένου Πελοποννήσιοι καὶ οἱ ξύμμαχοι (ii.47)

And as soon as the summer began, the Peloponnesians and their allies

οἱ δὲ Λακεδαιμόνιοι καὶ οἱ ξύμμαχοι τοῦ αὐτοῦ θέρους (ii.66)

In that same summer, the Lacedaemonians and their allies

κατὰ δὲ τοὺς αὐτοὺς χρόνους καὶ οἱ περὶ Σικελίαν Ἀθηναῖοι (iii.99)

Around the same time, the Athenians off Sicily

κατὰ δὲ τὸν αὐτὸν χρόνον Σιμωνίδης Ἀθηναίων στρατηγός (iv.7)

Around the same time, the Athenian general Simonides

2. A verb or participle generally descriptive of the activity:

ἐσέβαλον, "invaded" (ii.47, iv.2)

ἐστράτευσαν, "campaigned" (ii.66)

ἦλθον . . . ἐσβαλοῦντες, "went . . . to invade" (iii.89)

πλεύσαντες, "sailed" (iii.99)

ξυλλέξας, "collecting" (iv.7)

στρατευσάμενοι, "campaigned" (iv.49)

3. More detailed description of the activity:

ἐδῄουν, ἐδῄωσαν, "plundered" (ii.47 and iv.2, ii.66)

σεισμῶν δὲ γενομένων πολλῶν ἀπετράποντο πάλιν, "because there were many earthquakes they turned back" (iii.89)

ἐκράτησαν καὶ περιπόλιον αἱροῦσιν, "defeated . . . also capturing a fort" (iii.99)

κατέλαβεν, "seized" (iv.7)

ἔλαβον προδοσίᾳ, "took it with the help of traitors" (iv.49)

4. An indication of conclusion: [15]

ἀπέπλευσαν ἐπ᾽ οἴκου, "they left for home" (ii.66)

ἀπετράποντο πάλιν καὶ οὐκ ἐγένετο ἐσβολή, "they turned back, and there was no invasion" (iii.89—partly the same as element 3 above)

ἐξεκρούσθη τε καὶ ἀπέβαλε πολλοὺς τῶν στρατιωτῶν, "he was immediately booted out and lost most of his men" (iv.7)

ἔσχον τὸ χωρίον, "occupied the place" (iv.49)

The examples given above are drawn from simple picture units that concern military activity. The 13 developed units concerned with military aggression follow this same outline closely. The amount of detail that element 3, the focused description of the activity, includes is of course larger than in the 7 simple units, and the end sentence is more likely to include an indication of troop dispersal not necessary in the units only a sentence long. The progression within the unit, however, is the same.

Although all military picture units involve the same four-part outline this does not result in a repetitive or monotonous pattern. Interpretive material can be distributed in quite different ways within the general outline sketched above. Two general types of distribution occur.

The first, and more common, involves the selection of one aspect from the four-part outline for emphasis. In iii.1, for instance, (1) the time formula introduces the unit; the subject, Peloponnesians and allies, follows. Then comes (2) the general verb "campaigned" (ἐστράτευσαν), the customary mention of the general, and (3) the more specific activity: "They established their base and plundered the land" (καὶ ἐγκαθεζόμενοι ἐδῄουν τὴν γῆν). This material, all of it quite formular, is followed by a specific focus on Athenian strategy: "There were the usual attacks by the Athenian cavalry at every opportunity, and they prevented the main group of light-armed from going beyond the camp and damaging the areas near the city" (καὶ προσβολαί, ὥσπερ εἰώθεσαν, ἐγίγνοντο τῶν Ἀθηναίων ἱππέων ὅπῃ παρείκοι, καὶ τὸν πλεῖστον ὅμιλον τῶν ψιλῶν εἶργον τὸ μὴ προεξιόντας τῶν ὅπλων τὰ ἐγγὺς τῆς πόλεως κακουργεῖν). Then (4) the troops finally disperse: "After staying the length of time they had provisions for, the Peloponnesians withdrew and dispersed to their cities" (ἐμμείναντες δὲ χρόνον οὗ εἶχον τὰ σιτία ἀνεχώρησαν καὶ διελύθησαν κατὰ πόλεις).

Most of the other picture units of military aggression follow this first distribution of material within the four-part outline; one particular element in the outline is selected for a more detailed focus. Unit iii.88, for instance, provides a description of the setting of the activity, and even some mythological detail about it. Unit ii.31 describes the various forces drawn up, ii.58 isolates the plague as the determining element in the action, iii.96 emphasizes the motivation created by expectations about Lesbos, and so on.

The second subordinate pattern taken by developed military picture units occurs more rarely in the text of books ii.1–v.24. There are only two clear examples from the narrative of the Archidamian War, though, as we shall see below, in the later narrative of v.25–vi.7 this structure will be used more frequently.

The simpler of the two examples is ii.93. No single element is emphasized within the general four-part outline; instead, both the Peloponnesian plans to attack the Piraeus and the extensive Athenian reaction to the attempt are related in some detail. The impression given is not one of a single act of aggression but rather of two separate acts occurring in sequence, the second of which is a reaction to the first.

Unit iii.18 shows an even more elaborate form of an action-reaction pattern occurring within the general outline of military aggression. In its largest terms, the structure of the unit includes (1) the time formula and the initial subject, Mytileneans; (2) the general verb "campaigned" (ἐστράτευσαν), which introduces the action; (3) a description of more detailed activity ("After they attacked . . . they went away to Antissa," προσβαλόντες . . . ἀπῆλθον ἐπ᾽ Ἀντίσσης), and the succeeding movements of the Mytileneans, Methymnians, and Athenians; and (4) the concluding statement: "Mytilene was now forcibly [from both sides] . . . cut off" (καὶ ἡ μὲν Μυτιλήνη κατὰ κράτος ἤδη ἀμφοτέρωθεν . . . εἴργετο). But each of the three foci in 3 above can also be regarded as a partial outline formed on the same pattern. The first subject, Mytileneans, is followed by (2a) "campaigned" (ἐστράτευσαν), (3a) "After they attacked . . . they went away" (προσβαλόντες . . . ἀπῆλθον), and

(4a) "they hurried home" (ἀπῆλθον ἐπ' οἴκου). Then the pattern is repeated. The Methymnians in turn (2b) "made a campaign" (ἐστράτευσαν), (3b) "many of them were killed" (ἀπέθανόν τε πολλοί), and (4b) "and the remainder hastened back" (καὶ ἀνεχώρησαν οἱ λοιποὶ κατὰ τάχος). Finally, the Athenians enter the picture. They (2c) "sent out Paches" (πέμπουσι . . . Πάχητα), (3c) "arrived . . . and surrounded" (ἀφικνοῦνται καὶ περιτειχίζουσι), and (4c) settle in for the siege: "Forts were constructed at the stronger points" (φρούρια δ' ἔστιν ᾗ ἐπὶ τῶν καρτερῶν ἐγκατῳκοδόμηται).[16]

So far the subjects of 29 of the 33 developed picture units that occur in books ii.1–v. 24 have been considered: 3 that are not connected specifically to the theme of the war, 2 connected only in a general, descriptive fashion, 11 concerned with political decisions intended to affect the course of the war, and 13 that are directly military and are related by a specific and more detailed four-stage structure of their own. The subject matter of 4 developed picture units remains to be discussed.

As structures, ii.57, iii.17, iii.69, and iv.6 are not much more tightly arranged than the two general descriptive units concerned with Athenian administrative decisions and the plague (ii.24 and iii.87.1–3). In these four instances, however, the subject of the unit is not completely identified by the first sentence, as it is in all other picture units. In these four cases the unit itself is not independent; the subject of the unit is the connection in time among subjects of several other units. In ii.57, the relative chronology of several previous units concerned with invasion, the Athenian naval expedition, and the plague is made explicit.[17] In iii.17, Thucydides surveys the Athenian expenses incurred around Attica, in the Peloponnese, and in the north around Potidaea. The unit is not a completely successful survey, but it is meant to coordinate a series of actions, wherever it properly should have been placed in the text.[18] Likewise, iii.69 coordinates the Lacedaemonian plans for Corcyra with the activity of their fleet and anticipates the otherwise structurally unconnected events in Corcyra in iii.70–85. Finally, iv.6 joins two previously separate themes, the Peloponnesian invasion in the seventh year (iv.2.1) and the capture of Pylos by the Athenians (iv.2.2–5).

These four units alone anticipate a style of narrative that will be considered at greater length in chapters 5 and 6. These four units in effect are designed to overcome the divisions created by the unit structure. Units of action separate what were probably interconnected processes into discrete events that are related sequentially— the pattern that is the essence of the structure of Archidamian narrative. In many places in the Archidamian narrative, the way the units are arranged to form the year's sequence is itself an act of interpretation; this will be discussed at length in chapter 4. But ii.57, iii.17, iii.69, and iv. 6 go further, in that they suggest the possibility of moving out of the basic structural organization provided by discrete narrative segments following each other in an orderly sequence. Thucydides will take this development much further, as he writes up the narrative of later years of the war.[19]

Five developed picture units are over twenty-five lines long. Some structural anomalies do occur in these longest examples of the picture unit; they will be briefly noted here. But these five long units, like other developed picture units, continue to display a static relation between the introductory sentence, the body of the unit, and the end sentence that is very striking. Three of them are forty to forty-five lines long: ii.93–94 (the Peloponnesian attempt on the Piraeus), iii.92–93 (the foundation of Heraclea), and iv.76–77 (Demosthenes' plans for Boeotia).

ii.93–94 (forty-five lines):   the first sentence of this unit relates in five lines that Cnemus, Brasidas, and the other Peloponnesian leaders decided to make an attempt on the Piraeus. The next eleven lines describe their plans and give their reasons for attempting it. The action itself is related from line 16 to line 25. Then the Athenian reaction occurs from line 25 to line 35; the Peloponnesian dispersal and Athenian precautions taken conclude the unit. Here the unusual features are, first, the split of the Peloponnesian attempt into two stages, "wanted" (ἐβούλοντο, ii.93.1) and "proceeded immediately" (καὶ ἐχώρουν εὐθύς, ii.93.4),[20] and, second, the emphasis on not just one aspect—Peloponnesian or Athenian—but each in turn. The unit is one of military aggression and includes all four stages usually found in that type: (1) subject and time formula ("Cnemus, Brasidas, and the other Peloponnesian commanders, at the beginning of the winter," ὁ Κνῆμος καὶ ὁ Βρασίδας καὶ οἱ ἄλλοι ἄρχοντες τῶν Πελοποννησίων ἀρχομένου τοῦ χειμῶνος); (2) general description, though here in two stages ("wanted," ἐβούλοντο, and "proceeded," ἐχώρουν); (3) the specific details of this engagement ("They sailed . . . to the tip," ἔπλεον . . . ἐπὶ . . . τὸ ἀκρωτήριον, and so on), including the Athenian reaction; and (4) the conclusion stating details of dispersal ("[After] they reached Megara they went back on foot . . . the Athenians . . . sailed away in turn, and after this they kept the Piraeus more under guard from now on both by a closed harbor and by other precautions," ἀφικόμενοι δὲ ἐς τὰ Μέγαρα πάλιν . . . ἀπεχώρησαν πεζῇ· οἱ δ' Ἀθηναῖοι . . . ἀπέπλευσαν καὶ αὐτοί, καὶ μετὰ τοῦτο φυλακὴν ἤδη τοῦ Πειραιῶς μᾶλλον τὸ λοιπὸν ἐποιοῦντο λιμένων τε κλῄσει καὶ τῇ ἄλλῃ ἐπιμελείᾳ). The descriptive and motivational material is interspersed through all four parts of the outline.

iii.92–93 (forty-two lines):   the first and last sentences of this unit convey the rise and eventual fall of Heraclea, the Lacedaemonian colony established in the sixth year of the war at Trachis. But the unit itself does not set out the successive stages of the colony's existence. Instead it is shaped as a static picture unit; the body of the unit gives the cause for the colony (requests by the Trachinians and Dorians), the reasons why the Lacedaemonians accepted the colony, details of the foundation, reactions to it in Athens and Thessaly, and general reasons why the colony did not prosper. Although this unit is long and relates a temporal event, it resembles the static picture units iii.87.1–3 (the later plague) and ii.24 (Athenian preparations) in its conclusion, which is generally descriptive rather than a return to the time established in the first sentence.

iv.76–77 (forty lines):   this unit more closely resembles the temporal arrangement of iii.86 (the Athenian naval presence in Sicily). The first sentence relates the arrival of Demosthenes in Naupactus in three lines. The cause of his arrival is narrated in the next thirteen lines, the reason for it in lines 16 through 30. The last ten lines of the unit, less than one-quarter of it, relate Demosthenes' activities in attempting to carry out his plan. Although his arrival in Naupactus and his activities there provide the action of the unit, clearly the background material for it is more important; it looks forward to the disaster at Delium during the following winter (iv.89–101.4). The major difference between these three picture units forty to forty-five lines long and the shorter developed picture units discussed above lies in the more extensive interpretive detail added to several aspects of the longer units. This material is once more causal, motivational, or descriptive.

Two substantially longer developed picture units remain: iii.20–24 (the Plataean escape—119 lines) and iv.46–48 (the destruction of the oligarchic party in Corcyra— 60 lines). Units iii.20–24 and iv.46–48 are not, like the three above, merely slightly extended versions of picture units eight to twenty-five lines long. Instead, in each of these two cases, vivid narrative detail, sometimes of the most trivial kind, is added to the basic unit in such abundance that the original event with a single focus becomes a small story with a linear thrust of its own.

Units iii.20–24 (the Plataeans' escape) and iv.46–48 (Eurymedon in Corcyra), although lengthy, remain genuine picture units if one considers the relation between first sentence, body of the unit, and final sentence. List units follow a group of actors from place to place; extended narratives, often of about the length of iii.20–24 and iv.46–48, combine the detail of the picture unit with the abrupt change in setting of the list unit. In iii. 20–24 and iv. 46–48, however, an individual picture (described in such minute detail that a little story is created) is left largely unsupported

TABLE 3.2 Picture Units, ii.1–v.24

(number of units and percentage of units in each book)

	Book ii	Book iii	Books iv–v.24
Picture units	13 (37%)	18 (51%)	26 (53%)
Simple	5 (14%)	4 (11%)	15 (31%)
Developed	8 (23%)	14 (40%)	11 (22%)
Total units	35	35	49
Pages occupied by picture units (percentage of total pages occupied by such units)	8 (11%)	11.8 (17%)	8.7 (9%)

by any accompanying linear structure. Units iii.20–24 and iv.46–48 rather form scenes of particular vividness. We shall consider in chapter 4 how these two very long picture units enhance the importance of their topics, the fates of Plataea and Corcyra, as they are developed as part of a narrative thread through several years in the *History*.[21]

There are 57 picture units in ii.1–v.24 of the *History*. They range in length from 2 to 119 lines, although over 90% of them (52) are less than twenty-six lines long. They comprise almost half (48%) of all the units that make up the Archidamian narrative. Table 3.2 presents more detailed information about their distribution.

Several conclusions emerge from this table. In the first place, seen as a proportion of the number of units in each book, picture units show a steady increase in importance. Secondly, simple units in the last third of the narrative of the Archidamian War increase, while developed picture units decrease. This explains the apparent discrepancy displayed in the table, between a rise in the numbers of picture units and a decrease in the number of pages they occupy in books iv–v.24. The picture units in books iv–v.24 are more frequently seven lines long or less.

Other conclusions emerge from the discussions of simple and developed picture units above. In terms of their subject matter, 35% of the picture units in books ii.1–v.24 describe an act of military aggression. These demonstrate a more detailed formular structure within the general pattern of the picture unit: the causal, descriptive, or motivational material is organized in a four-part outline. The other two-thirds of the picture units display no distinctive structural pattern allied to subject.

The picture unit, as I have tried to show, focuses on a single activity, which is always introduced in the first sentence of the unit and is usually referred to again in the final sentence of the unit. The body of the unit contains material that describes, gives the causal background, or anticipates the intentions of the actors of the unit. In the case of the longer units, this material is carefully arranged to bring out particular elements for emphasis; the result is that each of the longer picture units is quite distinctive in its narrative appearance. One is tempted to speculate that an original briefer notation (the equivalent of many of the simple picture units) has perhaps been expanded by Thucydides in these instances into a small interpretive essay, with an analytic substance of its own.

The 5 long and elaborate developed picture units confirm that the single and rather static focus of the picture unit is not simply an accident of length; Thucydides has chosen in these longer units too to stay with a single focus and explore it in great detail. In the very long developed picture units, either one aspect of the analytic material is emphasized at much greater length (as iii.92–93 emphasizes the psychological reasons for the failure of Heraclea) or a picture of such fine detail is created that the unit becomes a small narrative of intensely concentrated vividness—the focus has sharpened from that of months or days to that of hours and minutes. But the supporting material, although increased in length, continues as in other picture units to provide descriptive or analytic support for the main topic set out in the introductory sentence.

The discussions here of simple and developed picture units have been somewhat longer and more detailed than those will be in the sections to come describing list, extended narrative, and complex units, since here I have been discussing some of Thucydides' basic narrative habits as well as those aspects of his style particular to the picture unit. General characteristics of the Archidamian unit occur in their simplest form in the picture units. Particularly noteworthy is the vigor imparted to the unit by verbs and participles conveying change and motion, even in the narrow confines of the simple picture unit. Also, the narrative of the picture unit is ordered so as to create a sharp, unquestioned single focus, even if it becomes one supported by a complex substructure of explanatory material. The outlines of iii.27–28 (Mytilene comes to terms) and iii.86 (the Athenian fleet to Sicily) in figure 3.1 above display how the first sentence of the picture unit provides the focal point around which the subordinate material is arranged. In the units to come, where more than one focus occurs in the unit, the effect of concentration is perhaps less striking, but it remains an underlying principle nonetheless.

Characteristics that are particular to the type of unit under consideration will be the focus in the three discussions to come. What we have seen here for the picture units will be largely taken for granted: the continuing emphasis of Thucydides upon verb-centered action and upon a clearly articulated set of foci, around each of which in turn a broad range of interpretive material is arranged to provide a highly individualized, specific description.

3.3 LIST UNITS (ii.1–v.24)

ii.25, ii.26, ii.30, ii.33, ii.69, iii.7, iii.19, iii.90, iii.91, iii.103, iii.115, iv.52.2–5, iv.75, v.4–5. Total: 14

Like picture units, list units are generally less than an Oxford page in length. There, however, the resemblance ends. While picture units contain the account of a single event, sometimes regarded from a variety of viewpoints, list units maintain a focus that is relatively stable upon a single group of men who move from place to place. The number of settings recounted in this linear fashion varies; list units range from very simple accounts of two consecutive actions to more extended portrayals like that of iii.91. The interpretive material included is very limited.

In terms of structure, what sets list units apart from picture units is the fact that the beginning sentence, the body of the unit, and the concluding sentence do not together construct a concentrated picture of a single activity. Instead, the body of the unit takes the introductory sentence as the starting point for a series of actions, related in the order in which they occurred, and including at least one change of setting. The end sentence concludes the series; the general effect is linear.

Fourteen list units occur in the narrative of the Archidamian War; they are the most rarely used of any of the five structural types. No list units occur in years three, five, seven, and nine. A military expedition is without exception the subject, and in 12 of the 14 the action is specifically naval. The list unit, in fact, is ideally suited for the narration of a naval expedition, since a voyage of a fleet can naturally be described as a progressive series of brief engagements or activities. Of the 2 nonnaval list units, iii.103 involves one land engagement and one landing of the Athenian fleet in Sicily; only iv.52.2–5 (attempts of the Mytilenean exiles to capture cities allied to Athens) involves a sequence of activities on land.

One example should suffice to reveal the basic pattern of the list unit. In ii.30, the first sentence identifies the subject of the unit and the first activity: "Meanwhile the Athenians in the hundred ships who were still around the Peloponnese took Sollium, a Corinthian town, and they gave the Palaerans of Acarnania exclusive rights to occupy the territory and the city" (οἱ δ' ἐν ταῖς ἑκατὸν ναυσὶν Ἀθηναῖοι ἔτι ὄντες περὶ Πελοπόννησον Σόλλιόν τε Κορινθίων πόλισμα αἱροῦσι καὶ παραδιδόασι Παλαιρεῦσιν Ἀκαρνάνων μόνοις τὴν γῆν καὶ πόλιν νέμεσθαι). The successive activities of this fleet are then recounted. First: "They overpowered Astacus . . . and brought the place into their alliance" (καὶ Ἀστακὸν . . . ἐξελάσαντες . . . τὸ χωρίον ἐς τὴν ξυμμαχίαν προσεποιήσαντο). Then: "Sailing to the island of Cephallenia, they brought it over without a battle. . . . " (ἐπί τε Κεφαλληνίαν τὴν νῆσον προσπλεύσαντες προσηγάγοντο ἄνευ μάχης. . . .). And finally: "Soon afterward they departed for Athens" (ὕστερον δ᾽ οὐ πολλῷ ἀνεχώρησαν αἱ νῆες ἐς τὰς Ἀθήνας).

Although the ordering of the body of the unit is very different in the list unit and the picture unit, the introductory sentence of list units often closely resembles that of the formular military picture units discussed above.[22] Elements 1 and 2 of the outline, the time formula and subject of the sentence and a general introductory verb, are present in 9 of the 14 list units in the text of ii.1–v.24. The exceptions are of two different types.

Units ii.25 and ii.30 are continuations of a voyage whose beginning had been announced in ii.23. In these two units, at least one of the verbs of the first sentence both summarizes and recapitulates previous activity. "The Athenians . . . together with [others] . . . damaged some places . . . and . . . [at Methone] they attacked the wall" (ἄλλα τε ἐκάκουν . . . καὶ . . . τῷ τείχει . . . προσέβαλον, ii. 25). Brasidas staves them off, but they then "take a town" (πόλισμα αἱροῦσι), Sollium, belonging to the Corinthians (ii.30). Unit iv.52 follows the same pattern, introducing the activities of the Mytilenean exiles rather abruptly: "Also, Mytilenean and other Lesbian exiles, setting out in most cases from the mainland with mercenaries they had hired from the Peloponnese and gathered locally, captured Rhoeteum. After receiving two thousand . . . staters, they returned it without doing damage" (καὶ οἱ Μυτιληναίων φυγάδες καὶ τῶν ἄλλων Λεσβίων, ὁρμώμενοι οἱ πολλοὶ ἐκ τῆς ἠπείρου καὶ μισθωσάμενοι ἔκ τε Πελοποννήσου ἐπικουρικὸν καὶ αὐτόθεν ξυναγείραντες, αἱροῦσι Ῥοίτειον, καὶ λαβόντες δισχιλίους στατῆρας . . . ἀπέδοσαν πάλιν οὐδὲν ἀδικήσαντες). The other exception to the military pattern is deliberative, resembling the picture unit ii.93–94. The verb of the first sentence is one of decision, not action: "Euarchus . . . persuaded" (Εὔαρχος . . . πείθει) in ii.33 and "[the Athenian commanders] thought" (ἐδόκει αὐτοῖς) in iv.75.[23]

The most basic difference between the 9 list units with formular military beginnings and the developed military units of the picture type, however, does not lie in their first sentences but in the behavior of element 3 of the outline. In the picture units, even in the two most complicated examples of ii.93–94 and iii.18, the setting of the activity remains the same. In the list units, the actors move from place to place, and the end sentence is less likely to complete the activity and sum it up. In 7 of the 14 list units the end sentence acknowledges termination of the series described.[24] The list structure, linear and lacking the extensive interpretive detail found in more developed picture units, tends to appear rather perfunctory.

The elements of the list unit nonetheless have an interpretive impact on the reader. In half of the 14 units Thucydides passes over some details that he seems to know and to have thought not important enough for inclusion: "They damaged some places" (ἄλλα . . . ἐκάκουν, ii.25.1), "Landing at some places along the coast, he ravaged them" (τῆς τε παραθαλασσίου ἔστιν ἃ ἐδῄωσε, ii.26.2), "some places elsewhere on the Acarnanian coast" (τῆς ἄλλης Ἀκαρνανίας τῆς περὶ θάλασσαν ἔστιν ἃ χωρία, ii.33.2), "the coastal areas" (τὰ ἐπιθαλάσσια χωρία, iii.7), "various [places]" (ἄλλα, iii.19.2), "plundered the coastal area" (τὰ ἐπιθαλάσσια ἔτεμε, iii.91.6), and "some landings" (ἀποβάσεις τινάς, iii.103.3). In iii.90 Thucydides articulates the principle that lies behind such statements: "But what I will mention is what was most notable among the Athenian and allied actions or counteractions against the Athenians" (ἃ δὲ λόγου μάλιστα ἄξια ἢ μετὰ τῶν Ἀθηναίων οἱ ξύμμαχοι ἔπραξαν ἢ πρὸς τοὺς Ἀθηναίους οἱ ἀντιπόλεμοι, τούτων μνησθήσομαι). We certainly would like Thucydides to be more explicit about the judgments underlying this principle than he is, throughout his text. It is clear, however, that just as the picture unit involves a single subject whose elements are deliberately selected for it, so too the list unit is the result of deliberate selection by the author, though it seems more than any other structure in the narrative to be merely a bare account of an expedition of some sort—where a given group of people went next and, very briefly, what they did when they got there.

Three structural subgroups can be distinguished in the list units in books ii.1–v.24. First, in 5 units the list structure occurs at its simplest; almost no interpretive material is added to flesh out the account of the single excursion.[25] The second group is very similar, but more interpretive material is added; 3 units fall under this category.[26] In ii.25, Brasidas's heroism is recounted as well as facts about the terrain in Elis; in iii.90, the Athenian attack on Mylae is described in detail; and in iv.52.2–5 (1 of the 2 nonnaval list units), the plan of the exiles from Mytilene occupies the last half of the unit. Six list units are more developed still.[27] In 5 of these, the list structure is only broken to a certain extent, since one set of actors is not simply being followed from place to place but is joined or supplemented by others. In ii.69, two fleets are actually discussed in turn, one under Phormio of twenty ships, and the other under Melesander with six. This is the only instance where no connection in activity links the two groups. In iii.7 Asopius sends some of his fleet back to Athens, raises an army from Acarnania, and proceeds on his journey; in iii.91 Hipponicus and Eury-medon with an army join Nicias; in iii.115 Pythodorus with a fleet joins the Athenians in Sicily; and in iv.75 the activities of Lamachus are mentioned in the first sentence as well as in the last seven lines of the unit.[28]

However, these 5 units also indicate how fine the line is between the most devel-oped of the 13 list units discussed above and the more numerous extended narrative units that will be discussed below. The list unit remains much more purely linear than the extended narrative unit; the subject of the unit stays the same, and the ac-tivities are told in a simple chronological order. Even the most developed list struc-tures do not contain the abrupt shifts of focus and the inclusion of interpretive ma-terial arranged around successive subjects that we shall see in extended narrative units. Unit v.4–5, the one list unit more than twenty-six lines long, comes the clos-est to including such material. In this unit, the first sentence relates that Phaeax was sent as ambassador from Athens to Sicily and Italy, and between that sentence and the straightforward, listlike account of his voyage occur thirteen lines of background, causal material. Except for this, however, the focus remains single, on Phaeax and his voyage—hence I have included it as a list unit.

Athenians provide the subject of 12 of the 14 list units in books ii.1–v.24; the two exceptions are ii.33 and iv.52.2–5. Quite possibly, list units represent Thucydides' decision about how to treat information about the Athenian navy that was at his dis-posal, of significance as part of the war effort and yet not deserving particular com-ment. One final observation about the distribution of the list unit is also worth not-ing. List units, like the developed picture units described above, tend to cluster in books ii (5 examples) and iii (6 examples). Moreover, the 3 list units that do appear in books iv and v are the most idiosyncratic. Unit v.4–5 is the rather longer unit dis-cussed above, which contains the shifts in time of a causal focus more commonly associated with the developed picture unit. Unit iv.52.2–5 contains a substantial de-scription of Mytilenean motives and depends on a very abbreviated list structure. Finally, iv.75 introduces the third commander of the fleet parenthetically in the first sentence and then returns to him for the focus of the last seven lines of the unit. The standard list structure in books iv and v.1–24 is modified more freely than it is ear-lier in the narrative.

List units provide just under 12% of all the units that make up the narrative of ii.1–v.24. Table 3.3 presents their distribution.

In some ways the list unit is a less subtle form than the picture unit. The general effect of the list unit is less like that of the developed picture unit comparable to it in

TABLE 3.3   List Units, ii.1–v.24

(number of units and percentage of units in each book)

	Book ii	*Book iii*	*Books iv–v.24*
List units	5 (14%)	6 (17%)	3 (6%)
Total units	35	35	49
Pages occupied by list units (percentage of total pages occupied by such units)	2.3 (3%)	3.3 (5%)	2.3 (2%)

length than it is like that of the simple picture unit, seven lines long or less. Like simple picture units, list units give enough information to tell the reader who is doing the action, and where. But frequently the bald series of actions holds little interpretive interest of its own. Its relative rarity in the text of ii.1–v.24 indicates its subordinate and accessory role in shaping the structure of the Archidamian narrative.

3.4 EXTENDED NARRATIVE UNITS (ii.1–v.24)

ii.2-6, ii.7-9, ii.18-23, ii.47.3-54, ii.55-56, ii.67, ii.80-82, iii.2-6, iii.33.2-35, iii.70-85, iii.94-98, iii.100-102, iii.105-114, iv.2.2-5, iv.24-25, iv.26-41, iv.42-45, iv.53-57, iv.66-74, iv.78-83, iv.102-108, iv.109.1-116, iv.120-122, v.2-3.4. Total: 24

To summarize briefly what we have seen so far: most of the three unit types already examined are less than a page in length. Their basic structures, however, are different. Simple picture units involve a single subject set out in seven lines or less. The developed picture unit contains within it interpretive material that explains the significance of the subject matter: it may refer to the past, in exploring the causes for the present action, or to the future, in analyzing the motives of the actors, what they hope to gain from the action; sometimes it is vivid present-oriented description. As figure 3.1 above suggests,[29] there is a large variety of possible arrangements of such material within the unit, and the shifts both in time and in viewpoint can give the more developed picture units a depth of interpretation that is extraordinary, given the number of lines involved.[30] List units are less static, but less analytic as well. Here the focus is not on a single action, but on a series of activities. The change in setting is accompanied by a simplicity of perspective; the shifting viewpoint of the developed picture unit is replaced by a straightforward focus upon a single group, usually a fleet, which is followed from place to place. Although these shorter units comprise 60% of the number of units in the narrative of the Archidamian War, they provide only 15% of the text in terms of its length.

The remaining two categories of units are generally over fifty lines long. Although there are many fewer of them, they comprise 85% of the narrative text of books ii.1–v.24. These are the most developed units of the Archidamian narrative. I have (somewhat prosaically, given their intensity and historiographical interest) called them here extended narrative units and complex units. Since extended narrative units are the simpler of the two in terms of their structural elements (although not in the resulting variety of possible arrangements), I will discuss them first.

The extended narrative unit combines elements of each of the two shorter structures to form a continuous narrative several pages in length. The shifting point of view and descriptive intensity of the picture unit are added to the progressive, linear series of actions of the list unit. Extended narrative units are found in every year of the narrative of the Archidamian War; one example occurs in years three, four, nine, and ten; two in year five; three in years one, two, and six; four examples in year seven; and five in year eight.

Extended narrative units resemble developed picture units in that they always focus upon some aspect of the war itself, but they are more difficult to define as purely military or political in subject. Where the developed picture unit shows a topical unity around which all the interpretive material is arranged, the extended narrative unit shows instead a series of interlocking but distinctive foci. One of the two very shortest extended narrative units demonstrates the differences in kind between this structural type and the simpler arrangements discussed above. Unit ii.67 is only thirty-three lines long; the actions described are almost exactly comparable to those of the developed picture unit iv.50. Both units concern the Athenian capture and disposal of a hostile embassy attempting to establish communication between the king of Persia and the Peloponnesians. In each case the embassy is captured in the north by the Athenians and brought to Athens, and the political problem created by the capture is resolved.

In iv.50 (the developed picture unit), the first sentence introduces the Athenians: "In the following winter, Aristides son of Archippus, one of the commanders . . . arrested Artaphernes, a Persian, at Eion on the Strymon when he was on his way from the king to Lacedaemon" (τοῦ δ' ἐπιγιγνομένου χειμῶνος Ἀριστείδης ὁ Ἀρχίππου, εἷς . . . στρατηγὸς . . . Ἀρταφέρνην ἄνδρα Πέρσην παρὰ βασιλέως πορευόμενον ἐς Λακεδαίμονα ξυλλαμβάνει ἐν Ἠιόνι τῇ ἐπὶ Στρυμόνι). The focus remains on Athenian activity for the duration of the unit. The Athenians translate the letter, decide what to do about it, and send a delegation themselves, which turns out to be fruitless. The emphasis is on a single event, the Athenian capture of the Persian and their resolution of the situation.

In the extended narrative unit ii.67, however, the actors of the first sentence are Peloponnesian. A Peloponnesian embassy is introduced and its motives are described:

> And at the end of that same summer, Aristeus the Corinthian, the Lacedae-
> monian envoys Anaristus, Nicolaus, and Pratodamus, the Tegean Timagoras,
> and in a private capacity the Argive Pollis, who were making the crossing
> to see the king in Asia in case they could persuade him to provide money and
> join them in the war, first came to Sitalces son of Teres in Thrace, wishing to
> persuade him, if possible, to abandon his alliance with the Athenians and go
> on a campaign to Potidaea, where there was a besieging Athenian army, and
> as their most urgent priority to cross the Hellespont with his help to Pharnaces
> son of Pharnabazus, who was to send them on to the king.

> καὶ τοῦ αὐτοῦ θέρους τελευτῶντος Ἀριστεὺς Κορίνθιος καὶ Λακεδαιμο-
> νίων πρέσβεις Ἀνήριστος καὶ Νικόλαος καὶ Πρατόδαμος καὶ Τεγεάτης
> Τιμαγόρας καὶ Ἀργεῖος ἰδίᾳ Πόλλις, πορευόμενοι ἐς τὴν Ἀσίαν ὡς βα-
> σιλέα, εἴ πως πείσειαν αὐτὸν χρήματά τε παρασχεῖν καὶ ξυμπολεμεῖν,
> ἀφικνοῦνται ὡς Σιτάλκην πρῶτον τὸν Τήρεω ἐς Θρᾴκην, βουλόμενοι πεῖ-
> σαί τε αὐτόν, εἰ δύναιντο, μεταστάντα τῆς Ἀθηναίων ξυμμαχίας στρα-
> τεῦσαι ἐπὶ τὴν Ποτείδαιαν, οὗ ἦν στράτευμα τῶν Ἀθηναίων πολιορκοῦν,
> καὶ ἧπερ ὥρμηντο, δι᾽ ἐκείνου πορευθῆναι πέραν τοῦ Ἑλλησπόντου ὡς
> Φαρνάκην τὸν Φαρναβάζου, ὃς αὐτοὺς ἔμελλεν ὡς βασιλέα ἀναπέμψειν.

Only after this lengthy first sentence does the focus of ii.67 shift to the Athenians: "The Athenian envoys Learchus son of Callimachus and Ameiniades son of Phile-mon happened to be with Sitalces and persuaded Sitalces' son Sadocus, the one who had become an Athenian, to deliver the men into their power" (παρατυχόντες δὲ Ἀθηναίων πρέσβεις Λέαρχος Καλλιμάχου καὶ Ἀμεινιάδης Φιλήμονος παρὰ τῷ Σιτάλκῃ πείθουσι τὸν Σάδοκον τὸν γεγενημένον Ἀθηναῖον, Σιτάλκου υἱόν, τοὺς ἄνδρας ἐγχειρίσαι σφίσιν).

This sentence is virtually the point in the action where iv.50, the picture unit, be-gins. But in ii.67, when the Athenians do finally enter the picture, they do so in a context of an already elaborated, complex set of political factors in Thrace. The fact that Sitalces' son had been made an Athenian citizen is presented as a major el-ement in the capture of the embassy. The shift to Athens itself is rather complicated, and causal motivations for the Athenian political decision to kill the prisoners are given. Moreover, the final sentence of ii.67 does not merely close off the activity at hand, as it does in iv.50. Instead, it gives a final shift in setting and one that broadens the subject of the unit once more, to include Peloponnesian political decisions too: "For at the beginning of the war, the Lacedaemonians had indeed killed as enemies all whom they caught at sea, both those allied with the Athenians and those belonging to neither side" (πάντας γὰρ δὴ κατ' ἀρχὰς τοῦ πολέμου Λακεδαιμόνιοι ὅσους λάβοιεν ἐν τῇ θαλάσσῃ ὡς πολεμίους διέφθειρον, καὶ τοὺς μετὰ Ἀθηναίων ξυμπολεμοῦντας καὶ τοὺς μηδὲ μεθ' ἑτέρων).

In other words, where the picture unit of iv.50 focuses on a single event, the extended narrative unit of ii.67 considers first the Peloponnesian embassy in isolation, then the Athenian ambassadors, then the political situation in Thrace and Sadocus's activities, the removal of the prisoners to Athens, their death without trial, and finally the behavior of the Lacedaemonians toward those captured at sea. The two units are not entirely dissimilar; clearly the narrative structure of ii.67 is more closely related in form to a developed picture structure than it is to a list structure. But the amount of complicated background and causal material contained lifts it to a new level of organization.

The wide variety of different possibilities of narrative development means that extended narrative units can differ greatly from one another in their varieties of structure. If the internal distribution of material in ii.67 were outlined, it would bear little resemblance to those extended narrative units that are almost completely listlike in structure, like iv.24–25 (Messina, the sea battle). Each of the 24 extended narrative units, in fact, exploits different possibilities of arrangement and distribution of material that are inherent in the type. The interest of this fourth structural category does not lie in the fact that narrative techniques from the list and picture types are combined, but rather in the variety of ways in which combination occurs, creating a new and idiosyncratic shape for each extended narrative unit. Although they are constructed from the same elements, similarity of structure does not define them, as it does the picture unit with its focus on a single event or the list unit with its continuity of actors followed through a sequence of activities; their shifting foci and variegated internal structures make these extended narrative units more challenging to interpret. The identity of an extended narrative unit is defined more by its thematic coherence than by observable regularities in its formal structure.

The thematic coherence is visible even in a rather short extended narrative unit like ii.67. In contrast to the picture unit iv.50, where the focus remains on the limited problem of the embassy itself, the shifting foci of ii.67, and especially its final sentence, draw our attention as readers not only to the fate of Aristeus but also to the international breakdown of trust and fair dealings, which Peloponnesians and

Athenians alike exacerbate. This developed sense of the unit's interpretive significance is sometimes (as in the discussion of Corcyra, iii.70-85) more explicit; it is sometimes (as in iv.24-25, where only the final sentence suggests it) much less. But as a facet of the longer narrative unit, the development of a relatively complex theme arising out of the idiosyncratic combination of the unit's individual narrative parts is an important addition to the range of interpretive possibilities offered in the simpler list and picture units.

Because the body of the extended narrative unit represents a longer and more complex presentation of events than that of either the list or the picture type, it is all the more necessary to continue to emphasize the aspect of the extended narrative unit whose similarity to the two simpler unit types is very striking: the introductory sentence. In all 24 extended narrative units, the initial sentence of the unit is formed on one of the patterns discussed in chapter 2.

Eighteen of the 24 extended narrative units in the Archidamian narrative, although in the development of the unit they may leave the military sphere, begin with one of the military introductory formulae.[31] They involve a general verb of military activity in the first sentence (11 examples) or the military action is introduced abruptly (4 examples) or they present a previous stage of deliberation before introducing the specific military action (3 examples).[32] We have seen introductory sentences of these kinds already in picture and list units with military subjects; they are neither unusual nor particularly ambitious. It is what Thucydides will do in the body of the extended narrative unit that distinguishes it from units of the three simpler types.

Of the 6 extended narrative units that do not begin with a sentence concerning military activity, 3 are political in subject: iii.2-6 is introduced by "Lesbos . . . revolted" ($\Lambda\acute{\epsilon}\sigma\beta os$ . . . $\dot{a}\pi\acute{\epsilon}\sigma\tau\eta$), iii.70 by "The Corcyraeans were in civil war" (oi . . . $K\epsilon\rho\kappa\upsilon\rho a\hat{\iota}o\iota$ $\dot{\epsilon}\sigma\tau a\sigma\acute{\iota}a\zeta o\nu$), and iv.120 by "Scione . . . revolted" ($\Sigma\kappa\iota\acute{\omega}\nu\eta$ . . . $\dot{a}\pi\acute{\epsilon}\sigma\tau\eta$). As in the majority of the military units, here too the introductory verb is again general and preparatory. One might also call ii.67 political in its introductory focus, though the verb does not generalize but in a neutral fashion (again as in some of the general military formulae) brings forward the Peloponnesian embassy: $\dot{a}\phi\iota\kappa\nu o\hat{\upsilon}\nu\tau a\iota$. One of the two remaining introductory sentences, ii.47.3, follows the same pattern. It links back to the previous unit, concerning the invasion: "And when [the Peloponnesians] had not yet stayed many days in Attica, the plague first began to occur in Athens" ($\kappa a\grave{\iota}$ $\check{o}\nu\tau\omega\nu$ $a\dot{\upsilon}\tau\hat{\omega}\nu$ $o\dot{\upsilon}$ $\pi o\lambda\lambda\acute{a}s$ $\pi\omega$ $\dot{\eta}\mu\acute{\epsilon}\rho as$ $\dot{\epsilon}\nu$ $\tau\hat{\eta}$ $A\tau\tau\iota\kappa\hat{\eta}$ $\dot{\eta}$ $\nu\acute{o}\sigma os$ $\pi\rho\hat{\omega}\tau o\nu$ $\check{\eta}\rho\xi a\tau o$ $\gamma\epsilon\nu\acute{\epsilon}\sigma\theta a\iota$). The other, ii.7, uses an imperfect to throw us into the midst of the activity, rather like the military units introduced in summary fashion: "After the action at Plataea occurred, flagrantly breaking the truce, the Athenians were making their preparations to go to war" (γεγενημένου δὲ τοῦ ἐν Πλαταιαῖς ἔργου καὶ λελυμένων λαμπρῶς τῶν σπονδῶν οἱ Ἀθηναῖοι παρεσκευάζοντο ὡς πολεμήσοντες).

Thus two-thirds of the extended narrative units in the text of ii.1–v.24 begin with one of the introductory patterns common to military list and picture units; the remaining 6, while not military in subject, also contain standard introductory formulae. Thucydides does not seek in the first sentence of the extended narrative unit to emphasize the unit's importance or its difference in kind from simpler narrative types. As the earlier contrast drawn between iv.50 and ii.67 made clear, the body of the extended narrative unit presents a very different impression from that of the developed picture unit, even when both concern Peloponnesian connections with Persia.[33] The complexity of the extended narrative unit's various structural combinations enables it to play a quite different interpretive role in the *History* from that of either the list or the picture units.[34]

Although the varieties of structural combination possible to this fourth, extended unit type are very numerous, the 24 extended narrative units in the narrative of the Archidamian War can be divided into three major subordinate patterns. The first, and in some ways the most intriguing, is also the rarest. In two cases, ii.7-9 and ii.47.3-54, the material of the unit is more like that of a picture unit than that of a list unit; that is, it is almost completely descriptive and analytic rather than narrative and chronological. Unit ii.7-9 shows the preparation of Athenian and Peloponnesian forces in anticipation of the war; ii.47.3-54 describes and analyzes the plague. The introductory sentence in each case does not just indicate the general direction the unit is to take but rather states its entire topic, like the first sentence of picture units. Only the large themes arising out of shifts of focus and setting within these units distinguish them, in fact, from picture units of a descriptive kind. Precisely the same two topics—preparation for the war and the plague—form the subjects of the two picture units discussed above as particularly static (ii.24 and iii.87.1-3). In no other extended narrative units is the role of analysis and description as extensive as in ii.7-9 and ii.47.3-54, although the more conventional treatment of Corcyra beginning in iii.70 also includes a substantial amount of the same sort of material, as does the description of Brasidas's march in iv.78–83.

The 22 extended narrative structures that remain may be separated into two other types, those in which the elements of list and picture are perfectly blended and form a long narrative of roughly the same degree of detail throughout, and those in which one part of the unit seems to be treated as a list, and another like a picture.

Eight units exhibit a fairly complete blending of list and picture attributes throughout the narrative, so that there is no sudden shift of style within the unit.[35] The subjects of these 8 units, selected solely on the basis of the internal coherence of style, fall into two clear groups in terms of their subject matter: those of major thematic significance to the *History*, and those concerning the campaigns in the northwest undertaken by Cnemus the Lacedaemonian and Demosthenes the Athenian. That is, the subjects of 5 of these 8 "blended" extended narrative units are Plataea, Lesbos, Corcyra, Pylos, and Amphipolis; it would be difficult to think of five other topics of greater weight in the development of the Archidamian War as Thucydides presents it.[36] But it is striking that military exploits in the regions of Acarnania, Aetolia, and Amphilochia in books ii and iii, and those alone, are treated in the same degree of narrative elaboration.[37]

The other 14 extended narrative units are neither purely analytic in form nor a perfect combination of linear progression and interpretive material spread evenly throughout the unit.[38] Sudden shifts of tone occur instead within the unit, so that one part of it is treated quite differently from another. Three of these units are almost completely like pictures in structure (ii.67, iv.66–74, and iv.120–122); one (iv.24–25) is almost completely a list. The others represent either a picture followed by a list (ii.19–23, ii.55–56, iv.42–45, and iv.53–57) or a list followed by a more developed picture (iii.33.2–35, iii.94–98, iv.2.2–5, iv.53–57, iv.109.1–116, and v.2.3–4). For instance, in iv.42–45 the Athenian campaign against Corinth is related in a long expanded picture (42–44), but chapter 45 adds onto this narrative a listlike naval excursion that begins where the picture part ends, with the Athenian fleet on the islands lying off the Corinthian coast. In iii.94–98, on the other hand, the list aspect precedes a picture. Chapter 94 begins with a rather abrupt account of towns attacked by the Athenian fleet in Leucadian territory, but it is further Athenian activity in Aetolia that receives the real attention in the unit, with multiple shifts of focus from Demosthenes to the Messenians to the Aetolians and back. The weight of the unit does not lie in its introduction but in its conclusion.

The fact that Thucydides uses long narrative units whose various parts are unequally developed is important. These passages are clearly units in the sense in which units are defined in this study, since an introductory sentence and general thematic coherence mark each of them off, just as they do for the simpler units of the list and picture type. If this is the case, however, it suggests that the degree and kind of interpretive detail added to the various parts of the individual unit are frequently one means adopted by Thucydides to indicate where the significance of the unit lies; they are not a sign of authorial inadequacy or incomplete or partial revision.[39] Thus in iii.94-98, the action in Leucas is demonstrably of less significance, since Demosthenes in iii.95 decides against its continuation; Thucydides has already indicated as much by the brevity and listlike description of the events given in iii.94.[40] On the other hand, only a perverse interpretation of iv.42-45 would claim that the landing in Epidaurus or Methana narrated at the end of the unit holds the same weight as the previously narrated Corinthian campaign. Extended narrative units of the most developed and completely integrated sort do represent actions of importance in the *History;* in the less evenly developed extended narrative units, brevity and a listlike appearance alternate with highly polished passages as one of the means adopted by Thucydides to emphasize which parts of the unit are more important in their own right, and which serve rather as background information of some sort or act as links to further activity elsewhere in the narrative.

Extended narrative units provide 20% of the units in the narrative of the Archidamian War, but they occupy 34% of the pages in the text. As the narration progresses, they are used more frequently by Thucydides, in contrast to list units, which are used much less frequently in books iv–v.24. Table 3.4 presents the distribution of extended narrative units in more detail.

To summarize: extended narrative units provide the most developed unbroken narrative stretches in books ii.1–v.24 of the *History.* The greater number of narrative techniques available in this longer unit type gives them a remarkable variety in appearance; some resemble fairly closely either the pure list or pure picture type, while others represent a combination of the two types. The shifts of focus and linear motion mean that significance is no longer a matter of a single action or a single progression; large themes rather develop out of the multiple shifts of focus and linear motion within the unit.[41]

Like developed picture units, extended narrative units cannot be narrowly defined in subject as either military or political. The events considered almost always have implications in both spheres. In over two-thirds of the extended narrative units in the text of the Archidamian War, however, the introductory sentence resembles the one often used in military units of the list or picture type. This indicates once more the extensive correspondences between Thucydides' simple and elaborate structures. He does not abandon his more primitive forms but instead builds on them.

As the narrative of books ii.1–v.24 progresses, extended narrative units become more numerous and represent a substantially greater proportion of the text. Again, this observation does not constitute an argument for a particular theory of how Thucydies wrote or rewrote his text. He could have gone back to revise and elaborate the more elaborately constructed extended narrative units, seeing their impor-

TABLE 3.4   Extended Narrative Units, ii.1–v.24

(number of units and percentage of units in each book)

	Book ii	*Book iii*	*Books iv–v.24*
Extended narrative units	7 (20%)	6 (17%)	11 (23%)
Total units	35	35	49
Pages occupied by extended narrative units (percentage of total pages occupied by such units)	19 (26%)	23.3 (33%)	40.7 (40%)

tance in hindsight. On the other hand, it is possible that they too were often written ἐξῆς ὡς ἕκαστα ἐγίγνετο (ii.1), and that, as the Archidamian War continued and Thucydides continued to write it up, events of major importance for the course of the war were happening whose details and implications Thucydides wished to portray at greater length than the list or picture unit would permit.[42]

3.5 COMPLEX UNITS (ii.1–v.24)

ii.10-12, ii.13-17, ii.29, ii.34-47.1, ii.59-65, ii.68, ii.71-78, ii.83-92, ii.95-101, ii.102-103, iii.8-16, iii.29-33.1, iii.36-50, iii.52-68, iii.104, iv.8-23, iv.58-65, iv.84-88, iv.89-101.4, iv.117-119, iv.124-132, v.6-11, v.14-20.1, v.21-24. Total: 24

The four unit types examined thus far involve unbroken narrative stretches whose actions develop out of the first sentence of the unit. I have called the fifth and final type of narrative unit complex because in it a more elaborate relation is established between the unit's introduction, body, and conclusion. The complex unit begins as a typical picture, list, or extended narrative structure, but, in the course of the narration, a new subject matter is abruptly introduced in an excursus. At its end, the earlier discussion resumes, so that the complex unit as a whole forms an *a-b-a* structure.

The two elements that form the complex unit are in this discussion called the frame *(a)* and the excursus *(b)*. These terms do not imply a judgment about the relative importance of the *a* and *b* material but merely describe their respective positions in the structure. In some instances the frame provides the more significant material for the larger thematic development of the *History,* while the excursus adds emphasis and detail, as in v.6–11, concerning the battle at Amphipolis and Brasidas's speech there. In other units the frame merely provides a setting while the excursus conveys the point of the unit, as in ii.34–47.1, the account of the funeral oration at Athens at the end of the first year of the war.

The frame, the element that always begins and ends a complex unit, is a narrative formed on one of the four patterns described above. It always concerns an event of the appropriate season and year, and it is introduced with one of the temporal formulae and introductory sentence patterns already discussed. The framing part of complex units is much more likely to be of the picture or extended narrative type than of the list type. Twelve complex units have frames like picture units; 10 complex units have extended narrative frames; only 2 have listlike frames.[43]

Several different sorts of excursus interrupt the framing part of the complex unit. In 18 of the 24 complex units the abrupt break in the narrative flow emphasizes form rather than content; a speech or quoted document is inserted.[44] Not all speeches summarized in the *History* create complex units, since many speeches are reported in an indirect discourse that does not break the flow of the narrative. It is the change in voice and tense that sets these 18 speeches and documents off from the surrounding narrative and makes the units in which they appear distinctive in their *a-b-a* pattern. In the other 6 complex units, all in books ii and iii, the subject matter of the excursus marks it as different from the surrounding narrative; it consists of antiquarian or geographical material only tangentially related to the matters of the year at hand.[45] Documents, speeches, and antiquarian paragraphs are very different kinds of material from one another, but Thucydides sets them all into the surrounding narrative in the same way, by the use of a complex unit of action.

The framing material is not the only structural constant. There occurs in every complex unit, either at the end of the excursus or at the end of the unit itself, a demonstrative (usually τοιαῦτα, or τοσαῦτα) that additionally emphasizes the unit's *a-b-a* structure. In 2 units containing an antiquarian excursus (ii.102-103 and iii.104), and 14 of the 15 units whose excursus is a speech, the demonstrative occurs just after the excursus, as in iii.29-33.1: "He did not persuade Alcidas with this short speech" (ὁ μὲν τοσαῦτα εἰπὼν οὐκ ἔπειθε τὸν Ἀλκίδαν, iii.31.1). A demonstrative ends the whole unit in the case of 1 speech (the funeral oration, ii.34-47.1), 4 units containing historical excursuses, all 3 units containing documents, and several units whose speech or speeches have already been set off by a τοιαῦτα.[46] The one complex unit not set off in either of these patterns is ii.68, containing the historical excursus on Ambracia, Amphilochia, and Argos. It concludes the account of a summer, so a demonstrative falls at the end of the unit here too: "All this took place during the summer" (τοσαῦτα μὲν ἐν τῷ θέρει ἐγένετο).[47] Of course, Thucydides does not use demonstratives to emphasize only the completion of complex units. Several long extended narrative units, like iii.105–114, finish in the same way. But the consistency with which the end formula is found in the unit containing an excursus suggests that Thucydides deliberately utilized it to emphasize the complex unit's formal *a-b-a* structure.

In their subject matter, the 24 complex units that occur in books ii.1–v.24 contain excursuses of four different kinds: military speeches, political speeches, epideictic excursuses that still concern the war, and epideictic excursuses only tangentially relevant to the events of the immediate frame material. The relation between frame and excursus is quite varied, but in every case the "foreign" material is embedded in an *a-b-a* structure and is emphasized at its conclusion by a demonstrative in an emphatic sentence.

Eight complex units are directed toward a military focus. In 7 of them, there are one or more military speeches, spoken by a commander before a battle and identifying the tactics and morale of one of the opposing forces. Unit ii.95-101 also belongs to this group; the action of the frame concerns Sitalces' muster and his great march. The excursus, though it resembles a *periplus*, is relevant to the frame in revealing the military might of the Thracian king, and the extent to which the Athenians miscalculated in strategy, when they failed to meet him.[48]

Of these 8 units, 1 (ii.10-12) begins and ends with a picturelike frame, another (iii.29-33.1) with a list. The other 6 frames consist of detailed extended narrative accounts in which the commanders' speeches serve to analyze some of the elements present. In 3 cases (ii.83-92, iv.8-23, iv.89-101.4) paired speeches are given, and the reader is thereby allowed to evaluate the respective acuteness and more general intellectual characteristics of the two leaders; in each of these pairs, one of the speeches is given by an Athenian. In the 4 units where only one military speech occurs (ii.10-12, iii.29-33.1, iv.124-132, and v.6-11), the commanders are the Spartan Archidamus, the Elean Teutiaplus, and (in 2 instances) the Spartan Brasidas. Thucydides uses the speech of military command in the narrative of the Archidamian War as one important means of conveying non-Athenian tactics and morale.

Seven complex units contain speeches that are political rather than military. Like the military units, they are spread fairly evenly through the Archidamian narrative. Of the 3 complex units with paired political speeches, 2 concern the fate of Plataea. Unit ii.71-78 contains a fourfold series of responses among the Plataeans, Archidamus, the Athenians, and Archidamus again; iii.52-68 depicts the debate between two Plataeans and the unnamed Thebans before Spartan judges. In each of these units, the speeches, though political, serve the same function as the military speeches above: they highlight certain aspects of the immediately surrounding unit. In the other political unit with paired speeches, however, the excursus has a different function. In unit iii.36-50, the immediately surrounding frame is not rendered more vivid or more significant; instead, contrasting aspects of Athenian theory about how to rule subject states are explored.[49] Units ii.59-65 (Pericles' last speech), iii.8-16 (the Mytileneans' plea at Olympia), iv.58-65 (Hermocrates' speech at Gela), and iv.84-88 (Brasidas's persuasion of the Acanthians) may be best understood in the same light. They are 4 politically oriented complex units, each of which contains a single speech illuminating not only the immediate frame that surrounds them, but also the larger issues of the war.[50]

While the complex units containing military speeches are themselves substantial pieces of narrative whose details the speeches develop, the politically oriented complex units contain a frame of little significance for its own sake, one that serves chiefly to set the stage for the more broadly significant excursus. Thus a relatively greater proportion of politically oriented complex units have a simple frame. Three units (ii.59-65, ii.71-78, iv.58-65) have a frame structured like an extended narrative unit, while the other 4 (iii.8-16, iii.36-50, iii.52-68, iv.84–88) are instead supported by a picture unit developed in just enough detail to introduce the excursus. Except in the Plataean episode, even the extended narrative frames are rather sketchily developed. Unit ii.59-65, Pericles' last speech, narrates a quite simple activity supplemented by a speech in indirect discourse and a concluding passage of analysis, while iv.58-65, the meeting of the Sicilian states, would certainly be thought to have a picturelike frame, except for the sudden change of focus at the end of the unit to the Athenian commanders exiled for their acceptance of the meeting's results.

In their immediate setting, all the speeches, military and political alike, aim toward an event still in the future. This invests the 14 complex units containing speeches with a certain narrative tension, resolved almost immediately in the military units but sometimes not resolved at all in the political ones.[51] Both these categories of complex units might be called deliberative, to the extent that they contain this forward-looking element. The two categories that remain to be discussed are, in contrast, epideictic in their nature. The frame of the unit is fashioned to display the excursus; the excursus itself does not point to a resolution of events still in the future.

The epideictic excursus still relates to the war at hand in 4 units: ii.34–47.1 (the funeral oration) and iv.117–119, v.14–20.1, and v.21–24 (the 3 units containing documents). The cease-fire, the truce, and the agreement between Athens and Sparta at the end of book iv and the beginning of book v are of course not as moving to the reader as the funeral oration. But structurally they serve a similar function. As E. Meyer has shown, they cannot easily be abstracted from their place in the text.[52]

Like Pericles' great speech, they make clear the elements of a situation at a certain moment. The three documents capture the precise balance of power in existence at the time of their writing; Pericles' speech captures the spirit and beliefs of the Athenians at the end of the first year of war.[53] Unit v.14–20.1 contains framing material extensive enough to be considered extended narrative in type; the other three are all framed by brief picture structures.

A final set of complex units also contains excursuses that are epideictic in function. The aspect of pure display is, in fact, even stronger than in the third type discussed above, since in ii.13–17, ii.29, ii.68, ii.102–103, and iii.104 the material contained in the excursus is not directly relevant to the war at all.[54] Unit ii.13–17 discusses the history of synoecism in Attica as an excursus within a picturelike description of Athenian preparations for the war. The excursus is not irrelevant; the fact that since Theseus's time the Athenians had been accustomed to a certain relation between city and country helps to highlight the distress felt as people poured into the city from the country. But more straightforward indications could have been found, and indeed occur within the same unit, in the vivid description of the crowding in Athens as well as in the description of the plague to come.

Often the material in the excursus must have seemed to Thucydides to be interesting for its own sake; this is even more apparent in the other historical and geographical excursuses. The difference between Teres and Tereus holds little relevance for the fact that Sitalces became an Athenian ally; the same could be said of much of the discussion of geography and mythology in ii.102–103 and iii.104. This last example contains a listlike frame; all the others have frames that resemble picture units. It is perhaps of significance that all these units occur in books ii and iii; Thucydides did not entirely lose his interest in antiquarian material, but later in the text he expresses it differently.[55]

Complex units account for 20% of all the Archidamian units, but they involve 50% of the text of ii.1–v.24 (see table 3.5).[56]

In sum, Thucydides uses an *a-b-a* structure to depict material of widely varying degrees of significance for the account of the war. In some complex units, the frame provides the major focus, and the excursus embellishes it; in some, the frame is very scanty and subordinate to the excursus within it. It is once more a sign of Thucydides' economy of method that one structure is used to convey an enormous range of material with varying degrees of interconnection and significance.

A complex narrative structure recounts but also interprets the events surrounding the excursus. In 9 units, the material in the excursus is almost purely epideictic

TABLE 3.5   Complex units, ii.1–v.24

(number of units and percentage of units in each book)

	Book ii	Book iii	Books iv–v.24
Complex units	10 (28%)	5 (14%)	9 (18%)
Total units	35	35	49
Pages occupied by complex units (percentage of total pages occupied by such units)	43.4 (60%)	30.8 (44%)	49.1 (48%)

and forms a static picture of more general import. Four of these units are directly concerned with the war; 5 seem superficially almost without relation to it. In all 9, the *a-b-a* structure provides a contrast to the continuous flow of activity represented in the surrounding narrative. In the remaining 15 complex units, the complex structure heightens the tension of the immediate account. Both units that contain military speeches and those with political speeches look forward, during the excursus itself, to a possible resolution of the factors presented there. The military speeches look less far ahead than the political ones; in almost all cases the military speech principally supplements an immediate extended narrative frame, and the resolution to the issues the speech raises is presented in the final *a* element of the unit. On the other hand, the frame of a political unit is often merely a picture, a bald description of the conference, congress, or assembly at which the speech was given. The issues discussed in the speech are relevant to the war as a whole and not just to the immediate frame.

This concludes the structural study of the five types of units of action. Short units fall into either the simple picture, developed picture, or list category, while with a very few exceptions long units follow either the extended narrative or complex *a-b-a* type. These categories will be important in the remainder of this study as a tool for discovering more exactly how Thucydides' narrative is put together and changes as the war continues. Chapter 4 will consider the way the 119 units of the Archidamian narrative combine to form year-long clusters, as well as the way in which large themes are developed over the course of several years, created from various combinations of unit types. Chapters 5 and 6 will sketch how the unit of action disappears eventually into a larger, more integrated and hypotactic narrative organization.

Throughout the narrative of ii.1–v.24, the units of action we have considered here remain the basic building blocks of Thucydides' narrative. They provide the foundation that underlies Thucydides' summer-winter scheme, and remind us of the extent to which he is a chronicler as well as a historian. The repetitive pattern established by first sentences sets each unit within the larger framework of the year. While this is not exact, as a calendar date would be, it helpfully establishes a rough relative chronology for the events of the season.[57]

Although the five types are distinct, their formation does not involve radically different elements, but rather simple elements combined in different ways. What principally defines the different unit types is the different relationship established between the introductory sentence and the body of the unit. The introductory sentence of the picture unit provides the entire topic of the unit, while in the list unit it supplies the subject of the unit but not the action, which proceeds chronologically from the point introduced by the verb in the first sentence. The extended narrative unit's introductory sentence is not in any complete sense the subject of the entire unit; it sets in motion an ongoing account and provides the first of several major foci that will be formed. Finally, in the relation of the first sentence to the body of the unit, the complex unit makes use of all of the other patterns, depending on whether the frame material is of the picture, developed picture, list, or extended narrative type.

Changes occur in Thucydides' choice of structure as the narration of the Archidamian War proceeds that may now be examined as various facets of a single phenomenon. In brief, Thucydides tends toward the end of the Archidamian narrative to use both more specific and more complicated structures. Picture units of the developed type and list units decrease in number in books iv–v.24. The functions that they played in books ii and iii are increasingly performed by simple picture units, those seven lines long or less; these show an increase in number. But this is only a subordinate facet of the more important development: the most elaborate continuous narrative forms, the extended narrative units, show a steady rise in importance. They become both longer and more numerous in the later narrative of the Archidamian War.

Some interpretation is required to reveal the significance of the corresponding changes in complex units. At first sight, the figures seem to show a decrease in their use over the course of the narrative, a trend not consistent with the general development mentioned above. But the high figures for complex units in book ii include 5 of the 6 that are purely epideictic, including an antiquarian excursus only tangentially related to the issues of the war. The decrease in this type later in the narrative is actually another aspect of the general development toward more unified,

TABLE 3.6   Proportions of all units, ii.1–v.24

Picture units	Book ii	Book iii	Books iv–v.24	% of ii.1–v.24
% of units	37	51	53	48
% of pages	11	17	9	12
List units				
% of units	14	17	6	12
% of pages	3	5	2	3
Extended narrative units				
% of units	20	17	23	20
% of pages	26	33	40	34
Complex units				
% of units	28	14	18	20
% of pages	60	44	48	50
Total units	35	35	49	119
Total pages	72.5	70.3	101.5	244.3

longer narratives and away from static, relatively simple patterns. Moreover, whereas 73% of the complex units in books ii and iii have a frame of either the list or the picture type, this proportion in books iv–v.24 falls to 33%. In the later narrative, two-thirds of the complex units have extended narrative frames. Again, there is a clear trend toward longer, more continuous narrative structures. The figures supporting these observations are summarized in table 3.6.

As the narrative of the Archidamian War continues, Thucydides relies less on units a third of a page or so in length, either of the developed picture type or of the list type. Instead, he tends either to use the very long extended narrative units or complex units, or to use the bald statement of fact seven lines long or less. That this development occurs is not in one sense surprising; naturally enough the events that come later in the war will be related in more complicated combinations, and will require more interpretation as well, if they are at all important. But it is also possible that Thucydides' prose habits, and his sense of historical causality too, change as the war continues. Events that in the early narrative are expressed in discrete short paragraphs are increasingly integrated instead into the context of larger developments. The discrete paragraph, represented by the list and developed picture unit, no longer plays as substantial a role in the narrative; in fact, it virtually disappears as an independent unit of action.

A second point must supplement this observation, however. It is not so much the fact of the shift from short units to long ones that encourages us to think in terms of a developing narrative style as it is the quality of the change. Examination of the extended narrative units in the Archidamian War has shown that for Thucydides, within the confines of a single and unified narrative, the choice of a more or less detailed account of a certain activity is an interpretive tool, and not a sign that the narrative is incompletely revised. In over half of the extended narrative units, one part is developed to a greater extent than others, and thus becomes the central focus of the narrative. In other words, brief narrative "paragraphs" are used throughout books ii–v.24 of the *History* to convey information that is useful but not of special significance. Later in the narrative, however, these short paragraphs tend to be integrated into a longer extended narrative unit, rather than being featured as an independent list or picture account.

One final observation should be made about the five types of narrative unit. A glance at table 3.6 reveals an obvious dichotomy in Thucydides' style: there are more of the shorter, more abrupt units, while the two longer types involve by far the greater proportion of the text. These two facts contribute significantly to the impression made by books ii.1–v.24 as an ongoing ten-year narrative: both the frequent repetition of introductory sentences (provided by the number of short units) and the shifting foci and interruptions for excursuses in the longer types bring to the narrative a sense of radical discontinuity as a fundamental, often-experienced, and therefore ultimately unifying element in the narrative. It also asks the reader in effect repeatedly to readjust his or her focus with the beginning of each new narrative thread, and to engage anew with the specificities of each new narrative unit.

CHAPTER FOUR

Patterns Formed by Units
of Action in the Archidamian
Narrative (ii.1–v.24)

Units of action in ii.1–v.24 fall into certain recurring types, and their first sentences too are distinctively formular. Both kinds of stylistic regularity help give the narrative a coherent, orderly but also highly episodic appearance. The units themselves have so far been treated in this study as discrete segments, arranged sequentially in the text. How does Thucydides also use them to build a larger story that traces out patterns of meaning for the first ten years of the Peloponnesian War?

This question has many different kinds of answer; here I continue to concentrate on structural issues, and in particular on the way that the units of the Archidamian narrative are arranged so that their sequence becomes a way of creating meaning as the *History* continues.[1] I argue that Thucydides intends us to notice and work with these patterns as part of our general skill as readers in interpreting the text. Significant juxtaposition is the first and most obvious kind of patterning he uses: contiguous units reverberate against each other to form sequences larger than those formed by the individual units taken separately. Next come the larger clusters that are defined by the year or last through several years or, finally, are formed over the continuous ten-year narrative regarded as a whole. At the end of this chapter we will consider some of the most general effects created by the overall progression of units of action in books ii.1–v.24.

Underlying these discussions are basic questions we have as readers: Why did Thucydides write the first ten years of his narrative in this way? Or, even more importantly, what historical judgments did he intend to use these specific narrative patterns to convey? The answers offered here continue to be more formal than philosophical. By looking at recurring structural patterns, I emphasize some of the ways in which Thucydides' vivid mosaic of units, large and small, simple or increasingly complex, vivid and expansive or brief and businesslike, form a kaleidoscope of continuously changing plot, argument, description, tempo, and mood. Thucydides demands that as we read we respond to its unrolling and changing shape as history, not as a bald chronicle or a severely annalistic record of events. That is, the ongoing narrative repeatedly reforms itself, as a succession of distinctive units that coalesce into larger patterns that stretch over several years' worth of events. As it does so, it requires that we too continuously reengage, remaining alert both to the distinctive structural patterning of each new narrated event of the war and to the ways that it resonates with other units that come before or after.

4.1 SIGNIFICANT JUXTAPOSITION (ii.1–v.24)

In considering the placement of units in the narrative, simple contiguity comes first, but the degree of significance to be attributed to individual instances of juxtaposition varies greatly. Sometimes Thucydides interrupts what might have been narrated as one long ongoing account with a unit of a quite different sort, making of the whole narrative sequence a larger version of the *a-b-a* pattern we have already seen within the structure of the complex unit.[2] Occasionally this Thucydidean use of a common archaic and Herodotean structuring device seems to provide little more than convenient points of narrative articulation. By inserting a second unit with a quite different content between two units on the same topic, Thucydides carefully distinguishes one discrete stage of an ongoing sequence of activities from the next. Sometimes, however, a pointedly judgmental meaning seems to arise out of the fact of the simple juxtaposition of units each of which has a different focus.[3] Irony seems to be present, which makes interpretation difficult. I am often less sure about the precise meaning of any significant juxtaposition of this type (in the sense of its capacity to make Thucydides' judgment on a particular issue clear) than I am in pointing to its pervasiveness as a feature of Thucydides' arrangement of his narrative units in the Archidamian narrative.[4]

4.1.1 LOOSE NARRATIVE CONTINUITY

Thucydides takes what could have been one continuous narration and breaks it into separate units, each with its own introductory sentence and distinctive structural pattern. The division into discrete units emphasizes different levels of meaning or subtle shifts in focus; for whatever reason, Thucydides chooses to structure several aspects of an ongoing nexus of events as discrete and separate narratives.

4.1.1.a Year One: ii.30, ii.31   A list unit about the Athenian fleet is followed by a picture unit that describes an attack on the Megarid by this fleet and other Athenian forces too. The introductory sentence of ii.31 stresses not the continuity but the new military action: "In autumn of this year, the Athenians invaded the Megarid in full force . . . under the command of Pericles son of Xanthippus" (περὶ δὲ τὸ φθινόπωρον τοῦ θέρους τούτου Ἀθηναῖοι πανδημεὶ . . . ἐσέβαλον ἐς τὴν Μεγαρίδα Περικλέους τοῦ Ξανθίππου στρατηγοῦντος). Probably one reason for the break and new first sentence is given in ii.31.3. Attacks on the Megarid occurred every year until its harbor, Nisaea, was taken in the eighth year.[5] Megara was thus too important a topic to be folded into the unit announcing the activities of the Athenian fleet in ii.30.

4.1.1.b Year Three: ii.83–92, ii.93–94   The naval battle between the Peloponnesian fleet and the Athenians in the Gulf of Corinth is described in a complex unit that is followed directly by a developed picture unit describing a daring attack on the Piraeus by the same Peloponnesian sailors, manning boats from Nisaea, the harbor of Megara. The change of season interrupts the two units, but we are missing an opportunity to think about the meaning of the text if we assume that the onset of winter forced Thucydides to arrange the two units in this kind of loose narrative connection. For one thing, the time formula introducing the second winter unit, ii.95–101 (Sitalces' great march), is "around the same time" (ὑπὸ δὲ τοὺς αὐτοὺς χρόνους): Thucydides could have begun the winter with it and then, as in so many unit juxtapositions of the a-b-a type, returned to the subject of the attack on the Piraeus. What comes through strongly in the loose narrative connection as it stands is the sudden change in Peloponnesian morale and attitude.[6] In the break between the two units, Brasidas, sent in iii.85.1 from Lacedaemon, has become a decisive voice shaping Peloponnesian strategy; the unit juxtaposition subtly highlights the drama of his importance to the Peloponnesian war effort, and the qualities he supplied that they normally lacked.[7]

4.1.1.c Year Eight: iv.78–83, iv.84–88   Brasidas may have been responsible for the daring maneuver in ii.93–94; he is certainly concerned in all three examples of loose narrative connection that occur late in the Archidamian War. In year eight, iv.78–83, an extended narrative unit, emphasizes the speed of his march Thraceward, the difficulties of the journey, and the degree of initiative required to achieve it. Unit iv.84–88, on the other hand, is a complex unit that includes his speech embodying the diplomatic skills necessary to make a success of winning over the Athenian allies in the North: "He was not an unskilled speaker for a Lacedaemonian" (ἦν δὲ οὐδὲ ἀδύνατος, ὡς Λακεδαιμόνιος, εἰπεῖν, iv.84.2).[8] By dividing the text into two units, Thucydides makes clear the versatility of Brasidas's talents. The march north requires initiative, the complete control of his troops (it was a dangerous march), and physical endurance. But when he arrives at Acanthus, the combination of the second half of the time phrase, "a little before vintage" (ὀλίγον πρὸ τρυγή-του), and the elaboration that follows, "in fear for the harvest" (διὰ τοῦ καρποῦ τὸ δέος), briefly sums up the inhabitants' dilemma. Brasidas becomes very subtle and diplomatic; he rejects the obvious use of brute coercion for much longer lasting gains. The Acanthians themselves are not completely swayed by his oratory, but the example becomes a potent one in other Thraceward cities (iv.81.2).

4.1.1.d Year Nine: iv.120–122, iv.123, iv.124–132   Here too, the division of Brasi-das's further activities into three contiguous units shows his versatility and the cumulative effect of his presence more clearly than a single long unit might have done.[9] Mende and Scione, treated separately, demonstrate in action the domino theory, success leading to more success, and also Brasidas's skill as a politician who understands how this principle works. His generalship and ability to inspire the troops are demonstrated in the final unit of the series.

4.1.1.e Year Ten: v.12, v.13   Ramphias's journey northward and his return after hearing of Brasidas's death are divided into two separate units. As in the case of ii.83–92 and ii.93–94 from year three (the naval battle in the Gulf of Corinth followed by the attack on the Piraeus, 4.1.1.b above), the change of seasons occurs as a separation of the two units but does not entirely explain it. As we saw schematically in figure 3.1 in chapter 3, Thucydides shows great flexibility in his ability to arrange subordinate material in a unit. Sometimes it supplies background information that occurred earlier in time (as in iii.86), or it can briefly anticipate events that come after those in the immediate season (as in iii.92–93). Thus he could have arranged in a single season either v.12 (which might have ended: "Later, when they discovered Brasidas's death, they went home") or v.13 ("At the beginning of winter, Ramphias, Autocratidas [Autocharidas], and Epicydidas, who had marched northward to support Brasidas"). That is to say, Thucydides is not compelled by the change of season to make two units here; presumably he has chosen to do so in order to emphasize both the significance of Brasidas's death and the inability of other Spartans to fill his shoes afterward.[10]

Brasidas plays a part in four of the five examples of loose narrative connection in books ii.1–v.24. In all five cases, the division into separate units creates more points of climax and thus multiple points of significance in the events related. As readers, we are encouraged by the changes that occur in the structure of the narrative of events (and more generally, by the intensity and precision of the narrative articulations) to regard individual details of the account as important and to look more closely at the meaning of what is under way.[11]

4.1.2 A-B-A FORMATIONS

A-b-a arrangements are more frequent than loose narrative connections. Although here again two units share the same subject, they do not follow directly upon one another; rather, a unit with a different subject is inserted between them. Sometimes, as in the first example below, the middle unit (the *b* element) overshadows the surrounding *(a)* units in importance; sometimes, as in the second and third examples below, the *b* element is very brief and seems to have as its only function the separation of the two units surrounding it. The *a-b-a* structures here discussed occur in years two, five, six, seven, eight, and ten.

A-b-a patterning is a very old arrangement for narrative.[12] As we have already seen in chapters 2 and 3, Thucydides uses it in a variety of ways. In introductory sentences, nine units insert mention of the setting between the article and noun of the subject; once the subject forms the *b* element placed between halves of the temporal phrase.[13] Within the unit, an *a-b-a* arrangement supplies the fundamental structure of complex units, and it also governs in a less formal way the relation between beginning, middle, and end of some picture units.[14] Here the same patterning device is taken up and applied on a larger scale to arrangements of contiguous units.

In general, the use of an *a-b-a* pattern of unit juxtaposition tightens the structure of the year and gives the reader a sense of familiar patterns transposed to larger narrative groupings. However, the familiarity of the structural pattern does not itself make its meaning in a particular situation obvious; it rather serves as a marker that something significant is here to be observed. Each of the six examples discussed below demonstrates Thucydides' imperious deployment of structure to achieve immediate interpretive ends of his own.

4.1.2.a Year Two: ii.47.2, ii.47.3–54, ii.55–56   Two units concerning the Peloponnesian invasion of Attica here frame a long extended narrative account of the plague. The *a* material, the invasion, is less compelling than the vivid central narrative, the *b* material concerning the plague itself. However, the mention of invasion before and after the central unit ii.47.3–54 adds formality and a framing emphasis to the account of the plague; conversely, the repetition of the fact of invasion at the end of the plague emphasizes how long the Peloponnesians were in Attica and how severe the depredations were that the Athenians suffered at their hands (ii.54.1); each element gains in impact by being part of the *a-b-a* pattern.[15]

This *a-b-a* cluster in year two provides one of the clearest examples of how unit contiguity can work on a variety of levels at once. Units ii.47.2, ii.47.3–54, and ii.55–56 stand in a relationship that goes beyond formal pattern alone. As ii.52.1 demonstrates, Thucydides was aware of the causal connections linking the invasion, the consequent overcrowding of the city, and the plague. The *a-b-a* pattern has been used here to bring out the causal connections linking these disparate phenomena.

4.1.2.b Year Six: iii.94–98, iii.99, iii.100–102, iii.103 *(a-b-a-b)*   Two units about Aetolia and Amphilochia here alternate with two units about Sicily. The material in iii.99 is of no special significance; it could easily have been explained in a subordinate clause in iii.103.3. As it stands, however, it does effectively separate the first series of major activities in Amphilochia, culminating with Demosthenes' defeat at Aegitium, from the second stage, Eurylochus's march against Naupactus. The formal elements in the *a-b-a-b* pattern in year six serve to mark off and clarify developing events in the west.[16]

4.1.2.c Year Eight: iv.102–108, iv.109.1, iv.109.1–116   This is a simpler example of the principle discussed above. The single sentence *b* unit (iv.109.1, about Megara) does not require its position for chronological reasons; its temporal formula, "in the same winter" (τοῦ δ' αὐτοῦ χειμῶνος), is very general. Its function is to provide a clear break between the two units about Brasidas surrounding it.

4.1.2.d Year Ten: v.2.–3.4, v.3.5, v.3.6, v.4–5, v.6–11 *(a-b-a-c-a)*   Cleon provides the subject of the *a* element in this series; Thucydides keeps him before our eye as he journeys toward Amphipolis in year ten. The stages of his voyage alternate with units about Boeotia and Sicily. The final unit, v.6–11, provides the climax of the whole cluster: Cleon dies at Amphipolis.[17]

4.1.2.e Year Seven: iv.1, iv.2.1, iv.2.2–5, iv.6, iv.7, iv.8–23, iv.24–25, iv.26–41 *(a-b-a(c)-b(c)-d-c-a-c)*   In year seven Thucydides puts together a remarkable narrative cluster that is climactic in its complexity.[18] The *a* and *b* elements, Sicily and the Peloponnesians, do not remain independent, as they do in most *a-b-a* series. They merge in the developing focus of *c*, Pylos.[19] The outline, *a-b-a(c)-b(c)-d-c-a-c*, conveys the progression of the unit arrangement that creates the effect discussed in other contexts by Gomme: Thucydides' ability to present events as they must have appeared at the time.[20] When Demosthenes first insisted on putting in at Pylos, it was seen as a way station on the journey to Corcyra and Sicily, and that is how it is presented in iv.2.2–5. Only after several more alternations of focus does it become the principal card in Athens's diplomatic hand. The series ends with Cleon's capture of the men on the island and Lacedaemonian reactions. A sense of developing drama and suspense is maintained throughout the eight units involved.

We may note in this context, as we have in several others, that a desire for chronological exactitude does not generally suffice to explain the end of one unit and the beginning of another.[21] The narrative about Pylos develops over the course of the summer; breaks in it occur where Thucydides wants them. They seem to occur at moments of high tension: the Athenian entrenchment (iv.5), the stalemate after the Athenians have gained control of the harbor (iv.23), and the final capture of the men on the island (iv.41).[22] We may call it dramatic, but it is drama of a very sophisticated type. How much more dramatic (and how much less effective) the narrative would have been if Thucydides had broken off just after the isolation of the men on the island (iv.14.3).[23] As it stands, the anxiety and growing frustration of the Lacedaemonians draw out the close of the second act; it is left for the bumptious Cleon to control the third. The drama of the narrative reflects not theater suspense, but the drama of events that must have been experienced in Athens at the time.

4.1.2.f Year Five: iii.69, iii.70–85   Strictly speaking, these two units do not form an *a-b-a* pattern. The elements of such a pattern, however, are present, and I have included them here to show once more, in Norden's phrase, the "Rücksichtslosigkeit eines Autokrators."[24] Thucydides is no slave to habit; here we see the subordination of a potential *a-b-a* pattern to other ends. Unit iii.69 portrays the Peloponnesian fleet on the way to Corcyra; iii.70–85 is a new unit whose initial focus falls much farther back in time. However, in the middle of this long extended narrative unit the Peloponnesian fleet is introduced again without any special fanfare (iii.76), as one of the elements that will play a role in the horrible events unfolding in Corcyra. A judgment, I think, is rendered by this structural technique: the military force that was earlier rather neutrally described in an independent unit and that provided the transition from the Aegean to Corcyra is subordinated in iii.70–85 to the theme of the growth of civic violence and the breakdown of corporate life. Thucydides does not declaim; he shows us the principle in action in his structure, as we watch the roles that both the Peloponnesian and the Athenian fleets of iii.69 play in exacerbating the carnage in Corcyra (iii.81).

4.1.3 CAUSAL CONNECTION

In years three, four, five, six, seven, nine, and ten, there is a connection between contiguous units that is not as explicit as that found in the loose narrative connections or *a-b-a* formations discussed above. The focus does not remain the same; major elements—actors, setting, or activity—have changed. The connection between the two units often suggests causality in an oblique and glancing fashion; if read closely, the second unit helps explain the first, or the first provides needed background for the second; sometimes the two together are the result of some other activity altogether. The introductory sentence of the second unit almost always makes the causal relationship between the units more explicit.

4.1.3.a Year Four: iii.18, iii.19   Unit iii.18 describes a series of military engagements in Lesbos that culminate in the Athenian establishment of a blockade around Mytilene. Unit iii.19 portrays a set of very different subjects: Athenian taxes, the collection of tribute from subject states, and the death of one commander in Caria. The first sentence of iii.19 provides the connection: "Since the Athenians needed more money for the siege" (προσδεόμενοι δὲ οἱ Ἀθηναῖοι χρημάτων ἐς τὴν πολιορκίαν). The Athenians needed money for the siege in Mytilene, and that is why they levied the taxes and sent out the ships.[25]

4.1.3.b Year Ten: v.13, v.14–20.1   The main reason for Ramphias's eager retreat from Thessaly in v.13 is given by the last sentence of that unit: "Above all, they went back because they knew that the Lacedaemonians, when they sent them out, were inclined toward a peace" (μάλιστα δὲ ἀπῆλθον εἰδότες τοὺς Λακεδαιμονίους, ὅτε ἐξῆσαν, πρὸς τὴν εἰρήνην μᾶλλον τὴν γνώμην ἔχοντας). This is elaborated in the first sentence of v.14: "The development . . . was that neither side resumed the war" (ξυνέβη τε . . . ὥστε πολέμου μὲν μηδὲν ἔτι ἅψασθαι μηδετέρους).[26] Both Athenian and Lacedaemonian reasons for wishing peace are then explored, as well as the actions taken that culminate in the treaty. The causal connection linking v.13 to v.14–20.1 forms part of a longer narrative complex that lasts through the latter half of year ten and brings the whole of the Archidamian War to its conclusion. Other parts of this cluster have been explored in subsections 4.1.1.e and 4.1.2.d above; it will be discussed as a whole in section 4.1.5 below.

4.1.3.c Year Seven: iv.2.2–5, iv.6   The long, developed *a-b-a* structure discussed above in subsection 4.1.2.e contains one smaller causal link within it. Unit iv.2.2–5 takes the Athenian fleet to Pylos; the first sentence of iv.6 begins: "When the Peloponnesians in Attica heard that Pylos had been occupied" (οἱ δ' ἐν τῇ Ἀττικῇ ὄντες Πελοποννήσιοι ὡς ἐπύθοντο τῆς Πύλου κατειλημμένης). The addition of the limited causal element tightens the developing *a-b-a* series and helps provide the sense of climax so impressive in the longer narrative.[27]

4.1.3.d Year Three: ii.80–82, ii.83–92   The first of these two units describes the failure of a Lacedaemonian offensive in Acarnania. The second, ii.83–92, begins: "The fleet from Corinth and the other allies on the Crisaean Gulf, which was supposed to join Cnemus to keep the Acarnanians from sending aid inland did not do so but was compelled, around the same time as the battle at Stratus, to fight a sea battle" (τὸ δ' ἐκ τῆς Κορίνθου καὶ τῶν ἄλλων ξυμμάχων τῶν ἐκ τοῦ Κρισαίου κόλπου ναυτικόν, ὃ ἔδει παραγενέσθαι τῷ Κνήμῳ, ὅπως μὴ ξυμβοηθῶσιν οἱ ἀπὸ θαλάσσης ἄνω Ἀκαρνᾶνες, οὐ παραγίγνεται, ἀλλ' ἠναγκάσθησαν περὶ τὰς αὐτὰς ἡμέρας τῆς ἐν Στράτῳ μάχης ναυμαχῆσαι). Thus this subsequent unit, whose main subject is Phormio's fight with the fleet from Corinth, also helps to explain Cnemus's defeat at Stratus.[28] See also subsection 4.1.1.b above for the continuation of this cluster; a loose narrative connection exists between ii.83–92 and ii.93–94.

4.1.3.e Year Six: iii.89.1, iii.89.2–5   The causal relation in year six is more subtle than those so far explored. Neither of the two units explains the other; a third element, expressed as a genitive absolute in each unit, explains them both. Both the Peloponnesian retreat from Attica and the inundations in different parts of Greece are caused by the earthquakes.[29]

4.1.3.f Year Nine: iv.117–119, iv.120–122   Unit iv.117–119 begins year nine and describes the approach to the armistice and then the armistice itself. The subject in iv.120–122 appears at first glance to have changed completely: Scione decides to revolt; both the decision to revolt and the violent reaction of Athens are described in some detail. Not until late in the second unit, iv.122, do we realize that the two units stand in a causal connection. That is, the armistice established in iv.117–119 explains not the first event of 120–122, Scione's revolt, but rather the consequent outrage of the Athenians: they (rightfully, Thucydides says) believe that Scione revolted after the treaty was in force, and—as we have learned in iv.117–119—they were a willing party to the agreement only in the belief that it would guard against such eventualities. The placement of the two units and the causal relation between the first unit and the second part of the second unit emphasize Athenian disillusionment and explain Athenian severity.[30]

4.1.3.g Year Five: iii.26, iii.27–28, iii.29–33.1, iii.33.2–35, iii.36–50   This is the most ambitious series of interlinked causal connections found in the narrative of the Archidamian War; together these five units tell the story of Mytilene.[31] In the first sentence of iii.26 the Peloponnesian fleet sets out for Mytilene. Unit iii.27–28 explains what happened because that fleet failed to arrive. Unit iii.29–33.1 explains why the fleet did not arrive; we see Alcidas behaving incompetently. Unit iii.33.2 shows Paches pursuing Alcidas and, finally, in iii.36–50, though the scene has shifted to Athens, it unrolls as the result of Paches' activities at the end of iii.35. The beginning of each of these units stands in an explanatory relation to some aspect of the previous unit. Although together these five units form a developing analytic narrative, each unit also has its own focus and is set off by a formular first sentence. As in subsections 4.1.3.e and f above from years six and nine, Thucydides does not force the connections in year five; as readers we must remain alert enough to see them ourselves.

In iii.26-50, the authorial decision to link the units together by causal connection creates and sustains a distinctive tone for the narrative as it develops. Following along as one unit gives way to the next, we see revealed before our eyes in slow motion, as it were, the human abilities and decisions that lead both to successful plans (Paches) and unsuccessful ones (Salaethus, Alcidas). Certainly the culmination of the episode is dramatic: "Mytilene's danger came this close" (παρὰ τοσοῦτον μὲν ἡ Μυτιλήνη ἦλθε κινδύνου, iii.49.4). But the glory of the passage, and its climax, lies in Diodotus's reasoned analysis and the consequent reversal of Athenian policy. The emphasis on chance and accident determining the Mytilenean posture throughout highlights the drama of the end of the episode, but it also makes clear the implicit contrast being drawn between Mytilenean politics and Athenian politics. To the end, the Mytileneans themselves are governed by "fate";[32] the Athenians, in contrast, make responsible decisions in their assembly that in this episode prove effective. The causal connections linking the whole passage together reinforce this impression.

The mood of the complex a-b-a sequence in year seven leading to the capture of Pylos (4.1.2.e above) is markedly different. The tacit differences of tone between the events of the Mytilene cluster and those of the Pylos cluster are reinforced by the differences in the kinds of narrative connection drawn between one unit and the next in each episode. In the Pylos episode (iv.1–41) the a-b-a connections are not causal but dramatic. The whole episode (including the conclusion) is emphatically fortuitous, as sudden alternating shifts of focus link together the picture of a largely accidental good fortune the Athenians experience at Pylos.[33] In Mytilene, on the other hand, causal connections link together a unit cluster whose high point is Athenian rationality—the Athenians themselves are trying to think through causal consequences, and the narrative connections linking this narrative sequence of units re-inforce the flavor of the logical connections they are drawing.[34]

4.1.4 THEMATIC CONTINUITY

The three kinds of significant juxtaposition examined so far are fairly straightfor-ward. To a certain extent, the distinctions established here for purposes of category definition have been drawn too sharply. I have already noted several points where the characteristics of two different types of connection are simultaneously present, and others certainly exist. The most important general point to stress is that for all three types of juxtaposition already examined, Thucydides himself establishes a de-liberate continuity of narrative line across units.[35]

In the clusters below, however, connections linking units to one another are more elusive. They rest on a subtler continuity of theme, one often merely suggested; we do not know if Thucydides intended them. He is, however, fundamentally respon-sible for our tendency to look for them, because a reader who has recognized even some of the connections drawn above cannot help but be aware of interstices be-tween units as potentially significant analytic points in the text. Loose narrative con-tinuities, *a-b-a* formations, and causal relations have taught us to look for connec-tion at these points, because it so frequently does exist and has some interpretive significance. Some of the following examples of thematic connection are widely ac-cepted; others are not. It is less important, however, to prove that any particular con-nection is valid than to see the procedures here as habitual ones on Thucydides' part—suggesting that Thucydides did not want our judgment to conform to his as much as he wanted us to begin to do the work of seeing connections for ourselves.[36] Thus the examples given here from years one and two, five, eight, and nine are not meant to comprise an exhaustive list, but to suggest an authorial habit of thought.

4.1.4.a Year Nine: iv.134.1, iv.134.1–134.2   Unit iv.134.1 states that Athens and Lacedaemon were at peace; iv.134.1–2 describes war between Mantinea and Tegea. The thematic connection, suggested by the particles μέν–δέ at the start of the episodes, is very low-key; from the similarity of theme we draw the causal infer-ence that the Mantineans and Tegeans went to war precisely because the larger war (in which they were allies) was in abeyance. Thucydides does not state the connec-tion overtly, but the existence of so many other significant connections between con-tiguous units encourages us at least to entertain the possibility.[37]

4.1.4.b Years One and Two: ii.34–47.1, ii.47.2, ii.47.3–54[38]   Here an almost Herodotean effect is gained from juxtaposition: success, however prudent, leads to downfall. Many have noticed the irony implicit in the juxtaposition of the funeral oration and the plague; the use of juxtaposition relieves Thucydides of the necessity of drawing lessons. The contrast between the unit about Athenian expansive self-confidence and the succeeding unit about complete civic demoralization is striking indeed, but Thucydides does not oblige us to think analytically about a specific lesson to be drawn. That is, the tone is ironic but not necessarily judgmental.[39]

4.1.4.c Year Eight: iv.53–57, iv.58–65   The high point of Athenian success in iv.53–57 (emphasized in 55) is followed by a unit about Gela, a foreshadowing of the Sicilian disaster to come.[40] We do not immediately realize the significance of the juxtaposition; the contrast is less stark than that between the end of year one and the beginning of year two. Here, though, a judgment is passed on the Athenians at the end of iv.65: "So extreme, in the midst of their current good fortune, was their conviction that nothing would stand in their way, that they would accomplish the practicable and the more problematic alike, whether with a great force or a weaker one. The cause was their extraordinary success in most respects, lending strength to their hopes" (οὕτω τῇ [τε] παρούσῃ εὐτυχίᾳ χρώμενοι ἠξίουν σφίσι μηδὲν ἐναντιοῦσθαι, ἀλλὰ καὶ τὰ δυνατὰ ἐν ἴσῳ καὶ τὰ ἀπορώτερα μεγάλῃ τε ὁμοίως καὶ ἐνδεεστέρᾳ παρασκευῇ κατεργάζεσθαι. αἰτία δ' ἦν ἡ παρὰ λόγον τῶν πλεόνων εὐπραγία αὐτοῖς ὑποτιθεῖσα ἰσχὺν τῆς ἐλπίδος).

4.1.4.d Year Five: iii.36–50, (iii.51), iii.52–68   The contrast in year five is not between the good fortune and bad of a single people, but between the eventual self-restraint and collective civic conscience of the Athenians, in their debate over Mytilene, and the deceitful and harsh treatment of Plataea that follows almost immediately.[41] Both the bitter vengefulness of the Thebans and the crass opportunism of Sparta are emphasized by the unflattering propinquity of iii.36–50 to iii.52–68. It is interesting that the one intervening unit contains the first mention of Nicias in the *History*, but it is not clear what interpretive value is to be assigned to this fact.

4.1.4.e Year Eight: iv.76–77, iv.7–83, iv.84–88, iv.89–101.4   An *a-b-b-a* juxtaposition is formed toward the end of the summer of year eight, as Thucydides shifts his focus from the preparations for Delium to Brasidas's march north, to the effects of that march, then back to the disaster at Delium. Again it is clear that Thucydides is presenting events as they appeared to the contemporary observer;[42] the unit contiguity itself becomes the judgment. As early as year three Thucydides criticizes Athenian strategic carelessness in the north;[43] in year eight the hitherto implicit portrait of dangerous carelessness emerges as a reality. By framing Brasidas's adventures with the elaborate and unproductive Boeotian scheme, Thucydides highlights the irony inherent in the events themselves.[44]

4.1.4.f Year Four: iii.20–24, iii.25   The connection here is also ironic. Unit iii.20–24 vividly describes continuing Plataean efforts to escape destruction at the hands of the Peloponnesians, while in iii.25 Salaethus the Lacedaemonian enters into Mytilene, and the Mytileneans believe his promises that help is coming from Lacedaemon very soon. The juxtaposition of the two units in this fashion draws our attention again to the magnitude of the task the Mytileneans have rather lightly undertaken (cf. iii.3.6, 4.2). Moreover, year four ends with iii.25, and the first two units of year five (iii.26, iii.27–28) will confirm how imprudent the Mytileneans were, trusting the Lacedaemonians with their lives.[45]

Other unit juxtapositions, too, may include causal, judgmental, and purely ironic overtones. Some possibilities include ii.83–92 and ii.93–94, from year three, discussed above as a loose narrative connection (subsection 4.1.1.b), and iv.42–45 in its relationship to iv.26–41 from year seven. In year three, we are tempted to link the new plan of attack in ii.93 causally with Brasidas's presence; in year seven, iv.42–45, the Athenian expedition to Corinth, which comes just after Cleon's success at Pylos, may suggest pique on Nicias's part and hence a motivation for his consequent attempts to show what he can achieve. Gomme mentions these possibilities.[46]

The various unit connections investigated so far encourage us to look for other intertextual reverberations. Thucydides does not do our work for us; by making a certain number of unit connections obvious, and by setting up others that are all but obvious, he demands that his readers become part of the process of making the *History*. Although this is not a new observation about Thucydides' style, we understand more of how it works by looking at Thucydides' use of the essentially paratactic, discrete nature of the units of action, often allowing the interpretation of connections between units to remain subtle and suggestive. We can never be sure of having established the full significance of what Thucydides meant by a given juxtaposition, or even whether he intended us to see it as interpretively significant in the first place.

4.1.5 INITIAL AND CONCLUDING CLUSTERS

Two rather special instances of significant juxtaposition remain to be discussed: the first six units of year one (ii.1, ii.2–6, ii.7–9, ii.10–12, ii 13–17, ii.18–23), and the last six of year ten (v.6–11, v.12, v.13, v.14–20.1, v.20.2, v.21–24). Like the extended clusters in years five and seven discussed above, these form two coherent series of events. They do not concentrate thematically, however, on certain aspects of the war to the immediate suppression of others. In year one, Thucydides takes the war from its inception to the point where the shifting focus from unit to unit is established as a pattern; in year ten, he does the reverse. The last hostilities are tied up, and the focus narrows gradually to the point of armistice and treaty. All the different kinds of link we have so far examined come into play in these two narrative stretches. [47]

In year one, Thucydides starts with a simple picture unit that is little more than a statement that the war began. Each of the stages in the narrative receives its full impact as an individual unit, each touching on a new aspect of the situation; the links between units reflect the variety in the units themselves. Unit ii.1 (a simple picture unit) identifies the beginning of hostilities as the time when exchange between Peloponnesians and Athenians ceased. Unit ii.2–6 (an extended narrative unit) explains why exchange stopped, by describing the entry of the Thebans into Plataea. That unit in turn becomes the cause for ii.7–9 (another extended narrative unit), the preparations, state of mind, and list of allies for each side in the impending conflict. [48] The focus has in three units broadened out to include/engulf the whole Greek world.

Unit ii.10–12 (a complex unit) stands in an *a-b-a* relation with the end of ii.6 and takes up the narrative of events after Plataea. Unit ii.13–17 (another complex unit) forms a thematic connection with ii.10–12; the same time period is covered from the Athenian side. [49] Unit ii.18–23 (an extended narrative unit) has a very loose narrative connection with both ii.10–12 and ii.13–17, since it takes the story from the point of invasion to the final Peloponnesian retreat. The links between units, as this analysis shows, are first predominantly causal and gradually become a mixture of looser types, thematic, loose narrative, and *a-b-a* formations. At the end of ii.23, the connection with the next unit, ii.24 (a developed picture unit), rests almost completely in the temporal phrase. The narrative is no longer a single thematic entity but has come to the point where the shifting focus and complete change of subject inherent in the ordinary paratactic unit structure can begin.

Year ten, on the other hand, begins with units rather loosely strung together and draws them together into a single focus upon the diplomatic maneuvers directly preceding the end of the war. Earlier in the year, the setting has shifted from Delos to Thrace to Boeotia to Sicily. Unit v.6–11 (a complex unit) is the long and decisive narrative that stands to the end of the war as the entry into Attica did to its beginning. The link between v.11 and v.12 rests purely in the temporal phrases; v.12 and v.13 (a simple picture unit and a developed picture unit) are linked by a loose narrative connection; v.13 is linked causally to v.14–20.1 (a complex unit), and v.20.1 is linked causally to v.20.2 (a developed picture unit). Unit v.21–24 (a complex unit) is linked in an *a-b-a* narrative connection with v.20.1 and takes the account to the final treaty between Sparta and Athens. The end of the war is expressed in four terse clauses: "This alliance was made soon after the treaty; the Athenians gave the men back to the Lacedaemonians, and with the summer the eleventh year began. The first war, which was continuous during the ten-year period, has been recorded" (αὕτη ἡ ξυμμαχία ἐγένετο μετὰ τὰς σπονδὰς οὐ πολλῷ ὕστερον, καὶ τοὺς ἄνδρας τοὺς ἐκ τῆς νήσου ἀπέδοσαν οἱ Ἀθηναῖοι τοῖς Λακεδαιμονίοις, καὶ τὸ θέρος ἦρχε τοῦ ἑνδεκάτου ἔτους. ταῦτα δὲ τὰ δέκα ἔτη ὁ πρῶτος πόλεμος ξυνεχῶς γενόμενος γέγραπται, v.24.2).

In these two pieces of narrative, for all their simplicity, Thucydides has accomplished a great deal. The central unit in each cluster, ii.7–9 and v.14–20.1, separates the first stage of the plot, the account of what happened, from the second one. Thus a broad and geographically sweeping analysis of the situation falls, in the first year, between the limited engagement at Plataea that first sets hostilities in motion and the formal beginning of an Athenian-Peloponnesian conflict. In year ten, the military account in the north, ending with Ramphias's hasty retreat, is separated from the implementation of the terms of the peace treaty.[50] In the two unit clusters, Thucydides has brought into play all the different types of link explored above. Years one and ten are not, as thematic wholes, as striking as some we have seen from the middle narrative. But they provide the mixture of analysis and narrative movement required to begin and end the narrative of the Archidamian War, in the one case creating an opening pattern that rapidly complicates itself, and in the other, a closing and simplifying movement that shuts the narrative down.

Four different kinds of significant juxtaposition have been discussed in this section. The story continues from one unit to the next, in loose narrative connections and a-b-a formations, or one unit explains developments in another, or a vaguer unity of theme suggests to the reader that the two units are to be compared or contrasted in some way. Sixty-four of the 119 units of action have been identified as part of at least one such cluster.

Each unit, as we have seen, is organized to produce a finished and self-contained whole; it is the unit's own depth that allows connections with contiguous units to be subtle and various. Each unit, with its neighbors, can set up a variety of connections all of which remain in play, so that we may read ii.47–56 as an emphatically formal a-b-a presentation of two disasters, invasion and plague, but at the same time we may read it as two causally connected events. The series of links between the events in the units of iii.26–50 show causal connections, but they may also be read as a way to show rather than describe the rationality and successful planning of the Athenians. Thucydides leaves it to us to articulate what the connections mean, or which of a variety of overtones to consider most significant. The isolation and paratactic progression of the units of action of ii.1–v.24 are what make possible the many levels of meaning that arise out of the multiple connections between units.

4.2 LARGER CONNECTIONS (ii.1–v.24)

The significant juxtapositions explored above play an important part in building the early narrative of the *History*. To be sure, they are not the only connections established across unit divisions in the text, but they form one important aspect of a very densely woven, richly textured narrative fabric. This section will first briefly discuss other types of connection found in the paratactic structure we have been examining in the Archidamian narrative: those created by the year, by cross-references among the individual units, by the reappearance of major themes, and in the Archidamian narrative as a whole. Many of these have already come up in previous chapters; the present discussion serves as a review that ties them to other patterns. Then, secondly, in summarizing how Thucydides individually patterns the ten years of the Archidamian War, year by year, I discuss how the various types of link considered separately up to this point work together as the yearly narratives continue, to create the impression of a cohesive ongoing narrative.

4.2.1 THE YEAR

The sequence of the formulae that begin the individual units and both begin and end the seasons and years is one structure that complements and offsets the interpretive impact of the unit clusters considered above. In terms of their first sentences, units that form part of a cluster remain structurally on a par with more isolated single units. Moreover, clusters rarely impinge on the yearly divisions. Years two through six in the ten-year narrative begin with introductory sentences announcing the same theme: the invasion of Attica by the Peloponnesians.[51]

Some of the unit clusters considered above help emphasize the structural integrity of the year over that of the season. In five of the ten years, an instance of significant juxtaposition links the last unit of summer to the first unit of winter; in three others, the first unit of winter is obviously the continuation of a subject already discussed in a summer unit.[52] Thus within the year, seasonal divisions are generally overcome by connections between the units; between years, divisions are emphasized.

4.2.2 CROSS-REFERENCES AMONG THE UNITS

Frequently, the unit itself includes elements that offset the effect of clusters by emphasizing ties of individual units with other units that are not in any sense contiguous. For instance, the reader of iii.87.1–3, the second outbreak of the plague in the winter of year five, is inevitably reminded of the major treatment of that theme in year two (ii.47.3–54). Sometimes Thucydides himself refers to the earlier passage; to the account of the purification of Delos in year ten he adds: "as I have described previously" ($\hat{\eta}$ πρότερόν μοι δεδήλωται, v.1; referring to iii.104).[53] Sometimes, however, the material is there for us to use, but we must make the connection ourselves. Both Eion and Heraclea, for instance, play significant roles in events in the north late in the Archidamian War (iv.107, v.6; iv.78, v.12); Thucydides has explained how they were enabled to do so in years six and eight (iii.100, iv.7, iv.106).

In general, it is the rare unit that has no ties of theme or causality to other units. The fourteen list units that occur in the narrative of ii.1–v.24 demonstrate this clearly. The list unit is ideally suited to convey a bald and isolated military account. It usually includes little interpretation, and its chief function seems to be to convey information Thucydides had about different Athenian fleets. However, eight of the fourteen list units form part of a narrative chain in their own years; the other six, too, are tied in different ways to the surrounding text. Sometimes, as in the case of iii.91, Nicias's voyage to Melos, Tanagra, and Locris, the reference is purely verbal, but even here the theme—Athens's attempt to subdue Melos—is significant in its own right as part of the larger pattern.[54]

4.2.3 MAJOR THEMES: CORCYRA, PLATAEA

In several instances, the connections established in the individual unit are neither to a contiguous unit nor to topics taken up in other units in the informal sense described above. Some themes are of major significance to the *History;* their stories are narrated with a great attention to detail and last through several years. Two such themes will be briefly described here, to convey a sense of how discrete units in different years nonetheless form part of a developing plot and bring a larger sense of continuity to Thucydides' depiction of the war as a whole.[55]

Corcyra has already been treated at some length in book i, since it is part of one of the causes of the war: "But for the Corinthians this became the first reason for war with the Athenians, that while they were under treaty obligations they fought with the Corcyraeans against them" (αἰτία δὲ αὕτη πρώτη ἐγένετο τοῦ πολέμου τοῖς Κορινθίοις ἐς τοὺς Ἀθηναίους, ὅτι σφίσιν ἐν σπονδαῖς μετὰ Κερκυραίων ἐναυμάχουν, i.55.2). However, it does not play a major role early in the narrative of the Archidamian War. After three brief mentions in year one (ii.7, ii.9, ii.25), we hear no more of the island until the major account of *stasis* in year five (iii.69, iii.70–85). In year six (iii.94–95) the Corcyraean democrats briefly support Demosthenes at Leucas. In year seven, the Pylos fleet is at first bound for Corcyra (iv.2.2–3.1). But later in year seven comes the final description of the island's savage breakdown in the narrative of the ten-year war (iv.46–48). A vivid and lengthy picture unit describes the final atrocities there: "In this way the Corcyraeans from the mountain were destroyed by the common people, and the civil war, which had been so extensive, ended here, at least as far as this war is concerned; for on one side there was nothing left to speak of" (τοιούτῳ μὲν τρόπῳ οἱ ἐκ τοῦ ὄρους Κερκυραῖοι ὑπὸ τοῦ δήμου διεφθάρησαν, καὶ ἡ στάσις πολλὴ γενομένη ἐτελεύτησεν ἐς τοῦτο, ὅσα γε κατὰ τὸν πόλεμον τόνδε· οὐ γὰρ ἔτι ἦν ὑπόλοιπον τῶν ἑτέρων ὅτι καὶ ἀξιόλογον, iv.48.5).

As we see in section 4.2.4 below, year six divides the first half of the war, in which one set of issues and concerns builds momentum, from the second, where the elements leading eventually to the unsatisfactory Peace of Nicias are forged. By dividing the narrative about Corcyraean civic breakdown into two units, one in year five and one in year seven, Thucydides has thematically bridged this gap very effectively. Moreover, the fact that iv.46–48 in year seven is a brilliant mosaic of description makes us, the readers, reach even more vigorously back in our own minds for the analysis in year five that explains the terrible events in year seven, and, further back still, the vivid description of Corcyraean opportunism in book i that sets the stage for the events of both years five and seven. The story of Corcyra itself becomes a linking device in the text.

The major stages of the account of Plataea occupy even more years than the account of Corcyra does. The Theban attack on Plataea in ii.2–6 is vividly narrated as an extended narrative unit. This event in year one is followed by ii.71–78, a complex unit in year three; iii.20–24, a long picture unit in year four; and the complex unit in year five, iii.52–68, which ends the account: "this was how matters ended for Plataea, in the ninety-third year after it became the ally of Athens" (καὶ τὰ μὲν κατὰ Πλάταιαν ἔτει τρίτῳ καὶ ἐνενηκοστῷ ἐπειδὴ Ἀθηναίων ξύμμαχοι ἐγένοντο οὕτως ἐτελεύτησεν).

Plataea does not, like Corcyra, bind together the two halves of the ten-year narrative; rather, it provides a focus that recurs throughout the first half. The vivid long picture unit, iii.20–24, is placed in the middle of the narrative sequence; it connects the initial investment in year three with the capitulations in year five. It emphasizes, as ii.71–78 did, the continuing courage and inventiveness of the besieged Plataeans and Athenians. The end of the story and the deception there practiced are correspondingly more pathetic.

Each of these two accounts, Corcyra and Plataea, lasts for several years. Thucydides has put care not only into their distribution and placement but also into the elements selected and the type of structure chosen in the successive stages of each story. Here again we see that events did not dominate the historian. A judicious selection of details, structures chosen for their narrative expression, and careful placement of the structures within the larger setting of summers and winters across a number of years have created these two compelling stories. Their unfolding as the narrative continues in turn helps bind the *History* together as a single although multivalent ongoing whole.

4.2.4 THE ARCHIDAMIAN WAR AS A WHOLE

Various kinds of connection between units have so far been considered: those of immediately contiguous units, those among units in the same year, and those linking units in different years. One final type of pattern needs discussion. In books ii.1–v.24 Thucydides uses all these connections, but he fits them into a unity that is larger still. In the narrative of the first ten years of the war, pattern and complex design find their complement in the parts of the narrative left much more simple and straightforward. All aspects of the ten-year account contribute to its shape. We will now consider this shape year by year. A complete list of the units that comprise these years is found below in appendix A.

Year One   The seventeen units of action in year one break the year into three distinct parts. First, six units form the initial cluster discussed above in section 4.1.5 (ii.1–ii.23); the war begins with a dynamic interlocking narrative. These units culminate in the account of the Peloponnesian entry into Attica. The units are distinct, in that each is introduced by a formular first sentence and contributes a new viewpoint and set of concerns, but the same topics recur repeatedly, and the general effect is of a unified and building set of themes. The passage comprising ii.1–23 takes up more than sixteen pages.

The second part of year one begins at ii.24. The tone of the narrative changes, since ten short and superficially unrelated units occur in four and a half Oxford pages. They are bald accounts, mostly of Athenian naval activity.

One unit eight pages long forms the third part of year one. The funeral oration, a complex unit, returns to the more spacious unit structures that began the year and sets a capstone on this first year of the ten-year account. As noted above, there is irony implicit in the placement of the funeral oration at the end of the year, where it immediately precedes an account of the plague.[56] But some of the force of ii.34–47.1 comes from its subtler placement within the year. For the ten small units in the middle of the year show, as an editorial analysis could not have done, the nature of the early conflict. A single extended narrative unit at the end of the first unit cluster (ii.18–23) describes the Peloponnesian act of aggression: a traditional land-bound march. The ten bald units in the center of the year in contrast portray a dazzling series of Athenian summer initiatives around the Peloponnese and in Locris, Euboea, Aegina; diplomatic coups in the north; the fleet around the Peloponnese again; and activity in the Megarid and Atalanta.

The final unit of this series shows an unsuccessful Corinthian attempt to counteract Athenian activity in Astacus. The cumulative impression of these ten brief units is of a flexible, confident, and very far-reaching sea power putting Pericles' strategy into action. Some of the force of the funeral oration comes from its placement at the end of this string of successes. It shows the spirit that moves and informs such activity.

Thucydides has managed in year one to vary the unit types considerably. The year begins with a string of long, interlocking units and ends with one very long complex one. In the center he provides a respite from challenging, analytic prose through a series of bald list or picture units. He has not, however, lost sight of the analytic function desired: these units supplement the Peloponnesian emphasis of the first cluster of the year by portraying in action the mobility and resourcefulness of Athens. Prose rhythm and interpretation complement each other. And although the initial units of the year focus on the might of the Peloponnese going to war, seen as a larger whole, the year steadily builds a picture of the glory of Athens.

Year Two   The eleven units of year two break the narrative into two unequal halves. Six units at the beginning of the year form a cluster, each in turn taking up different aspects of three related themes: plague, invasion, and Athenian attempts to carry on military activity. These occupy thirteen pages; ii.57, a picture unit whose integrating function was discussed in chapter 3, emphasizes how connected the three themes are.[57] The cluster ends with Pericles' third and final speech and a general evaluation by Thucydides of Athenian power and policy in the early war. The entire cluster stands in the strongest contrast to the picture of Athenian success depicted in year one; the plague has changed the shape of the war.

The five units that complete year two take up three and a half pages. They portray a variety of indecisive actions by Lacedaemonians, Corinthians, Ambraciots, and Athenians. Even the potentially positive effect of Athenian success at Potidaea at the end of the year is muted by Thucydides' emphasis on political dissatisfaction and disunity at home. Thus although structurally year two repeats the pattern of the first two-thirds of year one, the effect is very different. In year one, fragmented and isolated short units coming between two longer narratives convey the effect of power and confidence; in year two, the fragmentation completes the year and emphasizes the disorder and sense of unresolved issues articulated in the cluster that begins the year.

Year Three   Year three introduces a new set of relations between narrative units. The number of units goes down from year two, from eleven to seven; the number of pages goes up, from sixteen and a half to twenty-seven. Thucydides abandons the progression within the year from interlocking themes to individually isolated short military units. Instead, the seven substantial units of year three focus our attention upon a few military campaigns in much greater detail. The scene shifts from Plataea, to the north, to the west, to Athens itself, and to the north and west again. No one area dominates the year; fifteen of the twenty-seven pages concern the forces marshaled in the west by Cnemus or Phormio, but they are balanced by the complex unit about Plataea that begins the year and ii. 95–101, the long description of Sitalces' march.

The unit structure of year three supplements that of years one and two in a significant way. Military campaigning, a theme treated briefly and rather baldly in those years, is here taken up and analyzed in seven successive units. Thucydides in year three is concerned with the ingredients that go into military campaigns. Each of the campaigns considered is treated in enough detail that we understand the elements involved and the reasons for success and failure. And it is not just the general outcome that is considered. Thucydides is explicitly critical of the Athenian decision to send Phormio's reinforcements first to Crete, and he is subtly critical of their conduct of the war in the north.[58] He distinguishes the boldness and effectiveness of the Peloponnesian plan to attack the Piraeus from the elements that made it fail in practice. In year three, Thucydides is narrowing his focus, turning away from the general issues that shaped the early war and turning toward an underlying element, the combination of chance and technique that wins or loses a battle, or a campaign. He is giving us a tool for understanding and interpreting military units in general. The art of war becomes in year three a major theme in the *History*.

Year Four   Military activity continues to occupy a large portion of this year, but a very different aspect of it is emphasized. Instead of concentrating on the purely military details of several campaigns, six of the nine units in the year concern one topic: the impending revolt of Mytilene. Military actions are here shown to be part of a much larger set of factors, since political tensions and decisions stand behind events in the field. Unit iii.2–6 explores practical politics in Lesbos and Athens; iii.8–16 broadens the focus. At Olympia, before the assembled Peloponnesian allies, the Mytileneans consider the Athenian empire as a historical phenomenon, and they state in the most general terms their reasons for wanting to revolt. The year is shaped by this single developing story. The earliest stages of the revolution are followed, both as military and political acts, up to the final unit of the year, the modest picture unit about Salaethus's entry into Mytilene and the fateful decision there not to negotiate with Athens.[59] Year four is a shorter and denser narrative than year three and takes up fourteen pages.

Thus the overall impression created by the pattern of units in each of the first four years is quite different. In year one, far-reaching Athenian power is depicted; in year two, the plague and the subsequent loss of momentum. In year three, the details of military campaigning become the major focus; Thucydides here alternates between two fronts, in the north and in the west. In year four, though the geographical focus narrows to Mytilene, military maneuvers and decisions in the field are shown to be part of a larger political situation and set of attitudes and decisions.

Year Five   Of all the ten years in the Archidamian War, year five is treated in most detail. It is the longest, thirty-eight and a half Oxford pages, and it has thirteen units of action. The relation between military and political events we saw developing in year four is in year five brought to bear upon events in three cities: Plataea, Mytilene, and Corcyra. It begins like years one, two, or four, with a sequence of causally linked units, here about events in Mytilene. But instead of concentrating on this one topic for the rest of the year, or ending the year with a succession of small and unrelated units, Thucydides goes on to balance Mytilene with two other themes of equal importance: Plataea, in twelve pages, and Corcyra, in nine pages. Small and isolated units alternate with the larger ones: Mytilene is followed by Minoa, Plataea by the Peloponnesian fleet fleeing to Cyllene, Corcyra by the decision of the Athenians to send a fleet to Sicily.[60] Three picture units about unrelated events comprise the winter of the year.

Year five ties together three separate and vital chains of events, at the point when a developing depth of narrative has given the reader the background to appreciate them. Plataea has been considered in year one, year three, and year four; Corcyra has been effectively absent since the lengthy discussion in book i; the third topic, Mytilene, has been the object of rigorous scrutiny in the immediately previous year. In each context, year five brings to bear the sense of military technique articulated in year three, and the broader political implications articulated in year four. The problem of historicity and artfulness arises here. Does Thucydides, in a desire to make year five emphatic, sacrifice accurate reporting to the striking juxtapositions the present narrative displays?[61] I would argue not, and one of the reasons, it seems to me, lies deep in the structure created by units of action. It is the paratactic progression of units within the year and the variety of patterns available to the individual units that allow him to let the course of events disclose a significance for τὰ γενό-μενα. The text, of course, does not write itself, but Thucydides' apparent sensitivity, struggling to record both the precise shapes of individual events and the momentum underlying their increasing complexity, goes a long way toward giving the narrative its persuasive power.[62]

As we have seen in the first half of this chapter, significant juxtaposition is one technique that obviates the need for artificially tight analytic connections between units. Moreover, if year five had not been a year of great change, the loose progression of units that comprise the year would have encouraged Thucydides to postpone his discussion of stasis until iv.46–48 in year seven, or to anticipate the destruction of Plataea at the end of iii.20–24 in year four. The very flexibility of the unit structure is one of our best guarantees that Thucydides put every effort into trying to represent the shape of events as they evolved at the time.

Year Six   A lull in the narrative occurs here. The themes that have gradually been building in complexity and urgency in years one through five recede, and a simpler set of units, containing much vivid description but relatively little analysis, takes their place. The pattern formed by the thirteen units in year six bears some resemblance to that of year three, where Thucydides alternates between continuous narratives about Sicily and Acarnania. As we saw in chapter 1, the shift between these two foci in year six is interspersed with other units, most of them simple in structure and less connected to the ultimate tactical and political issues of the war: inundations, Heraclea, the purification of Delos, and the eruption of Aetna.[63]

Year six presents the effect of leisured simplicity. If we look at the Archidamian narrative as a whole, we understand better why. Not only is year six placed between two years that are themselves intense and demanding narratives, it is also in effect a lull between this early war's first and second halves. In years one through five the issues have been fairly clear-cut and understandable from the careful preparation for them at the end of book i. The contest has been between a land power whose chief initiative lies in yearly invasions, and a mobile and far-ranging sea power. But Pylos in year seven changes this situation. [64]

Year Seven   Year seven is nearly twice as long as year six, though the number of units is the same: thirteen. Here for the first time we see the change in the individual units discussed at the conclusion of chapter 3. Five units each occupy ten lines or less, and five units are over sixty lines long; only three units lie in between these two extremes.[65] The long and impressive *a-b-a* cluster about Pylos that dominates the year has already been discussed, in subsection 4.1.2.e above. Only at the end of the drama do we, like the Athenians, fully realize the role that the captured Spartans will play in determining the course of years eight, nine, and ten. The year is not allowed entirely to collapse at the end of iv.41; the compelling, long picture unit about Corcyra ties it thematically back to the first half of the war, and the ongoing references to Sicily (iv.1, 2, 5, 24–25, 46–48) tie it to years five and six as well.

Year Eight   The beginning of the year confirms that the war has changed. The Peloponnesians can no longer risk invading Attica. The narrative of year eight is almost as long as that of year five and takes up thirty-seven and a half Oxford pages. Again, as in year seven, the units tend to be very short or very long; eight units are over ninety lines long, four are fifteen lines or less, and only two units fall between these two extremes. Unlike most of the years so far examined, year eight contains its longer and more striking units toward the end of the year. It begins slowly, with an eclipse and then some plans of exiles from Mytilene, thwarted in another unit later in the summer (iv.75). The third unit of the year, iv.53–57, displays Lacedaemonian morale at its lowest. But from this point on things change: Gela, the failure of the Megarian revolution, Brasidas's march north culminating in the winter capture of Amphipolis, and Delium depict an almost unrelieved string of disasters for Athens.[66] While the early war presents the Athenians as versatile, having a great many possible courses of action, by year eight, the Athenians have only Pylos. The Peloponnesians, on the other hand, have set fire to a northern fuse too long ignored by Athens, one that will continue to burn for the duration of the war. Thus the heavy concentration of long narrative units at the end of the year, and Brasidas's important and rapid string of successes in the north, confirm our impression in year seven that the war has changed. Its dynamics are different from those of the early war, and the narrative structure formed by the sequence of units reflects that fact.

Year Nine   Year nine reminds us in structure of year two. It begins with four substantial units whose interconnections we have already explored;[67] these are followed by six units, each under ten lines long. The year as a whole occupies thirteen pages of text. Two developments seem to coexist and shape this unequally balanced year:

its first stage confirms the disastrous effect of the Athenian decisions witnessed in year eight, while its second stage begins a lull that will continue through the first several pages of year ten, until the start of the final tight unit cluster leading to the war's end.

Year Ten   The beginning of year ten continues the tone of year nine. The first six units are all moderate or short, and then comes the account of Amphipolis in 169 lines (v.6–11). We have seen how the alternation of units within the last cluster narrows the focus down to the final elements that need resolution before peace can come.[68] Year ten demonstrates, however, that Thucydides is unlikely to have published a separate "ten years' war" in anything like the present shape of the Archidamian narrative. Unit v.20.2 heightens the absence of finality; where we expect some summation of the events we have witnessed, Thucydides gives us instead a statement about his own technique in writing the *History* followed by an account of events whose spareness seems ironic. The ten-year narrative concludes with four paratactic statements, of which only the second has practical effects: "the Athenians gave the men back to the Lacedaemonians" (καὶ τοὺς ἄνδρας τοὺς ἐκ τῆς νήσου ἀπέδοσαν οἱ Ἀθηναῖοι τοῖς Λακεδαιμονίοις, v.24.2). But those effects, of course, will be enormous.

This concludes the discussion of connections between units of action, and here the consideration of the role of units of action in the narrative of the Archidamian War comes to an end too. In chapters 1 through 4, the object of this study has been twofold: to explore the implications of the unit structure in general, and to describe the narrative of the first ten years of the Peloponnesian War in terms of that structure. Chapter 1 describes the units of action of one rather simple year. Chapter 2 emphasizes continuity: the strongly formular introductory sentences of the units act as a device linking the units themselves together into a patterned sequence within the year, and the years together into a paratactically organized narrative of the ten-year Archidamian War. Chapter 3 considers the shape of the 119 individual units in ii.1–v.24 and describes change in their structures as the narrative progresses.

Chapter 4 has emphasized a deeper aspect of narrative continuity. I have tried to show something of the varied connections linking units to one another: connections of various types between contiguous units, thematic connection more or less explicit between units in the same year and units in different years, and finally the overall effect created by the years as they succeed each other in books ii.1–v.24. The total effect is complex and contrapuntal. No one pattern dominates the narrative.

At least at some points, Dionysius of Halicarnassus saw what I have described as the unit structure of the text of Thucydides. He saw, and heartily disapproved.[69] Here I have argued that the linear, paratactic progression of units within the year is, despite Dionysius's severe strictures, an essential strength of the early books of the *History*, because it allows Thucydides such enormous latitude in shaping the individual units, in each case letting the particular quality and impact of the event at hand emerge. The strongly formular first sentences link together units of action that are as individual narratives extraordinarily diverse and idiosyncratic in shape.

What emerges also from the way units succeed each other is a sense of years one through ten of the Archidamian War as a challenging and complex period. Thucydides does not force particular events into a frame determined by large-scale theories of interpretation; the larger meanings of the period rather seem to arise out of the individual units and the way they come together. The idiosyncratic shape of the units and the subtlety and variety of the links between and among different units suggest an author struggling to provide the closest approximation possible of the way events revealed themselves gradually to those participating in them. They are an essential element in that austere disinterestedness that Dionysius himself admired.[70]

PART TWO

CHAPTER FIVE

The Years of the Peace
(v.25–vi.7)

The Unit of Action Changing

In books v.25–vi.7, Thucydides is using units of action in new ways and for a new end. This chapter is an attempt to specify the details of how Thucydides' narrative technique changes as he moves into his account of the troubled years of the Peace, the uneasy interregnum that separated the Sicilian expedition of 415–413 B.C.E. from all that had gone before. Especially in comparison with the narrative of the Sicilian expedition and the Aegean War to come, many features basic to the earlier narrative remain. The building blocks of the years of the Peace continue to be units of action, each set off by a formular first sentence and a change of subject. But they are units often formed differently and for a different context: the narrative tends to alternate between extremely abrupt simple units and longer extended narrative passages that seem curiously flat in comparison with those of the first ten-year narrative stretch.[1]

The first three sections of this chapter, then, take up in turn the same three foci that we have already examined for the Archidamian narrative: the formular introductory sentences, the internal organization of the units of action, and the nature of the connections drawn between units. As in chapter 3, tables will be kept in the body of the chapter rather than relegated to an appendix; they depict most concisely the nature of the changes the narrative undergoes as Thucydides moves into the years of the Peace.

5.1 INTRODUCTORY SENTENCES OF UNITS OF ACTION (v.25–vi.7)

Here we continue on the whole to be in familiar territory. As in the earlier narrative, here too Thucydides sets new narrative units off and indicates their boundaries by placing at the start of each unit a sentence of the sort already familiar from years one through ten, identifying the new subject, verb, setting, and time.

The changes that do occur tend to be rather subtle. The order in which the first two formular elements of the sentence occur resembles that of years one through ten. Time and the subject of the sentence continue most frequently to stand at the head of the sentence: "In the following winter, the Lacedaemonians sent into Epidaurus a garrison of three hundred men commanded by Agesippidas who got past the Athenians by sea" (τοῦ δ' ἐπιγιγνομένου χειμῶνος Λακεδαιμόνιοι λαθόντες Ἀθηναίους φρουρούς τε τριακοσίους καὶ Ἀγησιππίδαν ἄρχοντα κατὰ θάλασσαν ἐς Ἐπίδαυρον ἐσέπεμψαν, v.56). However, the proportion of introductory sentences displaying this pattern has dropped from 55% of the total to 39%. Moreover, although Thucydides continues to use a wide range of the possible combinations of subject, verb, setting, and time as the first two elements of the sentence, combinations that include nonformular elements rise sharply. In v.25–vi.7, one of the first two elements is a dative, γάρ-clause, or direct object in 23% of the introductory sentences: these unusual elements are found at the start of 3% of the introductory sentences in books ii.1–v.24.[2] Thus although the pattern set in the earlier years remains dominant, Thucydides uses it here in a freer and bolder fashion. Table 5.1 sets out the extent of both similarity and change in the way first sentences are introduced.

The subjects in introductory sentences display the same mixture of stability and subtle transformation. Patterns from the Archidamian narrative remain, but Thucydides uses them in different proportions: Athenians are much less prominent, as are named individuals, while the use of Lacedaemonians and other collective nouns rises (see table 5.2).

Changes in subject are more obviously significant than changes in the order of the first two elements; they mark real changes that have taken place in the war itself.[3] Through most of the years of the Peace, as Thucydides narrates them, Athens appears to be playing a waiting game, while the Peloponnesians are active. The struggle for dominance between Argos and Lacedaemon is an important focus in these years; accordingly there is a shift in introductory sentences away from Athenian subjects, toward Lacedaemonians and others. When the narrative focus shifts back to Athens in year sixteen, Athenians are again the subject of four first sentences.[4]

TABLE 5.1 Order of first two elements in introductory sentences,
v.25–vi. 7 and ii.1–v.24

(number and percentage of total)

	Books v.25–vi.7	Books ii.1–v.24
Time, subject	19 (39%)	66 (55%)
Subject/time	4 (8%)	17 (14%)
Verb/subject	3 (6%)	5 (4%)
Subject/verb	4 (8%)	10 (8%)
Subject/setting	1 (2%)	6 (5%)
Setting/subject	1 (2%)	—
Setting/time	1 (2%)	1 (1%)
Time/setting	1 (2%)	4 (3%)
Verb/time	3 (6%)	4 (3%)
Time/verb	1 (2%)	1 (1%)
Verb/setting	—	1 (1%)
Setting/verb	—	1 (1%)
Other	11 (23%)	3 (3%)
Total introductory sentences	49 (100%)	119 (100%)[a]

[a] Because the number of instances is relatively small, this chapter occasionally adds up to 99% rather than 100%. Half percentages are not counted; rounding off the figures to the nearest full percentage is sufficient to draw the large-scale contrasts this chapter is concerned with.

Changes in verbs in introductory sentences also reflect the changed conditions in the years of the Peace. The rise in deliberative verbs parallels the heavy emphasis on diplomacy in these years; the decrease in initiatory verbs reflects the fact that many military units are extremely brief and no longer are introduced by the ἐστράτευσαν-type formulae from the early war (see table 5.3).

Within the category of introductory verbs of the summary type occurs one subordinate change that is of some interest; it points to changes occurring in the body of the individual unit that will be discussed below. The years of the Peace, with 49 units of action, contain five existential verbs in first sentences (εἶναι, γενέσθαι)—the same number as in the 119 units of the Archidamian narrative. As we shall see

TABLE 5.2   Distribution of subjects in
introductory sentences, v.25–vi.7 and ii.1–v.24

(number and percentage of total)

	Books v.25–vi.7	*Books ii.1–v.24*
Athenians	6 (12%)	32 (27%)
Lacedaemonians[a]	11 (22%)	13 (11%)
Others	18 (37%)	23 (19%)
Personal names	5 (10%)	25 (21%)
Concrete names	6 (12%)	21 (18%)
Place	3 (6%)	5 (4%)
Total units	49 (100%)	119 (100%)

[a] The "Peloponnesians" from the early war have disbanded. "Lacedaemonians and allies" have replaced them.

TABLE 5.3   Distribution of verb types in introductory sentences,
v.25–vi.7 and ii.1–v.24

(number and percentage of total)

	Books v.25–vi.7	*Books ii.1–v.24*
Initiatory	15 (31%)	49 (41%)
Deliberative	8 (16%)	13 (11%)
Summary	26 (53%)	57 (48%)
Total units	49 (100%)	119 (100%)

below, the shorter units in the years of the Peace are becoming swifter and less precisely focused as individual narratives; their verbs too are more often general and, in comparison with summary verbs from the early years, rather vague.[5]

Settings in the introductory sentences in v.25–vi.7 also suggest a less sharp focus for the unit as a whole. Sentences in which place is expressed by means of a prepositional phrase or a combination of phrases drop from 67% of the total number of sentences to 51%. The number of sentences with no identification of place has grown, on the other hand, from 24% of the total to 35% (see table 5.4). These changes are in one sense a natural reflection of the diplomatic cast to years eleven through sixteen, but they also have the effect of leaving a greater proportion of first sentences unspecific. As events, units are increasingly not assigned a definite location; stylis-

TABLE 5.4   Distribution of setting in
introductory sentences, v.25–vi.7 and ii.1–v.24

(number and percentage of total)

	Books v.25–vi.7	*Books ii.1–v.24*
Prepositional phrase	21 (43%)	60 (50%)
No setting	17 (35%)	29 (24%)
Object of verb	5 (10%)	7 (6%)
Subject of sentence	1 (2%)	2 (2%)
Other	1 (2%)	1 (1%)
Combination	4 (8%)	20 (17%)
Total units	49 (100%)	119 (100%)

TABLE 5.5   Distribution of time formulae in
introductory sentences, v.25–vi.7 and ii.1–v.24

(number and percentage of total)

	Books v.25–vi.7	*Books ii.1–v.24*
Simple season	15 (31%)	33 (28%)
Neutral prepositional phrase	7 (14%)	14 (12%)
Detailed season	5 (10%)	23 (19%)
Precise reference	10 (20%)	29 (24%)
Atypical	4 (8%)	6 (5%)
None	8 (16%)	14 (12%)
Total units	49 (100%)	119 (100%)

tically, the absence of a clear marker of place means the more frequent lack of one of the familiar formular signs that a new unit is beginning.

Time formulae continue to be a dominant element in first sentences of the years of the Peace; 59% of these sentences include time as one of the first two elements. Moreover, Thucydides uses the same formulae in much the same proportion as in years one through ten. Small changes, however, do occur; these are reflected in table 5.5.

The two exact categories of temporal identification—the detailed seasonal references ("In the following summer, as soon as it was spring," ἅμα δὲ τῷ ἦρι εὐθὺς τοῦ ἐπιγιγνομένου θέρους, v.40) and the mention of a previous event of the same season by name ("During the time the Argives were around Epidaurus," καὶ καθ' ὃν χρόνον ἐν τῇ Ἐπιδαύρῳ οἱ Ἀργεῖοι ἦσαν, v.55)—have fallen in years eleven through sixteen from a combined total of 43% to one of 30%. There is a slight corresponding rise in expressions of the simpler formular type, from 40% to 45%, as well as a larger proportional rise in the sentences whose time identification is odd or completely absent, from 17% to 24%.

In one sense, this is a natural change in years with only 4 or 5 units per year. Exact temporal formulae are not as necessary. But the rise in atypical time phrases or units with no time indication at all in the introductory sentence contributes to the impression that units are less crisply focused than in the earlier years, and therefore less sharply separated from one another.[6]

It is important not to overstate the differences between the introductory sentences of the years of the Peace and those of the Archidamian narrative. The key to the narrative change in v.25–vi.7 does not lie here. On the contrary, Thucydides continues to exhibit in the order of the first two elements of the sentence and in his choice of subject, verb, setting, and time the same varieties of expression, very often in the same proportions as in the earlier narrative. Subjects continue to be personal, summary verbs are most common, the single prepositional phrase describes setting most frequently, and simple seasonal phrases like τοῦ δ' αὐτοῦ θέρους continue to supply the largest percentage of expressions of time. The changes that do occur are in part attributable to the conditions of the period rather than to a profound stylistic reorientation on the part of the author. The Athenians are less active and therefore supply fewer subjects; diplomatic activity encourages the use of deliberative verbs. Diplomacy as a dominant topic also explains in part the drop in sentences identified by setting.

Nonetheless, some changes have taken place that cannot be explained by the demands of the material. There is an increase in the number of existential verbs in the summary category and in the number of sentences now without an identification by place or a time formula. The introductory sentences of the years of the Peace are not as consistently formular or as striking in their impact as are the introductory sentences in the Archidamian narrative.[7]

5.2 UNIT ARRANGEMENT (v.25–vi.7)

In the years of the Peace, the narrative is divided into units of action that continue mostly to be either under twenty-five or over fifty lines long, like those of the first

TABLE 5.6   Distribution of units according
to length, v.25–vi.7 and ii.1–v.24

(number and percentage of total)

	Books v.25–vi.7	*Books ii.1–v.24*
1–25 lines	39 (80%)	65 (55%)
26–50 lines	4 (8%)	13 (11%)
More than 51 lines	6 (12%)	41 (34%)
Total units	49 (100%)	119 (100%)

TABLE 5.7   Distribution of units according
to structural type, v.25–vi.7 and ii.1–v.24

(number and percentage of total)

	Books v.25–vi.7	*Books ii.1–v.24*
Simple picture	21 (43%)	24 (20%)
Developed picture	13 (27%)	33 (28%)
List	2 (4%)	14 (12%)
Extended narrative	9 (18%)	24 (20%)
Complex	4 (8%)	24 (20%)
Total	49 (100%)	119 (100%)

ten years of narrative.[8] One can still determine reasonably well whether a given unit is of the simple picture, developed picture, or list unit type (if it is twenty-five lines long or less) or an extended narrative or complex unit (if it is over a page in length).

Once we go beyond these preliminary observations, however, we are struck by the fact of change. Units no longer occur in the same proportions in the text as in the early war; they stand in new relations with the units surrounding them, and the emphasis within the individual unit is often unexpected.

The simplest difference is that of unit length. Short units, those twenty-five lines long or less, become much more frequent in v.25–vi.7, as table 5.6 makes clear. The rise in the number of short units principally reflects a great increase in the use of simple picture units, those seven lines long or less. Because there are fewer speeches, there are also fewer complex units in these years; this fact is largely responsible for a drop in units over a page in length (see table 5.7).

Tables 5.6 and 5.7 make it plain that Thucydides has substantially changed the way narrative units work in the years of the Peace. Other kinds of change occur that are less easy to quantify. Some occur in the interior of the unit and some in the way units come together to form a continuous text. In this next section of the chapter, the chief focus will be on change within the individual unit. Each of the five unit types will be considered in turn and compared with the equivalent type from the Archidamian narrative. No single change, we should note, is crucial in itself; it is the cumulative effect that creates the impression of change on the reader.

5.2.1 SIMPLE PICTURE UNITS

v.32.1, v.32.2, v.35.1, v.35.2a, v.39.1, v.50.5, v.52.1, v.56.4, v.56.5, v.81.1, v.81.2, v.82.1a, v.82.1b, v.83.3, v.83.4, v.84.1a, v.115.1, v.115.2–3, v.115.4, v.116.1, vi.7.3–4. Total: 21

As in the Archidamian narrative, these units are seven lines long or less; the subject of the unit is introduced in the formular introductory sentence and concluded in the briefest compass possible. Nonetheless, even in such short units, substantial change has taken place.

Three developments in the simple picture units of the years of the Peace are purely internal. First, there is less supporting detail, and what there is is less finished and less carefully positioned. In v.52.1, the account of the Boeotians in Heraclea, the first verb is repeated almost immediately: "The Boeotians took over Heraclea . . . and dismissed the Lacedaemonian Agesippidas for his poor leadership. They took over the place for fear that . . . " ($\tau\dot{\eta}\nu$ Ἡράκλειαν . . . Βοιωτοὶ παρέλαβον, καὶ Ἀγησιππίδαν τὸν Λακεδαιμόνιον ὡς οὐ καλῶς ἄρχοντα ἐξέπεμψαν. δείσαντες δὲ παρέλαβον. . . .) We might expect from the earlier narrative a more extensive use of subordination, in order to avoid such repetition. In v.32.1, the brief account of the end of Scione and the resettlement of the Delians in Delos, a time formula, object, and subject lead immediately to the verb, ἀπέκτειναν. The effect is very harsh; the reader is unprepared for the force of the impact. The Athenians provide the single subject for the sentence, so we are forced to consider Scione and Delos as aspects of the same unit, although two subjects so disparate are not linked together in this fashion in the earlier narrative.

Other simple picture units in years eleven through sixteen almost completely lack supporting detail: v.32.2, v.82.1a, v.82.1b, and v.35.1. None display the combination of brevity and exquisitely placed detail common in the simple picture units of the early war, like the description of the eclipse in ii.28 or even the capture of the fort in Locrian territory in iii.99.

The simple picture units that are not extremely brief in v.25–vi.7 emphasize action. While in the first ten-year narrative, only 1 of 24 simple picture units has more than three finite verbs, 6 simple picture units in years eleven through sixteen do: v.32.1, v.50.5, v.52.1, v.81.2, v.115.2–3, and v.115.4.[9]

The density of these units affects the reader's perception of events. In the Archidamian narrative, simple units convey relatively unimportant material. In the account of the Lacedaemonian expedition to Zacynthus (ii.66), for instance, enough detail is given that we understand the action, but it does not raise further questions. It concerns the number of ships, the nature of the inhabitants, and the composition of the invading force. The newly dense simple picture units of years eleven through sixteen, on the other hand, raise as many questions as they answer. In their four or five main verbs, an immense amount of information is given, very sparely described. In v.81.2 an event comparable in magnitude to the extended narrative unit iv.66–74, the Megarian revolution checked by Brasidas, is presented in the space of five lines: Argos becomes oligarchic. Here Thucydides does not give the impression of casual lack of interest, but rather of knowing more than he tells us, in the onrushing course of events.

Some of these units look like notes taken for a fuller, more developed account not yet written. Even when the unit might be presented more simply, Thucydides emphasizes the complexities involved. More certainly could have been added in v.115.2–3 about the political decisions in Athens leading to the raids at Pylos, and also about the background to the Lacedaemonian reaction. There is enough hinted at behind these brief, condensed accounts to suggest that a much more extended treatment could have been created from them.

The third interior change in simple picture units in years eleven through sixteen also contributes to the effect of intense activity conveyed in a very compressed form. The action-reaction pattern seen in some developed picture units from the Archidamian narrative is here employed in 5 extremely short units.[10] The fact that Thucydides has chosen to present both Athenian and Lacedaemonian involvement with Macedon in vi.7.3–4 suggests that the picture needs completion. What were Sparta's expectations from Perdiccas or the Chalcidians? Similarly, whom did the Argives suspect in v.116.1, and why? None of the two-stage simple picture units of the early war so vividly suggest an enormous range of diplomatic and military complexities lurking under the unit's surface. Thus the function of the simple picture unit has been transformed: brevity no longer automatically conveys the judgment that the unit is relatively straightforward or unimportant.

The relation of these units to those that precede and follow them is also different in the years of the Peace, emphasizing even more strongly the internal changes described above. The simple picture unit is no longer a relatively static and independent set piece but has become part of a rapidly moving narrative flow. Simple units in v.25–vi.7 are not placed with the same care at the beginning and end of seasons, and they are not contiguous only with longer units capable of setting them in bold relief. They occur instead now scattered throughout the narrative, often linked with other simple units. Unit v.32.1 is followed by v.32.2, and v.82.1a by v.82.1b. The focus moves in the one case from Scione to Delos to Phocis and Locris, in the other from Dium in Athos to Achaea.[11] The first sentences of simple units also contribute to the impression of a swifter, less deliberate narrative placement. While in ii.1–v.24 only 2 of 24 short units lack a time word, in the years of the Peace, 7 of the 21 do. The formular sentences standing at the head of the unit no longer so conspicuously check and break the narrative into discrete segments; transitions between units become harder to see.

The force of this change is strengthened by the final change to be observed in the simple picture units of years eleven through sixteen: 7 of the 21 are held in a loose narrative connection with at least one of the two contiguous units. This is a form of connection never used for simple units in the Archidamian narrative, perhaps because the requirements of unit integrity militated against it: in the space of seven lines or less, it is difficult to establish the distinctive focus that allows a unit in loose narrative connection at the same time to retain its own identity. In the years of the Peace, however, unit distinction does not seem to be a dominant aim in the construction of the narrative. The simple picture unit v.35.2 is virtually indistinguishable from the extended narrative unit that follows it, since both describe the status quo in the diplomatic maneuvers of year eleven. Only the two time words and repeated subjects in the space of two lines allow us to see the outlines of two units of action. Similarly, v.83.3 would be, but for the time formula μετὰ τοῦτο, the second half of a normal action-reaction developed picture unit begun in v.83.1–2. The Argives are clearly marching out to retaliate for Agis's actions at Hysia. Thucydides' placement of the simple picture unit is becoming much bolder and freer in the years of the Peace.

These three interior changes—the lack of descriptive material, the number of simple units with four or five verbs, and the increase in action-reaction connections between units—all suggest that the function of the simple picture unit is changing in the narrative of the years of the Peace. The unit has become spare, emphasizing action at the expense of description; it frequently suggests depths of activity without fully reporting them. The placement of simple units suggests a new desire for speed and potential narrative integration into larger patterns. They are frequently made part of loose narrative connections, they occur in clusters with other simple units, and more often than in the earlier narrative they lack the distinctive expressions of time. The relatively deliberate, descriptive, and static simple picture unit of years one through ten has vanished, and in its place are units that are often themselves denser and briefer, reported now as part of an ongoing, larger sweep of events.[12]

5.2.2 DEVELOPED PICTURE UNITS

v.25, v.26, v.34, v.39.2, v.49–50.4, v.51, v.53, v.54, v.56.1–56.3, v.83.1–2, v.116.2–4, vi.7.1b, vi.7.2. Total: 13

Density and comparative brevity characterize more developed picture units also. As the units become longer, however, these qualities are harder to quantify. Counting the number of main verbs, for instance, would not serve to capture the development in tone. The clearest sense of change is achieved by comparing individual units from v.25–vi.7 with units of roughly the same structure and subject from the earlier war. This is possible because the basic unit type remains. Developed picture units are still used in the years of the Peace to expand the theme stated in the first sentence of the unit; the last sentence still usually contains a verb that indicates that the unit is ending.

The topics covered in the developed unit of action in v.25–vi.7 are military, political, a mixture of the two, or finally some long narratives highly idiosyncratic in subject matter.[13] A comparison of each type in turn with units of similar topic and length from ii.1–v.24 should suggest both the extent of the changes and the continuity of basic narrative habits shaping the account of the Archidamian years and that of the years of the Peace.

5.2.2.a Military Units: v.51, v.53, v.54, v.83.1–2, vi.7.1b, vi.7.2   Half of the developed picture units in years eleven though sixteen are military in subject. Units v.51, v.83.1–2, vi.7.1b, and vi.7.2 are the most simply organized: the fact of the military initiative is stated in the first sentence, causal or descriptive material falls in the center, and a verb of retreat rounds off the final sentence. This is comparable to the arrangement, if not the elaboration, of ii.79 (the Athenians and Thrace) or iii.88 (the Athenian and Rhegian attack on Aeolus) from the early war.

The individual military unit, however, is no longer as static and self-contained. The subject of v.51 is the battle at Heraclea in which the Lacedaemonian commander and many colonists die. Although the unit contains explanatory material ("for it was unmistakably against their region that the place had been established and fortified," οὐ γὰρ ἐπ᾽ ἄλλῃ τινὶ γῇ ἢ τῇ τούτων τὸ χωρίον ἐτειχίσθη, v.51.2), the focus does not lie there. We are told neither about the battle itself, as, for instance, in ii.79, nor about the setting, as in iii.88.[14] Instead, the bare outline of events is presented, and the reader is carried immediately into v.52, which sets the battle and its consequences into the larger frame of political tensions between Boeotia and Lacedaemon. The contrast with the earlier narrative is accentuated by the fact that v.51 is the last unit of year twelve and v.52 the first unit of year thirteen. The isolation of the year, as well as that of the individual unit, is being eroded in v.25–vi.7.

Unit v.83.1–2, the Lacedaemonian invasion of Argos, is followed immediately by v.83.3, an Argive retaliation; vi.7.1b, another Lacedaemonian initiative, is followed by a developed picture about Athenian and Argive reactions to the settlement of exiles at Orneae. Such clusters almost become action-reaction units in themselves, since only the existence of a formular first sentence separates the second unit in the cluster from its predecessor. Description within the body of the unit no longer forms it into a rounded entity with its own internal dynamics; instead, the reader is rushed on to a resolution of the unit that lies outside the unit itself.[15]

In v.54 (the Lacedaemonian march and Argive response) action and reaction do occur within the confines of the same unit; the arrangement is similar to that of iii.18 in the early war (Mytilene fights Methymna). However, v.54 is a developed picture unit being used in a new way, like the other units so far discussed. A first sentence occurs at the beginning of v.54; we are given no indication at first that the unit is not completely self-contained. But as v.54 continues from the initial mysterious Lacedaemonian march to an Argive action clearly taken on the assumption that Argos was the target, a connection is retroactively established with v.53.[16] Just as the actors in the situation were uncertain where cause and effect fell, so Thucydides also obscures the distinction between units of action. Unit v.55, again set off formally by a first sentence, in some ways presents the resolution to the whole development, since the conference at Mantinea is called to deal with the tensions portrayed in v.53 and v.54. Thus although v.54 is technically, in terms of its own arrangement, an action-reaction developed picture unit similar to iii.18, it is not autonomous and self-contained. It is instead part of a larger account formed by loose narrative connections. In this larger account, v.54 does not have a thematic identity of its own; it is merely one stage in the developing chain of events.

Unit v.53 is structurally the equivalent of iii.86. It too is a military unit that does not depict a single activity or an action and the reaction to it but rather describes the initial act that will, in units to come, lead to an extended campaign. Unit iii.86 begins the account of Athenian involvement in Sicily and gives a concise but thorough summary of the extensive political and military background leading to Athens's engagement. In comparison, v.53 tells of the first aggressive action on the part of one of the members of the newly formed alliance of Athens, Mantinea, Elis, and Argos, but the background is explained only briefly. In terms of the unit itself, it is hard to accept Andrewes's comment in *HCT* IV: 13: "When he wrote book v, Thucydides had a clearer idea what needed communicating, and how to do it." As Andrewes indicates, we are not sure what the important phrase τῆς τε Κορίνθου ἕνεκα ἡσυχίας means; Lattimore translates it "to keep Corinth inactive." It looks as if Alcibiades and the Argives are inviting open war instead, and we would like to know more about it. The paucity of detail in v.53 has to do with the fact that it does not as a unit stand on its own. It is a continuation of the account of developing hostilities between Argos and Lacedaemon that will end with the battle of Mantinea in year fourteen. Unit v.53, like v.54, is not self-sufficient and does not provide a static, limited focus. It is narrated instead as part of a complicated developing sequence of events.

5.2.2.b Political Units: v.25, v.34   In tone, these two units resemble ii.24 from the earlier narrative (the description of Athenian preparations). Again Thucydides describes to the reader some important general developments without expressly tying them to an extended narrative or conveying them in a speech.[17] The fact that v.25 opens the years of the Peace sets the tone for the whole period; it is a proem whose argument is that the years of the Peace involved no true peace. If we compare it to ii.1, the stark announcement of the Archidamian War's beginning, again we see the narrative of years eleven through sixteen establishing a dominant focus larger than that of the individual units.[18]

Unit v.34 involves more action and less analysis: it concerns the Lacedaemonian reactions both to the helots who had fought with Brasidas and to the return of the soldiers on the island. It resembles ii.24 in that the arrangement of the sentences is paratactic. The first sentence only introduces the chain of thought leading to the last sentence; it does not sum up the entire narrative. Unlike most of the units discussed so far, v.34 (though perhaps rather simple in structure) would not appear out of place in the context of the Archidamian narrative.

5.2.2.c Developed Picture Units with Mixed Subjects: v.39.2, v.56.1, v.116.2–4
Each of these three units shows the same density of action and brevity found in simple picture units of the years of the Peace. Civic and military developments merge: the alliance of Lacedaemon and Boeotia in v.39.2 leads to the destruction of Panac-

tum, the Lacedaemonian aid sent to Epidaurus in v.56.1 leads to Alcibiades' insulting addition to the inscription of the peace treaty in Athens,[19] and the Melian capture of part of the Athenian investment results in the unconditional surrender and destruction of the Melians in v.116.2–4. Thus all three units contain both an action and the reaction to it. Thucydides does not describe in detail either the initial activity or the result, and the chief impression gained is one of increasing momentum. In the Archidamian narrative, the action-reaction structure is reserved for military picture units; in the years of the Peace, Thucydides has extended its sphere considerably.

Moreover, these units present a structural characteristic shared by almost all of the developed picture units of the years of the Peace. In the early war, especially in describing political developments leading to military results, Thucydides generally states the major action in the first sentence, and then goes back in time in the next few sentences to explain it. But 10 of the 11 developed units from the years of the Peace considered so far are temporally straightforward. The first sentence initiates the activity, the last sentence concludes it, and the material in the center leads directly from the one to the other. Once more, the resulting impression is one of speed and causal connections linking contiguous units, compared with the more static and elaborately patterned arrangement of units of the Archidamian narrative.[20]

5.2.2.d Long Developed Picture Units: v.26 (28 lines), v.49–50.4 (42 lines)   These two units do not especially resemble each other except that both maintain the focus on a single event of the picture unit. Both are rather longer than the other examples of this form. Unit v.26 contains a directly methodological discussion like v.20.2, while v.49–50.4 contains a descriptive narrative like ii.93–94 or iii.92–93. Each of these two long units stands out in the years of the Peace, since the beginning and end sentences for once enclose the detail normally displayed in the developed picture units of years one through ten.

Unit v.26 clarifies the implications of v.25. Thucydides gives his reasons for considering the Peloponnesian War a single twenty-seven-year war and the reasons why we should accept his judgment. Unit v.26 will be relevant to any attempt to form a picture of how the *History* was written; it is clearly not formed of layers written at different times but was written as a single whole sometime after 404.[21] As a developed picture unit, it stands in the same relation to v.25 as v.20.2 does to the whole ten-year account that precedes it. It shows the author stepping back and examining his data.

Unit v.49–50.4, the description of Elean-Lacedaemonian tensions at the Olympic games, is very different from the other action-oriented developed picture units in years eleven through sixteen. It contains an unusual degree of detail; it also contains a first sentence of the temporally staggered type common in the early narrative. The first sentence announces the Olympic games of 420; the narrative then doubles back to explain why the Lacedaemonians do not participate. Only in v.50.2 do we return to the scene at the games themselves and a dramatic incident in which Lacedaemonian intervention is feared.

This unit suggests that the speed, density, and brevity that have distinguished so many picture units of years eleven through sixteen are deliberate choices on Thucydides' part as narrator. Here he presents us with a unit as carefully worked out as any from years one through ten. The pause in the narrative sweep is certainly well timed; v.49–50.4 immediately follows the complex unit v.42–48.3, in which the fourfold alliance of Athens, Argos, Mantinea, and Elis is formed. The activity at Olympia shows as vividly as possible the anxiety felt in all of Greece as a result of the alliance. We are shown the fact that the participants at the games saw themselves on the brink of potential war, and that war might be precipitated by something as apparently random as an isolated beating administered to an individual Spartan. The narrative pace has slowed down to pause at this moment, and as readers, like the spectators at Olympia, we draw our breath in suspense.

Developed picture units in years eleven through sixteen are shorter, on the average, than comparable units in years one through ten. The average number of lines per unit has dropped from fifteen to eleven. The basic difference lies in Thucydides' changing conception of the role of this kind of unit in the larger narrative pattern. Most developed picture units, whether military, political, or mixed in subject, display in comparison with units of the Archidamian narrative less description and a greater emphasis on action. Action-reaction units are common, as are loose narrative connections in which the single developed picture unit represents only one stage in an ongoing account, not a distinctive focus as in the earlier years.

The units themselves are arranged in simple chronological order, with the earlier activity in the first sentence, and the later events rounding off the unit. Only in the two more extended accounts, v.26 and v.49–50.4, do we recognize the full, polished, and self-contained unit common in years one through ten.

5.2.3 LIST UNITS

v.33, v.52.2. Total: 2

No list units in v.25–vi.7 resemble those of the first six years of the Archidamian narrative. The Athenian fleet is less often visiting a series of places in order; in years eleven through sixteen Athens is relatively quiet, and its fleet is not engaged in direct military activity. Nonetheless, in two units, v.33 and v.52.2, a certain linear quality emerges. The Lacedaemonians march into Arcadia in v.33, first, to give help to some Parrhasians and, second, to destroy the fortress at Cypsela; they achieve both ends. Alcibiades in v.52.2 also has two objectives: he marches through the Peloponnese with special attention given to Patrae. He hopes to build a post near Rhium but cannot do so.

Although certain linear elements are obviously present, neither unit is constructed on the model of list units in the early war. The combination of foci that obscures the progression of some list units in years seven through ten is even more evident here. In v.33, the Lacedaemonian intentions are presented through a series of participles, and two main verbs describe actions of Lacedaemonians and Mantineans respectively. The Mantineans retreat without accomplishing their aim, and, finally, after two more participles, the Lacedaemonians too return home. The effect of the alternating foci resembles that of the action-reaction developed picture units.

Unit v.52.2 is similar in arrangement. The second activity, building the wall at Rhium, is expressed as an intent ($\delta\iota\epsilon\nu o\epsilon\hat{\iota}\tau o$). The whole journey is shaped into a single effort, undertaken to inspire the allies, that meets with indifferent success. The unit as a whole has more complicated narrative aims than those conveyed by the simple parataxis of comparable list units in the early war, like ii.33, iii.91, or even iv.75.

In v.33 and v.52.2, heavy emphasis is laid on what the actors—Alcibiades, the Lacedaemonians, the Mantineans—anticipate. The actions themselves are presented as aspects of the plans. This suggests once more that in years eleven through sixteen the whole unit organization is in the process of transformation. The stripped-down simple and developed picture units, less carefully organized to present a single effect, more oriented to conveying movement and activity, are not part of a naïve or imperfectly worked-out narrative stretch. Units v.33 and v.52.2 too display a sense of the coordination of planning and action, and a corresponding emphasis on causal connection rather than the string of activities narrated in the Archidamian narrative.

5.2.4 EXTENDED NARRATIVE UNITS

v.27–31, v.32.3, v.35.2–7, v.36–37, v.38, v.40–41, v.55, v.57–75, v.82.2–6. Total: 9

We move now to the longer units. Extended narrative units in years eleven through sixteen fall into three different subcategories. Two of the 9 extended narrative units are shaped in a familiar way, although they are quite short in comparison with those of the Archidamian narrative; 6 are rather spare accounts of diplomatic developments undertaken just after the establishment of the peace treaty; 1, which includes the battle of Mantinea, takes up the entire summer of year fourteen. In all 9 units, we still find the first sentence introducing a narrative that combines the concentration around one focus of the picture unit with the linear progression of the list unit.

Units v.55 and v.82.2–6 most closely resemble extended narrative units from the earlier war, like iv.42–45 (the Athenian expedition against Corinth).[22] One of the foci dominates the others in the unit. In v.55 the chief subject is the unsuccessful conference at Mantinea, to which Argive, Epidaurean, Lacedaemonian, and Athenian reactions are then appended. In v.82.2–6 the emphasis falls on the second half of the unit: the Lacedaemonian decision to count newly democratic Argos an enemy and the consequent wall-building. Although relatively brief, these units are reminiscent of many such in the early war, in which the focus of a picture unit is added to the sequentiality of a linear account.

The most substantial feature distinguishing v.55 and v.82.2–6 from comparable units in the early war has to do with how they are placed in the surrounding text. As we have seen, v.55 sums up the action that has been developing in the two preceding picture units, v.53 and v.54. A congress attempts to resolve Argive and Epidaurian differences, but hostilities immediately recommence, in which Lacedaemonians and Athenians are also involved. Thus in terms of the passage as a whole, formular first sentences and changes of focus have become comparatively insignificant as signposts to the dynamic movement of the narrative; there is no reason beyond the purely formal placement of first sentences for us to consider v.55 one unit and v.53 and v.54 two.

Unit v.82.2–6, the seizure of power by the Argive democrats and consequent renewal of hostility with Sparta, ends with the Argives building their wall. A change of season occurs, and the first account of winter is v.83.1–3, the Lacedaemonian destruction of the wall and slaughter of the Hysians, which is followed in turn by v.83.4, the Argive retaliation against Phlius. Again, the unit is part of a larger loose narrative connection. The brevity of v.82.2–6 is also striking. Tantalizing statements indicate whole areas of political and military activity that Thucydides will not elaborate. It is worth quoting in its entirety, to demonstrate the rapidity with which a complex set of heterogeneous material is unrolled in a single account:

> The people of Argos, gradually banding together and recovering their courage, fell upon the oligarchs after timing this exactly with the Lacedaemonian athletic festival for youth. A battle was fought in the city, which the people won, and they killed some and exiled others. The Lacedaemonians, after long unwilling-

ness while their friends were calling on them, postponed the festival and came to their aid. When they found out at Tegea that the oligarchs had been defeated, they were then unwilling to go any further, although the exiles pleaded with them, and they returned home and held the festival. Afterward, when representatives came from the city and messengers from those outside Argos, and the allies were also present, and a lot was said on both sides, they determined that those in the city were in the wrong and resolved to campaign against Argos, but delays and procrastination followed. Meanwhile the Argive common people were afraid of the Lacedaemonians and sought the return of the Athenian alliance in the opinion that this would help them the most, and they built long walls to the sea so that if they were cut off by land they would have the advantage of importing necessities with Athenian assistance. Some of the Peloponnesian cities also had complicity in building the walls. The Argives turned out in full for the work, including women and household slaves, and carpenters and stone-workers joined them from Athens. And the summer ended.

καὶ Ἀργείων ὁ δῆμος κατ᾿ ὀλίγον ξυνιστάμενός τε καὶ ἀναθαρσήσας
ἐπέθεντο τοῖς ὀλίγοις, τηρήσαντες αὐτὰς τὰς γυμνοπαιδίας τῶν
Λακεδαιμονίων· καὶ μάχης γενομένης ἐν τῇ πόλει ἐπεκράτησεν ὁ
δῆμος, καὶ τοὺς μὲν ἀπέκτεινε, τοὺς δὲ ἐξήλασεν. οἱ δὲ Λακεδαιμόνιοι,
ἕως μὲν αὐτοὺς μετεπέμποντο οἱ φίλοι, οὐκ ἦλθον ἐκ πλέονος, ἀνα-
βαλόμενοι δὲ τὰς γυμνοπαιδίας ἐβοήθουν. καὶ ἐν Τεγέᾳ πυθόμενοι ὅτι
νενίκηνται οἱ ὀλίγοι, προελθεῖν μὲν οὐκέτι ἠθέλησαν δεομένων τῶν δια-
πεφευγότων, ἀναχωρήσαντες δὲ ἐπ᾿ οἴκου τὰς γυμνοπαιδίας ἦγον. καὶ
ὕστερον ἐλθόντων πρέσβεων ἀπό τε τῶν ἐν τῇ πόλει [ἀγγέλων] καὶ
τῶν ἔξω Ἀργείων, παρόντων τε τῶν ξυμμάχων καὶ ῥηθέντων πολλῶν
ἀφ᾿ ἑκατέρων ἔγνωσαν μὲν ἀδικεῖν τοὺς ἐν τῇ πόλει, καὶ ἔδοξεν αὐτοῖς
στρατεύειν ἐς Ἄργος, διατριβαὶ δὲ καὶ μελλήσεις ἐγίγνοντο. ὁ δὲ δῆμος
τῶν Ἀργείων ἐν τούτῳ φοβούμενος τοὺς Λακεδαιμονίους καὶ τὴν τῶν
Ἀθηναίων ξυμμαχίαν πάλιν προσαγόμενός τε καὶ νομίζων μέγιστον ἂν
σφᾶς ὠφελῆσαι, τειχίζει μακρὰ τείχη ἐς θάλασσαν, ὅπως, ἢν τῆς γῆς
εἴργωνται, ἡ κατὰ θάλασσαν σφᾶς μετὰ τῶν Ἀθηναίων ἐπαγωγὴ τῶν
ἐπιτηδείων ὠφελῇ. ξυνῄδεσαν δὲ τὸν τειχισμὸν καὶ τῶν ἐν Πελοποννήσῳ
τινὲς πόλεων. καὶ οἱ μὲν Ἀργεῖοι πανδημεί, καὶ αὐτοὶ καὶ γυναῖκες
καὶ οἰκέται, ἐτείχιζον· καὶ ἐκ τῶν Ἀθηνῶν αὐτοῖς ἦλθον τέκτονες καὶ
λιθουργοί. καὶ τὸ θέρος ἐτελεύτα. (v.82.2–6)

Such a narrative in the earlier war might have been followed by a speech or two, so that we could better understand the arguments of the Argive democrats for Spartan acceptance of the fait accompli, or the grounds on which the oligarchs based their claims. Further, we would like to have information about the nature of the διατριβαί and the μελλήσεις, delays and procrastination. Was there disaffection at Sparta? Revolt and reluctance among Sparta's allies? Thucydides does not tell us.

Comparable instances of condensation and brevity in the narrative of years one through ten do of course occur.[23] But in ii.1–v.24, because of other activities fully elaborated by means of speech, analysis, or a very detailed narrative, it appears that selectivity has determined the focus; Thucydides simplifies and hurries over those events he considers less important. In the years of the Peace, however, the scale of Thucydides' view of what is important has changed. Even a series of events as complex as those of v.82.2–6 is not treated in the detail of the Archidamian years; almost the entire six-year account is narrated with the same quick and spare prose.

Six political extended narrative units occur in years eleven and twelve: v.27–31, v.32.3, v.35.2–7, v.36–37, v.38, and v.40–41. They create a masterly summary of tangled diplomatic developments, and they guide the reader through the period directly after the Peace when the new lines of power have not yet formed and a variety of potential alliances and interests are seeking expression. Similar narrative stretches occur in v.21 and 22 in year ten, although there they form part of a longer complex unit.

These 6 political extended narrative units set the tone for the narrative of the years of the Peace. They dominate year eleven and lead the reader swiftly toward the first major pause of the ongoing account: the formation of the alliance among Athens, Argos, Mantinea, and Elis in year twelve. That pause, as we have seen, is emphasized by the picture unit v.49–50.4 that directly follows.

In their internal structure, v.27–31, v.32.3, v.35.2–7, v.36–37, v.38, and v.40–41 emphasize many of the same qualities we have seen in simple and developed picture units. The impression is one of intense activity, related in the order that it occurs, with relatively little attempt to distinguish between events that produce large results (one of the most important of these, the dismantling of Panactum leading to the open break of Athens and Lacedaemon, is presented in one line at the end of the picture unit v.39.2–3) and those that eventually come to nothing, like v.38: "and there was a certain apathy and delay about the whole business" (ἀμέλεια δέ τις ἐνῆν καὶ διατριβὴ τῶν πάντων). It seems that here Thucydides is interested in the unfolding of processes, not in outcomes significant in themselves.

If this is so, it suggests as well a reason why, in this speech-ridden period, he has chosen to summarize arguments rather than repeat them directly. A speech, especially as part of a complex unit of action, is a static form of narrative. It slows the action down while the reader pauses over one point in time.[24] But in the years of the Peace, it is the quality of the period as a whole, and not the myriad small actions that go into its formation, that seems to be emphasized by Thucydides. The 6 extended narrative accounts in years eleven and twelve are themselves spare and quick-moving. The first sentences separating them have become largely formal breaks, since the point of the unit is no longer the development of an individual focus, a distinctive way of looking at something determined by the relation of first sentence, description, and action. Instead, each unit flows into the next so that a single evolution of Mantinean, Lacedaemonian, Corinthian, Argive, and Boeotian movements results.

It remains to discuss the long extended narrative unit v.57–75. The whole summer of year fourteen is taken up by a narrative that builds to the battle of Mantinea and the collapse of the Argive drive for supremacy over the Peloponnese. It is the longest unit of action in the *History*, with 362 lines, and it is the only unit that absorbs an entire season.

This discussion has noted several times that, in the years of the Peace, Thucydides treats the unit divisions, identified by the formular first sentence and a change of subject, as formal aspects of the narrative unrelated to the dynamics of the immediate passage. They have become conveniences rather than reflections of true breaks in thought. The lack of time words and casual placement of simple units, the extensive use of action-reaction picture units themselves in turn set into loose narrative connections, the general absence of description to round off the individual unit—all these techniques combine to neutralize the integrity of the unit as a separate structure. The extended narrative unit v.57–75 contributes strongly to the same impression. Throughout the summer of year fourteen, the subject does not change; a single account is in the process of unfolding. The impending conflict between Argos and Lacedaemon involves shifts of focus from Lacedaemonians to Argives to the battle itself and its aftermath; no contrasting topic is inserted, and no time formula of the seasonal type (τοῦ δ' αὐτοῦ θέρους) interrupts it in a formal sense. There are rudimentary first sentences at v.58, v.61, v.62, v.63, v.64, v.75.4, and v.75.5 that indicate the shifts in focus, but these are common also in the long units of the Archidamian narrative. Compare, for instance, iv.13 and iv.15 in iv.8–23 (the account at Pylos) or iv.67 in iv.66–74 (the abortive Megarian revolution).

The effect of this single long unit on the rest of the narrative of years eleven through sixteen is that of a magnet. In the summer of year fourteen, Thucydides *has* formed the various strands into a single account. It further weakens the effect of surrounding first sentences and shifts of focus: retroactively it encourages us to think of v.35.2–38, v.39.2–48.3, or v.82.2–83.3 as single narrative passages also. Thucydides is moving beyond the unit of action.

Extended narrative units in years eleven through sixteen, like shorter units, are less static, less self-contained, and less oriented to description than are the extended narrative units in years one through ten. The two shortest units are set in narrative contexts that make them into parts of a developing account rather than individual entities; this fact is even more marked in the succession of extended narrative diplomatic exchanges that take up most of year eleven and begin year twelve. And the sweep and cohesiveness of the long unit in year fourteen epitomize the qualities dominant in the narrative of the years of the Peace.

5.2.5 COMPLEX UNITS

v.42–48.3 (188 lines), v.76–80 (81 lines), v.84.1–114 (226 lines), vi.1–7.1a (141 lines). Total: 4

A complex unit by definition will constitute an exception to the narrative characteristics of speed and activity noticed throughout v.25–vi.7. The *a-b-a* pattern, with an excursus occupying the center and a picture or extended narrative unit surrounding it, brings the developing chain of events to a temporary halt.

The 4 complex units in years eleven through sixteen provide such halts at four very important points in the narrative. They suggest the delineation of the stages marking the narrative of the years of the Peace: v.42–48 pauses at the consolidation of alignments represented by the alliance of Argos, Mantinea, Elis, and Athens; v.76–80 pauses at the destruction of that alliance and consequent shift of Argos toward Lacedaemon after the battle of Mantinea; v.84.1–114 pauses as the indeterminate third period is coming to an end, and sums up the nature of the drives that have dominated these years; vi.1–6 turns the reader's attention toward Sicily.

Unit v.42–48 presents the culmination of the tensions described in the string of diplomatic extended narrative units in years eleven and twelve. The treaty between the four powers is given; it crystallizes the balance of power achieved. The *a* element, the narrative surrounding it, is for once vivid and suspenseful. Alcibiades' personality emerges very clearly as he maneuvers to achieve the alliance and to discredit the Lacedaemonians and Nicias. The deliberateness of the pause created in v.42–48 is emphasized by the nature of the succeeding unit, v.49–50.4.[25] A causal connection links the two units; Elis's squabble with Lacedaemon leading to the exclusion of the Spartans from the games is invested with tension because the treaty has just been achieved. Because of that treaty, the war that may break out is a Panhellenic one. But Thucydides does not make the two units into a single whole; as rarely happens in the years of the Peace, each unit preserves its individual focus. Units v.42–48 and v.49–50.4 complement each other but do not merge into one account.

Unit v.76–80 occurs at the conclusion of the next stage in the six-year period. The four-fold alliance formed in v.42–48 comes to grief, and v.76–80 displays the political adjustments made as a consequence of Mantinea. The *b* elements of this complex narrative, the texts of the Argive-Lacedaemonian agreement and alliance, show the importance of the battle more vividly than any amount of analysis would. Again the narrative comes to a halt, and the forward-moving momentum so often a part of the units of this period is replaced by a rounded single unit whose relatively static quality enables the reader to see that a second stage in the ongoing chain of events has ended, and a third has begun.

The role of v.84.1b–114 is more subtle. The Melian dialogue is the second unit in year sixteen, and it articulates the issues of political power that have implicitly dominated the entire six-year narrative of the years of the Peace. The third section of this chapter will consider its relation to the whole at greater length; here our concern is with its internal organization. As a complex unit, v.84.16–114 contains some unusual features, since the *a* and *b* elements are not clearly separated. In effect, the dialogue between Athenians and Melians, originally the *b* element, becomes the *a* element and carries the narrative along.

The unit itself is not a static arrangement of frame-excursus-frame. The verbal exchange that initially creates the excursus displays the swiftness and momentum that characterize these years. The dialogue itself sums up many of the issues we have seen in action; the urge to sovereignty of the Argives, the struggle of the Lacedaemonians to maintain their control, the rage of the Athenians at Lacedaemonian disregard of the treaty—these are all implied in the dialogue: "after all, those who do not yield to equals but comport themselves well towards superiors and treat inferiors with moderation are the most successful" (ὡς οἵτινες τοῖς μὲν ἴσοις μὴ εἴκουσι, τοῖς δὲ κρείσσοσι καλῶς προσφέρονται, πρὸς δὲ τοὺς ἥσσους μέτριοί εἰσι, πλεῖστ᾿ ἂν ὀρθοῖντο, v.111.4). It is an error to interpret this nexus of ideas too narrowly, as a judgment only on Athens, or on Athens and its subjects and would-be subjects. The overcoming of unit autonomy that we have noticed throughout this chapter should encourage us to interpret the Melian dialogue in the widest possible manner. The six years of the Peace show each of the sovereign cities of Greece trying to obey the "natural" law Thucydides articulates in v.111. The Melian dialogue as a whole makes the dynamic of these years explicit, before the narrative moves on to Sicily. Who is equal, who superior, who really inferior? That is the question that the narrative of the years of the Peace has posed.

Unit vi.1–7.1a, the fourth and last complex unit in the years of the Peace, brings to an end this period by beginning the next stage of the twenty-seven-year war: it introduces the Athenian expedition to Sicily. The geographic and historical excursus, set as the *b* element inside the *a* element of Athens's decision to go to war, in-

vests the entire topic with an appropriate solemnity, at the same time that it emphasizes the fact claimed in the frame material: the Athenians are taking on a realm whose
extent they do not know at all. The subtle transition to Sicily toward the end of year
sixteen resembles the earlier transition in year eleven found in v.25 and v.26. No clear
break between the years of the Peace and the Sicilian narrative occurs in the text,
because years eleven through sixteen are indeed part of one twenty-seven-year war
and are the bridge linking the Archidamian narrative to the grim events of years
seventeen and beyond.

The 4 complex units found in v.25–vi.7 complement the speed and density that we
saw in simple picture, developed picture, list, and extended narrative units. In these
four places, the narrative slows its pace, the unit again becomes self-contained, and
the reader is allowed a pause. These 4 units support the argument that Thucydides'
focus in these years is directed not toward the individual activities as they succeed
each other, but toward the period as a whole. It is the shape of the whole, at important transitional points, that the 4 complex units delineate.

If we compare individual units from years eleven through sixteen with similar
units from the Archidamian narrative, it is easy to feel some dissatisfaction with them.
We miss the abundance of vivid description of years one through ten: marvelous
scenes like iii.113, excerpts from the prehistoric past like ii.68, gemlike descriptions
like iii.88, or even unhurried, fully developed units like ii.70. In the 119 units of the
Archidamian War, we see a more expansive side of Thucydides as a man interested
in detail for its own sake (choosing, for instance, to narrate Nicias's operations at
Minoa, iii.51). But the spare, rapid units of the years of the Peace, though harder to
appreciate as individual pieces of narrative, coalesce into a swiftly moving dramatic
whole that does not analyze as much as imitate the experience of the years of the
Peace. The narrative explores how precarious the Peace is: as events rush onward,
it becomes increasingly strained and finally, with the beginning of the Sicilian expedition, breaks down. But before it has disappeared entirely, Thucydides pauses at
Melos to consider its inner workings.

5.3 CONNECTIONS AMONG UNITS (v.25–vi.7)

Chapter 4 showed that a variety of links occur between units in the Archidamian
narrative, creating larger clusters of meaning. *A-b-a* structures, loose narrative connections, thematic juxtapositions, and causal connections link contiguous units to
each other, while other ties are formed by units within the same year and stretch

from one year to others. Such a bewildering variety of connections and combinations in the early Archidamian narrative is made possible by the nature of the units themselves; as fully rounded, multifaceted entities, they are capable of forming links with other units on a variety of levels. As we saw, the resulting narrative as a whole resembles a carefully fashioned web in which the many strands interweave to form a single but complex fabric.

In the years of the Peace, most of the connecting patterns of the Archidamian narrative disappear. As we have seen, individual units emphasize action at the expense of description, even in the many units that are seven lines long or less. Thematic or *a-b-a* connections become very rare indeed. Almost the only link between units in v.25–vi.7 is the loose narrative connection; that is very common indeed. The effect created remains vaguely paratactic, but it is a parataxis that emphasizes the individual unit's place in a single developing story.

The loose narrative connections of v.25–vi.7 focus on the developing diplomatic alignments that point to Mantinea and beyond, thematically, to Melos. In year eleven, v.35.2a, v.35.2b–7, v.36–37, and v.38 begin a chain; v.39.2–3, v.40–41, and v.42–48 continue it in year twelve. At the end of the year, v.51 stands in loose narrative connection with v.52.1. In year thirteen, v.53, v.54, v.55, v.56.1–3, v.56.4, and v.56.5 portray the developing tensions between Lacedaemon and Argos. Again a connection is made over the yearly break, with v.57–75, v.76–80, v.81.1, and v.81.2 in year fourteen. Year fifteen does not take up the theme again until the third unit, but v.82.2–6, v.83.1–2, and v.83.3 all concern Argos and Lacedaemon. Only at the end of the period as a whole, in year sixteen, does the single developing theme resolve into alternating foci created by units about Argos, Melos, and Pylos, with whose type we are familiar from the early war. Even after the introduction of Sicily, the same focus on ongoing developments persists, in a series of picture units about a Lacedaemonian invasion of Argos, an Athenian reaction, and then a complete change of focus to Macedonia.

The direction given the narrative as a whole by this ongoing, dynamic chain of loose narrative connections is further emphasized by the number of action-reaction units that compose it. Five simple picture units, 4 developed picture units, 1 list unit, and to some extent all 9 extended narrative units display within the unit the same sense of chronologically straightforward progression. Events move onward very rapidly, both within the unit and from unit to unit. A reader who expects the leisure, the nuances, and the multidimensional meanings and combinations of meanings from the Archidamian narrative will be continuously disappointed by the years of the Peace. But they have their own integrity and purpose as a narrative, which the description of the narrative as a whole that concludes this chapter will try to emphasize.

5.4 THE NARRATIVE OF THE YEARS OF THE PEACE (v.25–vi.7)

Year eleven is the year of the Peace with the greatest number of units. In 15 units of action it sets the tone for the period. This is apparent in the first two developed picture units, v.25 and v.26. They are not merely introductory, like ii.1. Instead, they propose a thesis that the six years that follow will bear out. They argue, first, that the war under consideration in the *History* was a twenty-seven-year war, and, secondly, that Thucydides had access to the relevant information that equipped him to make this judgment. If these two units in one sense comprise a second proem, we must not forget that it is a proem that argues for continuity with the earlier period.

On a structural level, that continuity is established by the existence of units of action, still more or less individually set off from each other by a formular first sentence and a change of focus. But how differently the units come together! Now they do not linger on individual scenes but rather provide a succession of developing links in a chain; paradoxically, the overall effect is more paratactic on the whole than is the earlier Archidamian style, with its more completely discrete units. Seven units in v.25–vi.7 develop a quick-paced diplomatic account that lasts through the year: they display the maneuvers among Peloponnesians in anxiety over a possible Athenian-Lacedaemonian alliance that would overpower them and then, with the winter's change of ephors in Sparta, the beginning of a new set of political alignments.

The military events during this year are clustered together, and as simple picture units they are relegated to the status of brief interruptions in the political narration. Units v.32.1 (Scione, Delos) and v.32.2 (Phocis, Locris) come after the first extended narrative unit; v.33 (the Lacedaemonians in Arcadia) and v.35.1 (the Dians takes Thyssus) come after the second; and v.39.1 falls after the long loose narrative chain formed by four units and briefly mentions Olynthus.

By carefully separating the two kinds of event, Thucydides is initiating a pattern that becomes very powerful later, as the six-year narrative continues. To change the metaphor here, the political developments are presented as a long gunpowder train that Thucydides shows being laid down. The military actions, sporadic and transitory in effect, are the sparks that for the moment fall well off to one side. But the cautious reader begins to wonder, as political alignments become firmer, when one will light too close to the powder train. There is dramatic intensity in the narrative of the years of the Peace, but it is a very different kind from that found in the first ten years' account.

Year twelve brings to a climax the political tensions set out in year eleven. There are only 5 units in the year; the first two display the realignment of forces around Argos and Athens, and the Lacedaemonian attempt to maneuver between Boeotian and Athenian demands, an attempt that fails in v.42–48. The political account, which has for the most part remained on a very general level, becomes very vivid and immediate, with the picture of the Lacedaemonians tricked by Alcibiades, and the embarrassment and panic of Nicias. With the formation of the alliance, one powder train is complete. The third unit of the year, v.49–50.4, shows a spark falling very close: Elis has become part of a powerful group, and the account of tensions at Olympia manages to convey the sense that a potentially frivolous incident is feared to have the capacity to plunge all Greece again into open war. The danger passes, but Thucydides has demonstrated how fragile the Peace is now deemed to be.

The two final short units of year twelve begin another stage in the account. The unprofitable meeting between Argives and Corinthians and the battle at Heraclea are unrelated and portray a period of irresolution before open conflict to come. The first unit of year thirteen confirms the predominantly political cast of these years: the climax to the events at Heraclea is a political tension between Boeotia and Lacedaemon.

Unlike the years examined so far, year thirteen is not composed of long diplomatic passages alternating with extremely short military units, but of 8 units in two and a half pages, all of them small pieces of the picture, sparks, to continue the metaphor: Alcibiades in the Peloponnese, war declared on Epidaurus by Alcibiades and the Argives, and a series of mysterious near-conflicts between Argos and Lacedaemon, at which the rest of the Greeks seem to anticipate with dread the renewal of open conflict. The strong emotion underlying the speech of Euphamidas the Corinthian in v.55 is perhaps the more eloquent for remaining undeveloped in the text.

The picture of Alcibiades from these years is much more striking than the actual space devoted to his description would indicate. One brief passage (v.43) considers him directly; it is significant that Thucydides waits to put into the mouth of Nicias at the end of the six years of "peace" the criticisms commonly laid at Alcibiades' feet by his contemporaries, that he was expensive, a profligate leader (ἐλλαμπρύν-εσθαι, "to show off," vi.12.2). In v.43 Thucydides singles out only his youth, his ambition, his slighted pride that he had not been considered essential to the negotiation of the Peace in 421. This is the information about him necessary to understand the precarious pace of these years: Alcibiades marching in the Peloponnese, Alcibiades engraving inflammatory remarks on steles, Alcibiades encouraging the Argives to make war on Epidaurus. He adds to the powder trail and the sparks the further imponderable element of an ambitious young man playing with fire in pursuit of aims that are highly personal in nature.[26]

Year thirteen ends with 2 simple units about Argive-Epidaurian hostilities. Year fourteen begins with the Lacedaemonian retaliation that was bound to come. The summer has already been discussed as a single extended narrative unit; an Argive general avoids the first confrontation, but Alcibiades encourages the Argives and their allies to march on Orchomenus, and the decisive engagement at Mantinea occurs. The Lacedaemonians are described as formidable again, "since it appeared that they had been humiliated because of luck while still the same men in spirit" (τύχῃ μέν, ὡς ἐδόκουν, κακιζόμενοι, γνώμῃ δὲ οἱ αὐτοὶ ἔτι ὄντες, v.75.3).

As we have seen, the existence of one large unit taking up the whole summer of year fourteen also suggests that the extent to which other, smaller units in the ongoing narrative have merged together is not accidental. Thucydides has made the entire period, as it were, into a single story that builds to Mantinea. Events that do not affect this end are related as briefly as possible. Units follow one another toward a climax rather than focusing attention on themselves.

The first winter account of the year is the complex unit that includes the Lacedaemonian-Argive agreement and treaty. Two simple units then relate further consequences of the battle: Mantinea's retreat from alliance with Athens and the oligarchic coup in Argos. A second stage in the six-year "peace" has been reached: Argos has tried and failed in its bid for supremacy. In 4 units, year fourteen depicts that failure and its immediate consequences.

Year fifteen is described in one and a half pages of text; of all the years of the war it is the most briefly narrated. Two simple units begin the year; another two simple picture units end it. The third unit is an extended narrative about the recapture of power by the democrats at Argos, the fourth a picture unit ten lines long about the Lacedaemonian decision not to accept the Argive change of government. The third stage of the years of the Peace begins, as have the others, with a period of indecision.

Year sixteen provides a return to the proportions of year eleven: 11 units occur in thirteen pages. But the two years are differently distributed. While year eleven included a chain of extended narrative units in loose narrative connection, year sixteen is composed of picture units, none over ten lines long, and 2 complex units, v.84.1b–114 in 226 lines and vi.1–7.1a in 141 lines. Unit v.84.1b–114 (the Melian dialogue) forms, as we have seen, a summary of the whole six years of "peace": it represents the principles on which all states, Athens included, have been jockeying for position. The unit is not simply a ruthless exposition of "might makes right"; the one detail supplied us about the arrangement for the exchange between Athenians and Melians is the following statement: "The Melians did not bring them before the common people but told them to speak to the officials and a small group about their reasons for coming" (οὓς οἱ Μήλιοι πρὸς μὲν τὸ πλῆθος οὐκ ἤγαγον, ἐν δὲ ταῖς ἀρχαῖς καὶ τοῖς ὀλίγοις λέγειν ἐκέλευον περὶ ὧν ἥκουσιν, v.84.3). On each side, as Thucydides makes clear, those who have power are trying to keep it. The Athenians have faced a small island with the choice of extinction or loss of political autonomy; the governors of Melos, however, present those under them with no choice at all.[27]

The years of the Peace come to an end between the complex unit v.84.1b–114 and the second complex unit of year sixteen, vi.1–7.1a. Five picture units form this narrative stretch, whose focus shifts from Phlius to Pylos to Melos, to Lacedaemon and Argos, to Melos again. The passage teems with activity: 4 of the 5 units are action-reaction arrangements. It does not, however, build to a climax, as have the two earlier stages in the six-year span. Our attention, like that of the Athenians, is merely distracted: we turn abruptly to Sicily.

This is certainly one interpretive thread sustained in years eleven through sixteen. The speed and density of the individual units, the abandonment of the self-contained, inward-turning pattern of the early war, make us as readers of book v feel that we, too, are watching the powder train laid down in these years. It must have been hard to estimate the ultimate significance of these events: What would they lead to? Would the celebration at Olympia, for instance, plunge Greece into general war again? It is all very simple, if you are a ruthless egotist like Alcibiades. You will gain no personal advantage from peace; well then, you work for war. But for the rest, Thucydides seems to be saying, these years passed very swiftly. And living through them, one did not feel as though one were living in peace.

The presentation of speed and tension in years eleven through sixteen is subtle. One would think, offhand, that the way to prove the continuation of war would be to emphasize every military conflict strongly. But Thucydides chooses another vision. The battles—between Phocis and Locris in v.32.2, or in Arcadia in v.33, or Olynthus in 39.1, Dium's revolt in 82.1, Macedonia in 83.4—these are passed over as briefly as possible. Of much more interest to him are the developments that lead to major crises: the consolidation of the four-fold alliance in year twelve, the end of its momentum in year fourteen, the consequent recovery of prestige by the Lacedaemonians.

Issues are not simple in these years, as the Melian dialogue at the end makes clear. Freedom, autonomy, is a mysterious thing, less easy to define than physical safety and comfort. And yet, to preserve that autonomy, human beings are willing to risk everything. As vi.1–7.1 spells the end to the years of the Peace, so the Melian dialogue is also in a way the introduction to the Sicilian expedition. Freedom means different things, to be sure, to Athens and Melos. But just as the Melians are not willing to become a subject state, so Athens will refuse to tolerate more years requiring the passive endurance of years eleven through sixteen, even though men like Nicias assure them they must. One may call both Melians and Athenians self-destructive, but Thucydides lets us see the glory of risking all on a single throw, along with the foolishness. It is part of human nature, he seems to say, to seek for more than security.

In v.25–vi.7 the narrative arrangement does not break away entirely from the Archidamian model. Units of action with formular first sentences continue to exist. However, within this general similarity change has occurred. Units contain much less leisurely description. They are both sparer and denser; many actions are briefly mentioned that we would like to see developed at greater length. Units are very frequently in loose narrative connection with one another.

There is a purpose to this swift and compact narrative. In the years of the Peace, Thucydides selects and controls the contents of the units to emphasize those developments, principally diplomatic, that lead again toward open war. The four points where a complex unit occurs and the narrative slows down, becoming more detailed and descriptive, represent conclusions to four stages involved in years eleven through sixteen: the period dominated by the alliance of Argos, Mantinea, Elis, and Athens; the period in which the battle of Mantinea breaks that alliance; the general conclusion to the whole period represented by the Melian dialogue; and the turning toward Sicily in vi.1–7.

CHAPTER SIX

· Years Seventeen through
Twenty-one (vi.8–viii.109)

The Unit of Action Transformed

This chapter examines the disappearance of the unit of action as a structuring principle, in the five years of the *History*'s narrative that remain to be discussed. I will
argue that, viewed in the light of the kinds of analysis used so far in this study, the
narratives of the Sicilian expedition (books vi.8–vii.87) and of the Aegean War
(book viii) exhibit some profound structural similarities that distinguish them from
the earlier accounts of the Archidamian years and the years of the Peace. Thucydides is now choosing a very different way of telling the ongoing story of the Peloponnesian War.

These two last stretches of narrative in the *History* are generally thought of as
two separate and very different accounts. The Sicilian narrative (in years seventeen through nineteen, vi.8–vii.87) forms a polished essay. It includes speeches,
passages of intense pathos, and a clear dramatic shape that prepares the reader for
the tragic conclusion at the end of book vii, the destruction of the Athenian fleet
in the harbor of Syracuse.[1] The Aegean account that follows it and constitutes the
bulk of book viii, on the other hand, is unfinished. It ends abruptly, in the middle
of a summer and even a sentence.[2] There are no speeches,[3] and sometimes it is hard
to follow the chain of events.[4] Major events, like the Athenian change of government recounted in viii.63.3–77, are introduced abruptly, and, in contrast to events
of comparable magnitude in Sicily, they are rather dryly reported.[5]

Such differences in style between the two accounts have long been recognized.[6]
Not so frequently recognized are profound structural similarities between the Si-

cilian books and book viii that indicate, first, that the last five years of the narrative of the *History* are formed on comparable narrative principles, and, second, that these principles are very different from those that lie behind the narrative of years one through sixteen.

This chapter will explore two major structural changes that take place in Thucydides' late narrative. First, individual units of action (or scenes, as I will now call them) are no longer clearly separable from those that precede and follow them, since the narrative as a whole now develops as successive and interlocking aspects of one complex picture, focusing on the war in Sicily in books vi and vii and the Aegean War in book viii. Scenes in books vi.8–viii.109 do not resemble either the rounded, descriptive units of action of years one through ten or the more abbreviated, momentum-driven units of years eleven through sixteen. Instead, highly diverse elements of place, subject, and even time are considered together (and make sense together) as complementary aspects of a larger general focus, which dominates the entire account. Second (and this plainly is related to the changed nature of the scene), formular introductory sentences setting out a change of subject, action, place, and time at the head of each scene have largely disappeared. As a result of these two changes in structure, the *History* in books vi.8–viii.109 cannot be analyzed as a paratactic progression of independent units. The narrative has become a more organically structured whole, in which each new scene is intricately interconnected with those that precede and follow it.

The chief concern of the discussion that follows is to show the extent to which Thucydides abandons his earlier narrative structures in books vi.8–viii.109. The discussion is based on a series of examples, rather than the quantitative technique used in earlier chapters, because the aspects of the narrative previously measured—the formular first sentence and the discrete, autonomous structure of the individual unit—are no longer there to be measured.[7] Although aspects of Thucydides' earlier narrative habits can still occasionally be identified, they have now become virtually irrelevant to the narrative's large-scale organization. Successive scenes can be distinguished from each other by changes in setting, actors, the action, or even occasionally a time formula. But these elements no longer mutually reinforce each other by occurring simultaneously and thus demarcating a unit of action. Instead, Thucydides deliberately uses them to offset each other, so that each scene to some extent merges with those before and after it.

The winter of year eighteen in the Sicilian narrative provides a good example. The scene of vii.10 begins like a complex unit of action from the Archidamian narrative, with a formular first sentence that includes an indication of time, subject, setting, and verb: "In the following winter, when the men from Nicias reached Athens, they stated what they had been told orally, answered any questions that were asked, and delivered the letter" (τοῦ δ' ἐπιγιγνομένου χειμῶνος ἥκοντες ἐς τὰς Ἀθήνας οἱ παρὰ τοῦ Νικίου ὅσα τε ἀπὸ γλώσσης εἴρητο αὐτοῖς εἶπον, καὶ εἴ τίς τι ἐπηρώτα ἀπεκρίνοντο, καὶ τὴν ἐπιστολὴν ἀπέδοσαν). But the reading of Nicias's letter in Athens is not the *b* element in a unit centered on the meeting in Athens at which the letter was read, as one would expect, according to the Archidamian model. Instead, the scene glides into the consideration of further political issues in Athens (vii.16.1b) to steps then taken as a result of those decisions (vii.16.2b) to the reasons for those steps that involve Corinth (vii.17.2) to Corinthian action, first generally (vii.17.3) and then in Naupactus (vii.17.4).

If we examine in detail the five points at which these partial shifts in subject occur, the difference from the unit structure of years one through sixteen becomes obvious. The first shift, at vii.16.1b, occurs in the middle of a sentence: "When the Athenians heard it, they did not release Nicias from his command, but . . . they voted to send another land and naval force" (οἱ δὲ Ἀθηναῖοι ἀκούσαντες αὐτῆς τὸν μὲν Νικίαν οὐ παρέλυσαν . . . στρατιὰν δὲ ἄλλην ἐψηφίσαντο πέμπειν καὶ ναυτικὴν καὶ πεζήν). The second shift, in contrast, appears at first to be introduced by a formular first sentence: "They sent Eurymedon to Sicily . . . immediately, around the winter solstice . . . to announce . . . " (καὶ τὸν μὲν Εὐρυμέδοντα εὐθὺς περὶ ἡλίου τροπὰς τὰς χειμερινὰς ἀποπέμπουσιν ἐς τὴν Σικελίαν . . . ἀγγελοῦντα . . . , vii.16.2). The second half of the sentence, however, deliberately draws the reader back to the original first subject of the scene, since what Eurymedon is to announce (ἀγγελοῦντα) concerns the decision taken at the meeting in Athens and the help that would be forthcoming in consequence.

The third shift of subject is only a slight extension of the idea of the previous one; we move from Athenian ships being sent to Sicily to ships being sent around the Peloponnese. Then the fourth and fifth shifts, which involve Corinth, are presented as the causal background that makes vii.17.2 necessary. But, unlike such causal material in an earlier unit of action, the background material is not now carefully framed and identified as subordinate in importance to the surrounding context. Rather, it ends the scene and thus provides an easy transition to the next subject, since the Lacedaemonians have already been introduced as the subject of one sentence in vii.17.3. The beginning of vii.18 is a natural extension.

The sentence that introduces vii.18, the general discussion of Lacedaemonian thoughts and strategy, is formular, but not so obviously as the sentence in vii.16.2b quoted above. The time expression emphasizes relations with the scene just discussed: "The Lacedaemonians were also preparing for an invasion of Attica, as they had already resolved and also with the Syracusans and Corinthians urging them on, after they had found out about the reinforcements for Sicily" (παρεσκευάζοντο δὲ καὶ τὴν ἐς τὴν Ἀττικὴν ἐσβολὴν οἱ Λακεδαιμόνιοι, ὥσπερ τε προυδέδοκτο αὐτοῖς καὶ τῶν Συρακοσίων καὶ Κορινθίων ἐναγόντων, ἐπειδὴ ἐπυνθάνοντο τὴν ἀπὸ τῶν Ἀθηναίων βοήθειαν ἐς τὴν Σικελίαν, vii.18).[8]

Thus in the winter of year eighteen, the one formular sentence that might divide the narrative occurs at vii.16.2b, and even here the second half of the sentence makes it obvious that no clean break has taken place. The one strong shift of subject occurs at vii.18, where the Lacedaemonian preparations and plans are introduced. But the end of vii.17 works against a sense of division, as does the sentence that introduces vii.18. A provisional separation of the winter of year eighteen into two scenes can be made, one scene loosely dominated by the Athenians, the other summing up the Lacedaemonian state of mind. But because the structural signals of change now do not reinforce but rather contradict each other, the division seems one of editorial convenience rather than a genuine division between two separate narrative units; it does not reflect the basic structure of the passage.[9] In subject, Corinth forms a bridge as a topic linking Athens and Sparta. The only apparent formular first sentence occurs in the middle of the first scene and does not break the narrative.

The start of viii.60 within the Aegean narrative shows the same refusal of distinctive unit boundaries. The previous scene has focused on the problem of pay for the Peloponnesian army and Tissaphernes' desire to lure the Peloponnesians back from Rhodes (viii.57). The scene of viii.60 begins: "When the winter was already ending, the Boeotians used treachery to capture Oropus, where the Athenians had a garrison" (Βοιωτοὶ δὲ τελευτῶντος ἤδη τοῦ χειμῶνος Ὠρωπὸν εἷλον προδοσία, Ἀθηναίων ἐμφρουρούντων). The change in setting from the Aegean to Boeotia appears to be absolute.

However, viii.60 does not remain at Oropus. Within eight lines, the narrative continues: "Accordingly, now that they held Oropus, the Eretrians went to Rhodes, calling the Peloponnesians into Euboea" (ἔχοντες οὖν ἤδη τὸν Ὠρωπὸν ἀφικνοῦνται ἐς Ῥόδον οἱ Ἐρετριῆς, ἐπικαλούμενοι ἐς τὴν Εὔβοιαν τοὺς Πελοποννησίους). And the next sentence goes on to add that the Peloponnesians choose to go to Chios: "But they were more intent on coming to the aid of Chios, since it was in difficulty, and they put out from Rhodes and sailed with all their ships" (οἱ δὲ πρὸς τὴν τῆς Χίου κακουμένης βοήθειαν μᾶλλον ὥρμηντο, καὶ ἄραντες πάσαις ταῖς ναυσὶν ἐκ τῆς Ῥόδου ἔπλεον). Both the scene and the winter then end with an account of an engagement the Peloponnesians encounter on their way to Chios from

Rhodes; no time words occur to interrupt this development. As in vii.10–17 discussed above, the stages in the account are all gradual, but the scene that begins near the boundaries of Attica ends at Rhodes and Samos. Setting, actors, and action have all gradually changed without the aid of a structural division in the narrative; no break, complete with formular first sentence or change of subject, has occurred. The Peloponnesians here provide the pivot, since we see them requested to come to Euboea, and deciding to go to Chios instead.[10]

As in vii.10–17, the changing subject within viii.60 implies links between scenes too. The end of the unit, with its emphasis on the Peloponnesian fleet, approaches if it does not completely join with viii.57–59. That is, the Peloponnesians of the previous scene, who have been driving a very hard bargain with Tissaphernes, are the same group who in the middle of viii.60 go to Chios rather than Euboea.[11]

The scenes of vii.10–17 and viii.60, then, demonstrate one important structural change that has taken place in the *History*. As appendix A's list of narrative segments for years seventeen through twenty-one indicates, books vi through viii can be divided into scenes as much as possible like the previous units of action, but the attempt does not now lead to an understanding of the narrative's underlying structure; it is precisely in trying to define the boundaries demarcating individual scenes that we realize the extent of the change. To be sure, Thucydides continues to use certain aspects of familiar techniques, like introductory sentences indicating temporary shifts of subject. However, such sentences no longer divide the narrative into discrete, paratactic segments. They work instead contrapuntally, each offsetting the impact of the others. The narrative flows from place to place, from actor to actor, from one activity to the next, without establishing a series of complete breaks separating one scene cleanly from the next.[12]

Almost any passage from books vi, vii, and viii would demonstrate the individual scene's now permeable boundaries. The narrative of viii.29–43 is a passage composed, in my reading of it, of eleven scenes. One further point about the difficulty of distinguishing scenes emerges when a passage of this sort is considered in its entirety. Six of the eleven scenes in viii.29–43 are introduced by formular first sentences of the type books ii.1–vi.7 have accustomed us to; the range of subjects displayed in each scene is briefly indicated in table 6.1.[13]

In these eleven scenes, not only is there a blending of subject within the individual scene; the same topics are repeatedly reintroduced throughout the passage, which further serves to break down any remaining sense of boundary between scenes. The elements shared by any two scenes constantly change: sometimes it is setting, sometimes actor, sometimes activity. Some of the topics repeated in viii.29–43 are listed in table 6.2.

TABLE 6.1   Subjects of eleven scenes, viii.29–43

Scene	Subject
Scene 1: viii.29	Tissaphernes, Hermocrates, Therimenes, and problem of pay
Scene 2: viii.30	Athenians at Samos decide on plans against Chios and Miletus
Scene 3: viii.31–33	Astyochus at Chios, Therimenes, Chians, Lesbians to Miletus by way of Corycus
Scene 4: viii.34	Athenians at Corycus, Chios
Scene 5: viii.35	Lacedaemonians to Cnidus, Athenians at Samos
Scene 6: viii.36–38.1	Astyochus at Miletus, problem of pay discussed with Tissaphernes and Therimenes
Scene 7: viii.38.2–5a	Athenians against Chios, and difficulties of Chians
Scene 8: viii.38.5b	Athenians at Samos against Miletus, Peloponnesians refuse battle
Scene 9: viii.39–42	Lacedaemonian advisers for Astyochus sent out, Chians ask Astyochus for help against Athenians, Astyochus journeys to meet advisers and sails against Athenians at Syme, then to Cnidus
Scene 10: viii.43.1	Athenian fleet from Samos sails to Syme and back to Samos
Scene 11: viii.43.2–4	Peloponnesians together at Cnidus, problem of pay, Tissaphernes

TABLE 6.2   Subjects in common among scenes, viii.29–43

Subject	Scenes
Astyochus	3, 6, 9
Tissaphernes and pay	1, 6, 11
Athenians at Chios	2, 4, 7, 9
Athenians stationed at Samos	2, 5, 8, 10
Chios	2, 3, 4, 7, 9
Cnidus	5, 9, 11

The scenes in viii.29–43 are thus interdependent to an extent unknown in the earlier narrative of the *History*. It is as if the different kinds of link that earlier provide a sense of narrative patterning and suggest connections to be drawn among different contiguous units of action—loose narrative connections, *a-b-a* patterns, thematic echoes, and so on—are all being used at once, to the extent that the very integrity of the narrative blocks so linked has melted away. The effect is cumulative.

TABLE 6.3 Distribution of subjects of scenes, vi.8–viii.6

	Year seventeen	Year eighteen	Year nineteen
Athenians	13	5	10
Syracusans	3	2	9
Both of above	2	1	3
Peloponnesians	1	4	5
Non-Sicilian	0	4	1
Total scenes	19	16	28

Thucydides is no longer using the Archidamian unit of action as the basic building block of his narrative. The narrative of viii.29–43 is rather a single and ongoing passage, without clear separations among its various component parts.

Thus a larger and more complicated kind of narrative unity has transformed the structure of the account in books vi.8–viii.109. For the Sicilian books, the point does not really have to be proved in great detail; most scholars would agree that almost all scenes in vi.8–viii.6 contribute to the development of a single plot, the fate of the great Athenian army sent off to conquer Sicily in year seventeen.[14] One of the elements that create this impression can be seen in a table. Of the sixty-three scenes that comprise years seventeen through nineteen, only five (seventy-one lines, or a little more than two pages of text) are not dominated by one aspect or another of this larger plot. The remaining fifty-eight have as their subject the Athenians engaged in trying to dominate Sicily, the Syracusans defending themselves, the two in combat, or the Peloponnesians coming to help the Syracusans (see table 6.3).[15]

On the surface it seems surprising that the structure of book viii can be analyzed in the same terms. Events in the Aegean War seem chaotic, in contrast to those of Sicily; Ionia is a vast area, and successive scenes occur at widely different places and in what looks like a random order. For instance, in viii.19–22, in the space of fifty-three lines (approximately five scenes), our attention is drawn from Chios to Anaia, to Teos and Ephesus, to Samos, to Spiraeum, to Cenchriae, to Teos, Aerae, Samos, and again to Chios.

However, just as in the Sicilian account, scenes with very different settings, actors, and actions are nonetheless linked together to form a continuous, ongoing story. Thus Chios in viii.14–16, Miletus in viii.17, Samos in viii.21, and Lesbos in viii.22 are not treated as separate topics, as they might have been in the Archidamian account. The Chians have been instrumental in starting the revolt of Miletus in viii.17

TABLE 6.4   Distribution of subjects of scenes, viii.7–109

	Year twenty	Year twenty-one
Athenian fleet	9	5
Peloponnesian fleet	9	3
Both of above	11	3
Tissaphernes	7	8
Total scenes	36	19

and the revolt in Lesbos in viii.22 (Thucydides explains why in viii.22). The ships in Cenchriae are getting ready for Chios in viii.20. The Athenian fleet, on the other hand, brings about the democratic revolution in Samos in viii.21; later, the change of government in Athens itself takes its starting point and much of its direction from this same fleet.[16] Tissaphernes will play a role here (viii.56.1b–5), as well as in determining the fortunes of the Peloponnesian fleet (viii.78).

In other words, as in the Sicilian narrative, the scenes that follow each other in book viii are structured to represent different facets of a single question about winning and losing. Here the question is, Will the Peloponnesian or the Athenian fleet dominate the eastern Mediterranean? Like the Sicilian account before it, book viii can be described in terms of a few main foci.[17] The fifty-five or so scenes of viii.7–109 emphasize the Athenian fleet and the various personalities who control it; various Ionians and their competing factions; the Peloponnesian leaders and fleet; the two fleets in conflict; and the influence on the shape of the conflict exerted by Persian satraps, notably Tissaphernes and Pharnabazus. Table 6.4 presents the distribution of these subjects in the year and a half narrated in book viii.

The extent to which book viii follows the integrating and interlocking narrative style of books vi and vii is all the more striking in that events themselves do not seem naturally to lend themselves to forming a single, ongoing development. As we have already seen, viii.60, the account of Oropus, leads back to the Peloponnesians at Rhodes.[18] Other scenes revealing that the focus now lies on the Aegean as a whole would be viii.45–54, where the political coup at Athens is presented as the direct outcome of Alcibiades' machinations with Tissaphernes, and viii.63.3–77, where the remainder of this account begins at Samos and continues with a strong emphasis on the roles of Alcibiades, Tissaphernes, and the fleet at Samos. Thucydides prevents us from viewing the events at Athens, important as they are, as unrelated and isolated phenomena. Instead, like accounts of events in other cities, such as Samos,

Chios, and Teos,[19] the upheavals at Athens are presented as aspects of the single convulsive power struggle dominating the Aegean as a whole.

Book viii thus resembles the Sicilian account in the extent to which scenes that succeed each other take up the same few foci repeatedly. Yet in another respect the two accounts still appear to be very different. The Sicilian account is understandable on a level that book viii lacks; we know in books vi and vii what Thucydides thinks about the events unfolding as well as what occurred, because the narrative as a whole is shaped—on the most obvious level, it has a beginning, middle, and end. This is not true of book viii, the account of the Aegean War. However, the fact that we do not fully understand where viii.7–109 is going does not mean that lines of interpretation are absent. Lacking the larger controlling structure, however, the reader cannot assign interpretive weight with any certainty that the narrative's own lines of power are being honored.

Let me begin with one season of the Sicilian expedition in some detail, as illustration of what I mean. The winter of year seventeen is formed by seven scenes occurring in Syracuse, the region of Messina and Naxos, Camarina, Athens, and Sparta (vi.63–93). All of them concern the development of the Sicilian expedition: an Athenian victory at Syracuse is followed by Syracusan reflections afterward, subsequent Athenian preparations for spring, the Lacedaemonian assembly in which Alcibiades persuades the Peloponnesians to send reinforcements to Sicily, and a final brief scene at Athens, where more money is voted for the expedition. If we look at this sequence of scenes closely, we see two simultaneous and contradictory interpretive developments emerging; it is the way they are arranged that allows both to remain, as it were, in suspension for the moment.

On the most obvious level of the narrative, the Athenians are still in control. They dominate four of the seven scenes and occupy a large part of a fifth (vi.75–88.2). The winter begins with an account of their victory and ends with a brief statement of the support their expedition still receives at home. Thus from one viewpoint, year seventeen ends with Athens's control of the situation unshaken. But within this large-scale picture of Athenian optimism, Thucydides has placed a second, subtler development designed to cast doubt on all the Athenian plans. The victory in vi.63–72.1a is followed by a scene in Syracuse, where Hermocrates criticizes Syracusan mistakes in terms that leave hope for future improvements and eventual success, a critique later indeed confirmed by events. As threatening to Athens on a subtler level, though, is the fact that the meeting takes place at all. The scene of vi.72.1b–73 demonstrates that the Syracusans have in Hermocrates a formidable leader even in defeat, and their acceptance of his advice in vi.73 is one sign that in Syracuse the Athenians have unwittingly taken on an enemy equal to themselves.[20]

The debate at Camarina within the fourth scene (vi.75–88.2) is hard to judge as a set of issues, though in comparison with Hermocrates, Euphemus the Athenian speaker appears defensive;[21] certainly the Camarinaean decision to choose neutrality is more of a clear defeat for Athens than it is for Syracuse. Athens needs support in the winter of the expedition's first year not only for practical reasons but even to render its mission legitimate. The Athenians cannot claim to have been called to Sicily if no Sicilian city agrees with them.[22]

Finally, the sixth of the seven winter scenes of year seventeen is the most devastating of all for Athens. Alcibiades in exile is shown here to be still significant—now even dangerously significant—as an element in the Sicilian account as a whole.[23] In vi.88.7–93.3, Alcibiades alone is responsible for the Peloponnesian decision to support Syracuse with arms, and he is the determining factor in their decision to fortify Decelea. Gylippus, who will play such a large part in the military success of Syracuse, is selected largely as a result of Alcibiades' urgings. The brief scene about Athenian finances (vi.93.4) that ends the year is anticlimactic after this picture of resolution and energy. Although Athens's mastery of the situation in Sicily has not been physically threatened, the narrative of the winter of year seventeen already signals to the attentive reader that Athens faces great future difficulties.

Thus the winter of the first year of the Sicilian expedition presents a subtle interpretive ambiguity: two conflicting lines of development that only the end of the account in year nineteen will put in correct perspective. But if we lacked the end of the Sicilian account, and the series of judgments related there,[24] we would not see the winter of year seventeen as the masterly performance it is. That is, we would be unable to distinguish between the more obvious and superficial set of developments, those in which Athens still appears successful, and the more restrained but compelling indications that weaknesses are already appearing. We would see the winter's various developments in one sense as coherently interlinked, because of the set of causal connections obliquely binding the seven scenes together as aspects of the general Sicilian focus, but the knowledge to interpret each scene in the light of the meaning of the whole would be missing.

Turning now to book viii: again, the linear links, the causal connections, are in place. As in year seventeen above, the narrative in years twenty and twenty-one moves rapidly from one focus to the next, from the Peloponnesians to Tissaphernes to the Athenians and Ionians and back to the Peloponnesians again. The outlines for drama exist in Tissaphernes' growing vacillation, the increasing demoralization of the Peloponnesians, the astonishing resilience of Athens, and the very complexity of the situation created as each of these forces alone or in combination acts as a chemical catalyst upon innumerable small cities and towns along the Aegean coastline. But just as the lines of tension within the winter of year seventeen could not be accurately drawn without reference to the end of the account in year nineteen, so our feeling for the architechtonic quality of book viii is necessarily faint. We do not know where or how Thucydides would have brought to a close the picture that we see developing over two years and fifty-five scenes, in the extant last chapters of the *History*.

So we come to the end, as the *History* breaks off in the summer of the twenty-first year of the war. The unit of action disappears in books vi.8–viii.109. It is superseded by the use of scenes that frequently are not confined to one setting, actor, or action and often lack a formular first sentence. A series of such nonunitary scenes forms an ongoing narrative; because the narrative moves fluidly among a limited number of topics that blend together in different combinations within successive scenes, it must be made sense of as an ongoing single, if complicated, account. Because the Sicilian narrative comes to a conclusion, as readers we can see that it is clearly organized to form an interpretive whole. Our view of book viii, however, must remain one of a linked series of scenes that still lack the inner coherence of a completed narrative, despite their obvious connections to each other. If we were missing the latter half of book vii, the Sicilian narrative would disappoint and mystify us in some of the same ways that book viii currently does.

This new, more integrated narrative structure found in both the Sicilian narrative and the account of the Aegean War in book viii represents a very great change in Thucydides' narrative habits. The paratactic succession of discrete units of action found in years one through sixteen of the *History* has been superseded in both the Sicilian and Aegean portions by a more ambitiously organized single narrative, several years in length, whose scenes are mutually dependent on each other and whose interlocking repetitive themes create the ongoing account. In the earlier books we see a historian interested in the discrete event that happens to a particular group of people at a given place and point in time, narrated for its own sake and then arranged as well as one element in a chain of separate similar events. In the last three books one might say that the war itself occupies his attention, as a subject all of whose parts are meaningful with relation to the whole. So book viii, the narrative that is the most difficult for us to understand and appreciate, is also the one that most fully demonstrates in action the proud claim of i.1.2: "This was certainly the greatest disturbance to affect the Hellenes and a considerable number of barbarians—one might say the majority of mankind" (κίνησις γὰρ αὕτη μεγίστη δὴ τοῖς Ἕλλησιν ἐγένετο καὶ μέρει τινὶ τῶν βαρβάρων, ὡς δὲ εἰπεῖν καὶ ἐπὶ πλεῖστον ἀνθρώπων).

CHAPTER SEVEN

· Some Conclusions

Thucydides' Narrative Structures
(ii.1–viii.109)

This study of the *taxis* or narrative arrangement of Thucydides' *History*, ii.1–viii.109, leads to two broad areas of conclusion concerning the narrative organization of the Archidamian War and the ways in which the narrative patterns established there are transformed as the *History* progresses. I will summarize these matters first, and then return to some more general and impressionistic arguments raised at the end of the introduction, about the mind of the man who wrote the *History* and about the genre his history helped fashion.

Books ii.1–v.24 are organized as a paratactic sequence of units of action. Each unit is introduced by a distinctively formular first sentence that emphasizes both radical discontinuity with what has immediately preceded it and a larger sense of connection with the narrative as a whole, since the same formulae are repeated at the head of every unit in the progression; the expressions of time are particularly important in anchoring these formular sentences to Thucydides' larger summer/winter schema. Each unit of action has a distinctive shape of its own, and the material is carefully organized so that some units, or even parts of units, receive more detailed, explicit consideration, while other contiguous material is treated quite summarily. The unit structure itself is often an interpretive choice. List units, for instance, often convey information about Athenian naval maneuvers that do not lead to immediate results of much importance but provide part of the general strategic picture of the early war; the spare, linear quality of the unit itself emphasizes the kind of attention Thucydides places on the event recounted.

The absolute separation of contiguous units, each set off by its own first sentence and distinctive shape, gives the Archidamian account as a whole both subtlety and resonance. As chapter 4 shows, each unit offers the possibility of a variety of connections to be made with other units. In some cases, the relation is analytic, in that one unit gives background or explains causes lying behind the other; in some, the relation is purely linear, since a single development occurs, and two or more units merely present earlier and later aspects of it. Sometimes the link is more loosely thematic or even ironic, requiring the reader's awareness of possible connection or significant contrast rather than an obvious stated relationship of subject, setting, or action. Connections can be explicit or implicit, and can occur between two contiguous units, between units separated by the interjection of a third unit, or between units widely separate in the text. All these patterns of connection together form the web of meaning that we call the Archidamian War; by writing it as he has, Thucydides requires his readers to do much of the work of making meaningful connections among units for themselves.

Even if units of action per se have not been traditionally identified as the building blocks for Thucydides' early narrative, their effect has long been recognized. Most readers learn to read Thucydides by beginning at the beginning; judgments about later books of the *History* are often based on expectations aroused by how the narrative of the earlier Archidamian account in books ii and iii is formed. Books v and viii have often been considered incomplete and uneven drafts, almost collections of notes, and the Sicilian narrative of books vi and vii superficially appears to be a monograph originally written to be independent from the larger twenty-seven-year war.[1] But the kinds of changes that occur in the *History's* narrative structure and have been examined in this study make it clear that books v–viii are not merely imperfect sketches of something whose finished version would resemble books ii.1–v.24, but rather present new kinds of narrative organization, quite different from those used to structure the story of the early years.

Three stages of change in the *History's* structural organization have been described in this study. The first is a gradual process within the ten–year account of ii.1–v.24. Units of action in these books, though they continue throughout to display the same range of internal patterns, show some changes in the relative frequency with which the five patterns explored here occur. Early in the Archidamian War, the developed picture unit and the list unit, each eight to twenty-five lines in length, are very common, as prominent in the text as very short or very long units. But in the last four years (books iv–v.24), both developed picture units and list units are progressively neglected in favor of units that are either very short or very long. The simple picture unit, seven lines long or less, usually conveys the material not found in an extended narrative or complex account.

Thus instead of being a progression of units more or less equivalent in length, the narrative is in iv–v.24 composed of several long passages, punctuated occasionally by simple picture units.[2] Brasidas's journey north is told in three sets of contiguous units linked in loose narrative continuity;[3] in contrast, in books ii and iii *a-b-a* patterns usually break up such chains of extended narrative units, which might otherwise dominate the years in which they occur.[4]

Books v.25–vi.7 provides a second change in narrative structure. While in the Archidamian years, simple picture units, extended narrative units, and complex units each provide one-fifth of the total number of units, in the years of the Peace 43% of all units are of the simple picture type. List units (4%) and complex units (8%) almost disappear. The narrative shows the tendency described for the later Archidamian years, but in a more extreme form; the focus of the six years of v.25–vi.7 remains upon one set of elements, the various political developments that might threaten the unstable Peace. Units themselves more frequently lack descriptive detail and much more frequently are linked together to form ongoing accounts that overcome unit boundaries.

So although units of action exist in v.25–vi.7, they are becoming harder to identify. The characteristic shape of the five unit types is present only in an attenuated form. For example, the features in the Archidamian narrative that distinguish a simple picture unit from a developed one become much harder to see. Simple picture units in the years of the Peace are often condensed accounts of complicated actions and seven lines long, while developed picture units are equally spare and dense and usually now occupy only eleven or twelve lines. The increasing number of loose narrative connections between contiguous units often makes the identification of units an increasingly arbitrary process. One must depend on the presence or absence of the formular first sentence to decide where the unit's boundaries lie, rather than on the shape of the unit or the distribution of detail within it, as in the Archidamian narrative. A linear momentum that points one unit on to the next now becomes common, creating an effect quite different from the more static analytic effect of the Archidamian units.[5]

A third change in narrative arrangement occurs within books vi.8–viii.109 and represents the final stage of the trends discussed here. The whole narrative has become a single, unified account, and all actions are described as parts of it. The natural concomitant of this increasing narrative integration is the absence of the limited account with its own beginning, middle, and end. Units of action have disappeared.

Certain aspects of the unit remain in these late books. Formular sentences of the type familiar from the earlier narrative certainly occur, but they are no longer introductory; they do not mark distinct changes of setting, actor, and action. Shifts of focus occurring within the ongoing narrative are more subtle and often gradual, and their effect is often deliberately minimized, as emphasis is placed on narrative continuity rather than on a sequence of independent and discrete events.[6] In some ways, books vi, vii, and viii represent an amalgam of features used in ii.1–vi.7, adding the selective distribution of detail of ii.1–v.24 to the more ambitiously linear impetus of v.25–vi.7.[7] Structurally, the Sicilian books and book viii resemble each other; book viii suffers from being an ongoing account whose end or interpretive cornerstone is missing, and in consequence it is much harder to see where all the various interconnected threads of activity are heading.

The arrangement of books ii through viii of the *History*, then, displays a gradual development from simple parataxis, short narrative passages succeeding each other and connected by the repetition of their formular first sentences, to narratives of increasing length and integrated organization. The first stages of this development already occur late in the Archidamian account, where extended narrative units are frequently contiguous. In book v, much descriptive material disappears, and the account itself becomes a linear chain. The unit of action becomes harder to define. In books vi through viii this process accelerates; Thucydides has in a sense made the entire narrative in these books into a single extended narrative or complex unit. All the different kinds of linkage used earlier here are employed in an overlapping fashion, so that the reader's attention shifts from one aspect of the war to another, presented now as a continuous unfolding of interconnected elements.

The development of Thucydides as a historian and writer suggested by this data that seems the most likely to me is, like all such views, an argument from probability. It is easy to imagine the historian, with no clear idea at the beginning of how to proceed, but understanding that the war would be worthy of record, "beginning his work as soon as the war broke out in expectation that it would be a major one and notable beyone all previous wars," ἀρξάμενος εὐθὺς καθισταμένου καὶ ἐλπίσας μέγαν τε ἔσεσθαι καὶ ἀξιολογώτατον τῶν προγεγενημένων (i.1). He would begin by recording events taking place in various sectors, uncertain at first whether they would lead to significant further developments or not. The unit of action in books ii–v.24 (already undergoing modification toward the end of the Archidamian War) was a brilliant choice of initial narrative organization for such a historian. Important connections, because they occur again and again in the paratactic progression, would gradually emerge into prominence. Important patterns and developing trends would not be lost because the historian had at first failed to see their potential significance, but would rather become obvious from the way they kept reappearing within the succession of ongoing narrative units.

A historian capable of fashioning such a narrative, however, would not be content to remain a recorder of a sequence of discrete individual developments. As the war continued and became more complicated, he would come to see in a different way how apparently unrelated events or movements were intimately linked together—particularly since he himself was no longer principally based in Athens. At the same time, major trends in the war's development would become more obvious and more limited in number. Prominent themes—the emergence of Brasidas in books iv–v.24, the political tension threatening to disrupt the Peace in books v.25–vi.7, the Sicilian expedition in books vi.8–viii.6, and the Aegean naval conflict in book viii.7–109—would dominate the narrative as a whole, while other events that in his authorial judgment were less important accordingly would need to be integrated as subordinate aspects of the main account. One of the most important truths emerging about the war for Thucydides was, precisely, that it was *one* war, and that events, decisions, and even beliefs were both part of it and simultaneously influenced its course.[8]

As I said in the introduction, it is important to emphasize that the investigation of narrative structures undertaken in this study does not allow us confidently to state that Thucydides wrote any given passage at a particular date; in this sense, it is not a solution to the composition question but rather reveals how extensively his narrative habits changed as the *History* continued. Both the nature of the sentences introducing the units of action used in the early years and the structures of the units themselves make plausible the portrait of the *History*'s transformation advanced here: a journal-like format adopted by Thucydides for recording the early years of the war, severely modified as he took a more integrated, hypotactic approach to his subject in the years of the Peace, and abandoned altogether as he wrote up the Sicilian narrative and book viii, in favor of a more flexible, integrated, and ongoing narrative that emphasized links among superficially disparate movements.[9]

The question of how Thucydides wrote up his version of the Peloponnesian War encroaches on but does not answer the question of why he wrote as he did. Many aspects of this larger central question will remain unanswered. We will never know, for instance, why Thucydides did not write up the last six years of the war, even though ii.65, v.26, and vi.15 make it clear that he was still writing after the war ended; ii.100 perhaps suggests that he wrote down into the 390s.[10] Perhaps he was still carefully revising the units of action from the early years of the war, and polishing up the Sicilian narrative; perhaps he was now gathering information in Athens and elsewhere unavailable during the war years themselves; perhaps, like many Athenians after 404, he was almost fully occupied (both personally and as a wealthy citizen from a politically important family) with the political and economic issues entailed by the need to attend to his own fortunes in a changed Athenian infrastructure, in the wake of the brutal last years of the war and the uneasy years of amnesty that followed. Perhaps he was writing up or polishing book i.

This brings me to a few thoughts, mostly tentative, on how book i fits into this study of Thucydides' war narrative in books ii–viiii. On the most obvious structural level, book i resembles the narrative of books ii and iii more than it does the more complex, integrated narrative of the later *History*, since it too is composed of a series of discrete and polished independent narrative segments. I list them here as Simon Hornblower identifies them:[11]

i.1–23: introduction (Archaeology and Chapter on Method) (a)

i.24–55: the Corcyra episode (b)

i.56–67: the Potidaea episode (c)

i.67–88: debate at Sparta (d)

i.89–117: the Pentecontaetia or 'fifty years' (e)

i.118: recapitulation; Athenian consolidation of their power; the Spartans consult the Delphic oracle (f)

i.119–125: meeting of the Peloponnesian League (g)

i.126: the Cylon affair (h)

i.127: the Spartan motive (i)

i.128–135: the curse of Taenaron; the curse of Athena of the Brazen House (the Pausanias excursus) (j)

i.135.2–138: the story of Themistocles (k)

1.139: final diplomatic exchanges (l)

i.140–144: Pericles' first speech (m)

i.145–146: the Spartans rebuffed; recapitulation (n)

Viewed as an overall structure, book i resembles the Archidamian narrative that follows directly upon it. Most obviously, the narrative segments that comprise it are as discrete and distinctively organized as the units of books ii–v.24. Moreover, the paratactic sequence of segments creates a main movement that looks forward, tracing a variety of developments that lead up to the war itself, in approximate chrono-logical order (segments a–d, f–g, l–n above). Segments e, h, j, and k look back-ward in time, but like many excursuses in the Archidamian narrative, they identify the discrete issues from the past narrated here as causally important for understanding current events. Segments f, i, and n perform the same narrative function as those few Archidamian units that do not narrate new activity but rather sum up and inte-grate threads earlier treated separately.[12] On a more global and impressionistic level, too, the way Thucydides deploys excursus and juxtaposition to tell the story of book i (particularly in chapters 118.3–145, f–n) reminds us both of the construction of the longer complex units of actions in the Archidamian narrative and the construc-tion there of long multi-unit sequences through loose narrative continuity. Much meaning in book i also arises out of juxtapositions that ask us as readers to supply the interpretive connections ourselves—for instance, concerning the significance of the placement of the portraits of Themistocles and Pausanias as paradigmatic Athenian and Lacedaemonian characters, just before the narrative of the final diplo-matic exchanges on the eve of war.[13]

On the other hand, none of the narrative segments in book i listed above begin with a first sentence at all resembling the formular introductory sentences that mark the commencement of each new unit of action in the Archidamian narrative. The first sentences of i.56 and i.118 come the closest, and they, like the other first sen-tences of the narrative segments of book i listed above, rather stress the connec-tions between these narrative segments and those that precede them. Like the other narrative segments of book i, i.56–66 and i.118 are treated as separate but related aspects of an ongoing and systematic exploration of a single topic: the various factors that together led to the beginning of war in 431 B.C.E.[14] The assurance with which Thucydides identifies separate and multiple strands of narrative, and then weaves them back together, and the variety of different kinds of narrative he uses (includ-ing some strikingly Herodotean ones!),[15] suggest that although some version of in-troductory material was probably conceived early, and even perhaps written up as part of his initial introduction to the Archidamian narrative, the final version that he produced may well have also been substantially revised, by an author now de-ploying many years of knowledge, both about the war itself and about how to write up a lengthy and multifaceted introduction to a long and complicated story.[16]

One issue remains to be discussed. I ended the introduction and the brief dis-cussion of the "linguistic turn" in contemporary historiography given there with a general argument about the theoretical usefulness of Bakhtinian dialogism for iden-tifying the principles underlying and shaping a historical narrative. I claimed that although any historian of course relies on the ideas of *to prepon* and *to eikos* prevalent in his or her culture to construct his or her historical account, an analysis of the narrative arrangements of Thucydides, at any rate, would make it clear that he uses literary techniques in a distinctly idiosyncratic way, as they suit his own purposes as a historian, trying to record as best he can "what really happened." The kinds of narrative structure considered in this study show what I had in mind. As the narrative of the twenty-seven-year war continued, we have seen that Thucydides first developed narrative techniques of some precision, creating the Archidamian unit of action, but also that he later abandoned them in favor of a more fluid ongoing and complex account, not now dealing unit by unit with isolated occurrences, but rather weaving everything together into a single ongoing narrative frame.

Tim Rood's recent analysis of the narrative focalization found in books vi–viii shows the interpretive advantages gained by Thucydides' decision in the *History*'s later books to abandon the more static narrative structures used to describe the events of the early war, in order to convey the convulsive and virtually simultaneous, rapid-fire, mental engagement of many different actors and groups of actors, from many different cities, all increasingly caught up in a single overarching experience.[17] Indeed, in the more finished Sicilian narratives of books vi and vii, one might point to Demosthenes' famous night sortie on Epipolae (vii.42–44), and even the battle for the great harbor of Syracuse (vii.59–71), as descriptions of Bakhtinian dialogic polyphony itself: multiple actors from different cities, not even speaking the same dialect, giving the paean and mishearing its significance, with lethal consequences for the expedition of the Athenians (vii.44.6); or crowds of Athenians looking on at the ships battling in the harbor, with different parts of the action visible from different parts of the shore, and variously shouting, depending on what they saw, "We have won!" "We have lost!" (vii.71.4). Meanwhile, the voice of the author, Thucydides himself, constructs the whole account by negotiating the various perceptions and consequent actions of the individuals involved, weaving them together into a single, ongoing and complicated, multivoiced narrative. It is significant that the newly fluid, continuous structures of Thucydides' later narrative deploy such vivid scenes not merely as set pieces within discrete units of action, but as temporary climaxes within an ongoing and complex chain of events that is itself created and sustained by the multiple decisions and actions of the participants themselves.

Although it lacks the brilliant and detailed finish of the Sicilian narrative, Thucydides' narrative in book viii employs the same polyphonic interweaving of many voices and many points of view. This is what makes the genre of narrative history, at least as practiced by Thucydides, profoundly dialogic, in ways that Bakhtin himself was not at liberty to explore. Thucydides' own changed perception of the war, as the narrative continues, is mirrored by the changed perceptions of its various participants. In book viii these too all seem to be struggling with its totalizing, engulfing energy, and it is the quality of Thucydides' prose that makes us participate, as readers, in what this must have meant, both to the participants and to the historian himself.

As we follow the unrolling narrative of stasis at Athens, we see how Alcibiades, various Athenian aristocrats, the Athenian navy, the Athenian demos, several parts of the Samian citizen body, some Spartan and Syracusan generals and Spartan kings, and even two Persian satraps all play a part in an intricately structured single web of unrolling meaning, no part of which can be understood in isolation from the others. This is an achievement made possible by Thucydides' development of specific choices of narrative structure late in the narrative. Thucydides could not have written up the war he saw unrolling in 411, using the units of action that he used to tell the story of the Archidamian War. Instead, he fashioned a new and much more complicated kind of narrative in the service of getting down for us, his readers, what he saw, in all its multiple interconnections. The magnitude of his achievement may be gauged by the fact that his account of a long, complicated regional war in the later years of the fifth century B.C.E. still seems important to us almost two and a half millennia later, as he anticipated it would be.

· Narrative Units and Narrative
Scenes (ii.1–viii.109)

Note: For ease of consultation, arabic rather than roman numerals have been used
for the book divisions within the table.

TABLE A.1   Archidamian War: Narrative units

W = beginning of winter

Unit	Lines	Type	Topic
Year one: ii.1–ii.47.1 (431/430 B.C.E.)			
2.1	5	Simple picture	Introduction
2.2–2.6	124	Extended narrative	Events in Plataea
2.7–2.9	58	Extended narrative	Preparation and allies of both
2.10–2.12	69	Complex	Lacedaemonian preparation
2.13–2.17	126	Complex	Athenian preparation
2.18–2.23	109	Extended narrative	Lacedaemonian invasion
2.24	11	Developed picture	Description of Athenian preparation
2.25	26	List	Athenian naval expedition to Peloponnese
2.26	6	List	Athenian naval expedition to Locris, Euboea
2.27	13	Developed picture	Athenians expel Aeginetans

Unit	Lines	Type	Topic
2.28	4	Simple picture	Eclipse
2.29	31	Complex	Nymphodorus and Tereus
2.30	10	List	Athenian fleet
2.31	17	Developed picture	Fleet of 100
2.32	5	Simple picture	Athenians fortify Atalanta
2.33 W	16	List	Euarchus, Acarnanians, and Corinthians
2.34–2.47.1	243	Complex	Funeral oration
Total: 17			
Year two: ii.47.2–ii.70 (430/429 B.C.E.)			
2.47.2	4	Simple picture	Invasion of Attica
2.47.3–2.54	157	Extended narrative	Plague
2.55–2.56	25	Extended narrative	Invasion and Athenian expedition around Peloponnese
2.57	9	Developed picture	Juxtaposition of invasion, expedition, and plague
2.58	17	Developed picture	Athenians in Potidaea
2.59–2.65	193	Complex	Assembly and Pericles' third speech
2.66	7	Simple picture	Lacedaemonian expedition against Zacynthus
2.67	33	Extended narrative	Corinthian embassy to Asia
2.68	31	Complex	Ambraciot-Amphilochian history
2.69 W	12	List	20 Athenian ships round Peloponnese; 6 to Ionia
2.70	22	Developed picture	Potidaea
Total: 11			
Year three: ii.71–ii.103 (429/428 B.C.E.)			
2.71–2.78	171	Complex	Plataea resists
2.79	22	Developed picture	Athenians against Thrace
2.80–2.82	83	Extended narrative	Ambraciots and Cnemus
2.83–2.92	274	Complex	Fleet from Corinth and Phormio fight
2.93–2.94 W	45	Developed picture	Cnemus and Brasidas on Piraeus

Unit	Lines	Type	Topic
2.95–2.101	164	Complex	Sitalces' call-up
2.102–2.103	44	Complex	Athenians in Naupactus into Acarnania
Total: 7			

Year four: iii.1–iii.25 (428/427 B.C.E.)

Unit	Lines	Type	Topic
3.1	9	Developed picture	Peloponnesian invasion of Attica
3.2–3.6	85	Extended narrative	Revolt of Lesbos
3.7	22	List	Fleet around Peloponnese
3.8–3.16	149	Complex	Peloponnesian decision about Lesbos
3.17	15	Developed picture	Numbers of ships
3.18	20	Developed picture	Mytilene fights Methymna
3.19 W	8	List	Tribute collected
3.20–3.24	119	Developed picture	Plataean escape
3.25	12	Developed picture	Mytilene
Total: 9			

Year five: iii.26–iii.88 (427/426 B.C.E.)

Unit	Lines	Type	Topic
3.26	16	Developed picture	Invasion of Attica
3.27–3.28	25	Developed picture	Mytilene comes to terms
3.29–3.33.1	55	Complex	Fleet of Peloponnesians
3.33.2–3.35	42	Extended narrative	Paches chasing them
3.36–3.50	347	Complex	Mytilenean debate
3.51	16	Developed picture	Nicias's expedition against Minoa
3.52–3.68	361	Complex	Plataeans come to terms
3.69	13	Developed picture	Peloponnesian fleet to Corcyra
3.70–3.85	279	Extended narrative	Corcyra
3.86	19	Developed picture	Athenian fleet to Sicily
3.87.1–3.87.3 W	9	Developed picture	Plague
3.87.4	3	Simple picture	Earthquakes
3.88	14	Developed picture	Athenian and Rhegian attack on Aeolus
Total: 13			

Year six: iii.89–iii.116 (426/425 B.C.E.)

Unit	Lines	Type	Topic
3.89.1	5	Simple picture	Invasion of Attica

Unit	Lines	Type	Topic
3.89.2–3.89.5	17	Developed picture	Inundations
3.90	17	List	Sicily
3.91	20	List	Nicias for Melos
3.92–3.93	42	Developed picture	Heraclea
3.94–3.98	103	Extended narrative	Demosthenes against Aetolia
3.99	4	Simple picture	Athenians in Sicily to Locri
3.100–3.102	50	Extended narrative	Aetolians
3.103 W	15	List	Athenian activity in Sicily
3.104	42	Complex	Purification of Delos
3.105–3.114	204	Extended narrative	Demosthenes in Ambracia
3.115	20	List	Athenian activity in Sicily
3.116	6	Simple picture	Aetna
Total: 13			

Year seven: iv.1–iv.51 (425/424 B.C.E.)

Unit	Lines	Type	Topic
4.1	17	Developed picture	Messina revolts from Athens
4.2.1	4	Simple picture	Peloponnesians invade Attica
4.2.2–4.5	53	Extended narrative	Athenian fleet for Sicily goes to Pylos
4.6	10	Developed picture	Peloponnesians withdraw from Attica
4.7	6	Simple picture	Athenians capture Eion in Thrace
4.8–4.23	329	Complex	Peloponnesian relief for Pylos
4.24–4.25	72	Extended narrative	Messina, sea battle
4.26–4.41	308	Extended narrative	Pylos
4.42–4.45	78	Extended narrative	Athenian expedition against Corinth
4.46–4.48	60	Developed picture	Eurymedon and Sophocles in Corcyra
4.49	6	Simple picture	Athenian expedition against Anactorium
4.50 W	15	Developed picture	Athenians capture a Persian at Eion
4.51	5	Simple picture	Chian fortifications demolished
Total: 13			

Unit	Lines	Type	Topic
Year eight: iv.52–iv.116 (424/423 B.C.E.)			
4.52.1	3	Simple picture	Eclipse of sun
4.52.2–4.52.5	15	List	Exiles from Lesbos in Rhoeteum
4.53–4.57	93	Extended narrative	Athenians in Cythera, etc.
4.58–4.65	139	Complex	Conference in Gela
4.66–4.74	200	Extended narrative	Megarian revolution stopped by Brasidas
4.75	20	List	Athenian fleet against Antandros; in Pontus
4.76–4.77	40	Developed picture	Demosthenes, Hippocrates plotting against Boeotia
4.78–4.83	111	Extended narrative	Brasidas through Thessaly
4.84–4.88	104	Complex	Brasidas's further advance in Thrace
4.89–4.101.4 W	258	Complex	Athenian defeat at Delium
4.101.5	5	Simple picture	Death of Sitalces, Seuthes succeeds
4.102–4.108	138	Extended narrative	Brasidas captures Amphipolis
4.109.1a	2	Simple picture	Megarians recapture long walls
4.109.1b–4.116	116	Extended narrative	Brasidas in Thrace
Total: 14			
Year nine: iv.117–iv.135 (423/422 B.C.E.)			
4.117–4.119	81	Complex	Athenian-Lacedaemonian armistice
4.120–4.122	58	Extended narrative	Scione revolts
4.123	19	Developed picture	Mende revolts
4.124–4.132	221	Complex	Brasidas and Perdiccas against Arrhabaeus
4.133.1	4	Simple picture	Thebans demolish Thespian wall
4.133.2–4.133.3	9	Developed picture	Hera's temple at Argos burned
4.133.4	4	Simple picture	Blockade around Scione
4.134.1a W	2	Simple picture	No fighting between Athenians, Lacedaemonians
4.134.1b–4.134.2	9	Developed picture	Mantineans and Tegeans fight
4.135	8	Developed picture	Brasidas attempts Potidaea
Total: 10			

Unit	Lines	Type	Topic
Year ten: v.1–v.24 (422/421 B.C.E.)			
5.1a	2	Simple picture	Treaty until Pythia
5.1b	7	Simple picture	Expulsion of Delians
5.2–5.3.4	35	Extended narrative	Cleon sails to Thrace
5.3.5	3	Simple picture	Boeotians capture Panactum by treachery
5.3.6	3	Simple picture	Cleon around Athos
5.4–5.5	38	List	Athenians and politics in Sicily
5.6–5.11	169	Complex	Amphipolis
5.12	6	Simple picture	Lacedaemonian reinforcement
5.13 W	8	Developed picture	Lacedaemonian reinforcement leaves
5.14–5.20.1	154	Complex	Reaction of both sides and treaty
5.20.2	13	Developed picture	Chronological method
5.21–5.24	68	Complex	Disagreements among Peloponnesians, alliance

Total: 12

TABLE A.2   Years of the Peace: Narrative units

W = beginning of winter

Unit	Lines	Type	Topic
Year eleven: v.25–v.39 (421/420 B.C.E.)			
5.25	14	Developed picture	Description of the period
5.26	28	Developed picture	Methodology
5.27–5.31	109	Extended narrative	Political details
5.32.1	6	Simple picture	Scione, Delos
5.32.2	1	Simple picture	Phocis and Locris
5.32.3	23	Extended narrative	Politics
5.33	13	List	Lacedaemonian march into Arcadia
5.34	14	Developed picture	Return of helots and Spartans from Sphacteria
5.35.1	2	Simple picture	Dians take Thyssus

Unit	Lines	Type	Topic
5.35.2a	2	Simple picture	Suspicion, treaty not being honored
5.35.2b–5.35.7	30	Extended narrative	Description of political arrangements, Boeotia and Lacedaemon
5.36–5.37 W	45	Extended narrative	Continuation of political maneuvers
5.38	25	Extended narrative	Continuation of political maneuvers
5.39.1	2	Simple picture	Olynthus
5.39.2–5.39.3	16	Developed picture	Discussion about Panactum
Total: 15			

Year twelve: v.40–v.51 (420/419 B.C.E.)

5.40–5.41	41	Extended narrative	Continuation of political maneuvers
5.42–5.48.3	188	Complex	Athenian decision for alliance, text of treaty
5.49–5.50.4	42	Developed picture	Olympic games, fear of conflict
5.50.5	5	Simple picture	Argives try to get Corinthians to join
5.51 W	10	Developed picture	Heraclea
Total: 5			

Year thirteen: v.52.1–v.56 (419/418 B.C.E.)

5.52.1	6	Simple picture	Heraclea continued from v.51
5.52.2	9	List	Alcibiades in the Peloponnese
5.53	10	Developed picture	Alcibiades and Argos declare war on Epidamnus
5.54	14	Developed picture	Lacedaemonians march and Argives react
5.55	19	Extended narrative	Political developments
5.56.1–5.56.3 W	12	Developed picture	Lacedaemonians into Epidaurus, Argives react
5.56.4	4	Simple picture	Skirmishes between Epidaurus, Argos
5.56.5	4	Simple picture	Argive attempt to enter Epidaurus
Total: 8			

Year fourteen: v.57–v.81 (418/417 B.C.E.)

5.57–5.75	362	Extended narrative	Battle of Mantinea

Unit	Lines	Type	Topic
5.76–5.80 W	81	Complex	Agreement between Spartans and Argives
5.81.1	4	Simple picture	Mantineans leave Athenian alliance too
5.81.2	5	Simple picture	Suppression of democracy at Argos
Total: 4			
Year fifteen: v.82–v.83 (417/416 B.C.E.)			
5.82.1a	2	Simple picture	Dium revolts from Athens
5.82.1b	2	Simple picture	Lacedaemonians in Achaea
5.82.2–5.82.6	23	Extended narrative	Democrats at Argos regain control
5.83.1–5.83.2 W	10	Developed picture	Lacedaemonians against Argos
5.83.3	3	Simple picture	Argives march out to Phlius
5.83.4	7	Simple picture	Athenians declare war on Perdiccas
Total: 6			
Year sixteen: v.84–vi.7 (416/415 B.C.E.)			
5.84.1a	5	Simple picture	Argos and Alcibiades
5.84.1b–5.114	226	Complex	Melos
5.115.1	3	Simple picture	Argives invade Phlius
5.115.2–5.115.3	7	Simple picture	Raids on Pylos and consequences
5.115.4	6	Simple picture	Melian defense
5.116.1 W	5	Simple picture	Lacedaemonians plan to invade Argos
5.116.2–5.116.4	10	Developed picture	Melos surrenders, is destroyed
6.1–6.7.1a	141	Complex	Sicilian history
6.7.1b	8	Developed picture	Lacedaemonian invasion of Argos
6.7.2	8	Developed picture	Athenian and Argive reaction
6.7.3–6.7.4	6	Simple picture	Athenian skirmishes with Perdiccas and reaction
Total: 11			

Narrative segment	Lines	Topic
Year seventeen: vi.8–vi.93 (415/414 B.C.E.)		
6.8–6.26	369	Athenian assembly, three speeches
6.27–6.29	38	Affair of the Hermae
6.30–6.32.2	70	Preparations for sailing and the embarkation
6.32.3–6.41	210	Syracuse: speeches of Hermocrates, Athenagoras
6.42	11	Athenian preparations in Corcyra
6.43–6.44	40	Sailing for Corcyra
6.45	9	Reactions at Syracuse
6.46–6.50.1a	73	Athenians at Rhegium realize deceit of Egestaeans
6.50.1b	5	Alcibiades sails to Messina and back
6.50.2–6.52	62	Unproductive Athenian voyage, return to Catana
6.53–6.61	198	There they find the Salamina, orders for Alcibiades
6.62	22	Short Athenian voyages
6.63–6.72.1a W	173	Athenian victory against Syracuse
6.72.1b–6.73	34	Syracusan assembly, speech of Hermocrates
6.74	13	Various Athenian activities (Messina, etc.)
6.75–6.88.2a	258	Syracusan activity and two speeches at Camarina
6.88.2b–6.88.6	23	Athenian preparation for spring
6.88.7–6.93.3	150	Lacedaemonian assembly, Alcibiades' persuasion
6.93.4	4	Athenian trireme arrives in Athens, money voted
Total: 19		
Year eighteen: vi.94–vii.18 (414/413 B.C.E.)		
6.94	19	Athenians in Sicily
6.95.1	5	Affairs in Argos
6.95.2	4	Thespiae
6.96–6.103	182	Epipolae, beginning with Syracusan focus
6.104	22	Help coming from Gylippus
6.105	19	Embroilment of Athens in Argos
7.1–7.2	51	Gylippus and Corinthians come just in time
7.3	20	Athenians react
7.4.1–7.4.3	13	Syracusan wall

Narrative segment	Lines	Topic
7.4.4–7.4.7	23	Athenian activity: Nicias fortifies Plemmyrium, sends twenty ships
7.5–7.6	33	Gylippus foils Athenian investment
7.7	14	Twelve Corinthian ships come
7.8	16	Nicias sends letter home
7.9	5	Euetion, Athenian general, marches against Amphipolis with Perdiccas
7.10–7.17 W	119	Nicias's letter reviews the situation
7.18	30	Lacedaemonians prepare to invade Attica
Total: 16		

Year nineteen: vii.19–viii.6 (413/412 B.C.E.)

Narrative segment	Lines	Topic
7.19.1–7.19.3a	12	Lacedaemonian fortification of Decelea
7.19.3b–7.19.5	19	Ships sent from Lacedaemon to Sicily
7.20	16	Athenians send ships to Peloponnese and Demosthenes to Sicily
7.21–7.24	79	Gylippus and Hermocrates capture Plemmyrium; decline in Athenian morale
7.25	44	Various results after battle
7.26	17	Demosthenes sails toward Sicily
7.27–7.30	103	Decelea and Mycalessus
7.31	28	Demosthenes' voyage continued
7.32	14	Nicias ambushes support coming to Syracuse
7.33.1–7.33.2	9	Camarinaeans arrive with reinforcements for Syracuse
7.33.3–7.33.6	21	Demosthenes continues voyage
7.34	38	Peloponnesians in Naupactus fight Athenians
7.35	13	Demosthenes and Eurymedon refused passage at Croton
7.36–7.41	125	Syracusan victory before Demosthenes' arrival
7.42–7.45	136	Demosthenes' failure to take Epipolae
7.46	8	Syracusan activity after victory
7.47–7.49	78	Athenian generals evaluate situation
7.50.1–7.50.2	14	Gylippus and Sicanus return
7.50.3–7.54	75	Syracusan attack

Narrative segment	Lines	Topic
7.55–7.56.3	32	Syracusan high spirits and hope for future
7.56.4–7.59.1	88	Survey of forces on both sides
7.59.2–7.71	294	Great sea battle, generals' speeches
7.72–7.87	388	Athenian retreat, including Nicias's speech
8.1	30	Reception of news at Athens
8.2 W	23	Reaction in other cities, including Sparta
8.3	17	Preparation in Lacedaemon as a result
8.4	8	Preparation in Athens
8.5–8.6	67	New allies for Lacedaemonians
Total: 28		

Year twenty: viii.7–viii.60 (412/411 B.C.E.)

Narrative segment	Lines	Topic
8.7–8.12	96	Abortive beginning of revolt in Chios
8.13	7	Sixteen Peloponnesian ships from Sicily
8.14–8.15	37	Chian revolt and Athenian reaction
8.16	15	Strombichides' activity
8.17.1–8.17.3	17	Lacedaemonians pursue Strombichides
8.17.4–8.19.1a	19	Text of first treaty between Lacedaemonians and the king of Persia
8.19.1b–8.19.4	15	Chians sail, happen on Athenians
8.20.1	8	Twenty Peloponnesian ships in Spiraeum joined by Astyochus
8.20.2	7	Tissaphernes and Athenians successively in Teos
8.21	10	Democratic revolt in Samos
8.22	13	Chians and Peloponnesians bring Lesbos into revolt
8.23.1a	3	Astyochus goes from Cenchriae to Chios
8.23.1b	4	Three days later, Athenians sail to Lesbos
8.23.2–8.23.5	29	Athenians take Mytilene, Astyochus on to Eresus, Lesbos, and Chios
8.23.6	7	Athenian activity in Clazomenae, after Lesbos
8.24.1	7	Athenians at Lade
8.24.2–8.24.6	32	Athenian war against Chians, Chian decision
8.25–8.28	97	Miletus, Phrynichus's character, Amorges and Tissaphernes

Narrative segment	Lines	Topic
8.29 W	14	Astyochus and problem of pay
8.30	12	Athenian preparations at Samos for naval expedition against Miletus
8.31–8.33	50	Astyochus against Clazomenae, anger at Chians
8.34	11	Athenian force sailing around Corycus, storm, most get to Miletus
8.35	18	Lacedaemonian Hippocrates to Cnidus, joins those at Miletus; Athenians capture lookout ships
8.36–8.38.1	35	Astyochus to Miletus, another agreement between Lacedaemonians, Darius, Tissaphernes
8.38.2–8.38.5a	15	Athenians resume attack on Chios, Astyochus refuses to help Chians with Pedaritus
8.38.5b	4	Athenians from Samos cannot draw fleet at Miletus into battle
8.39–8.42	114	Voyage of Lacedaemonian commissioners and Astyochus
8.43.1	6	Athenians after battle
8.43.2–8.43.4	17	Spartan commissioners do not like treaty
8.44	22	Peloponnesians persuade Rhodes to revolt, Athenian response
8.45–8.54	234	Beginning of Athenian oligarchic conspiracy
8.55.1	8	Leon and Diomedon make attack on Rhodes
8.55.2–8.56.1a	15	Desperate situation at Chios reported to Peloponnesians on Rhodes; events at Chios
8.56.1b–8.56.4	24	Athenian representatives with Pisander talk with Tissaphernes and Alcibiades
8.57–8.59	45	Tissaphernes wants Peloponnesians to return to Miletus; a third treaty
8.60	17	Boeotians capture Oropus, Peloponnesians decide to go to Chios and not Euboea
Total: 36		

Year twenty-one: viii.61–viii.109 (411 B.C.E.)

Narrative segment	Lines	Topic
8.61.1a	4	Dercyllidas the Spartan sent to revolt of Abydus
8.61.1b	15	Chians fight sea battle

Narrative segment	Lines	Topic
8.62	14	Dercyllidas marches and Strombichides sets out against him
8.63.1–8.63.2	8	Astyochus at Miletus tries to fight Samians, who refuse to sail out
8.63.3–8.77	302	Problem in Samos because of oligarchic revolution
8.78–8.79	38	Discontent in Miletus; sea battle sought at Samos
8.80.1–8.80.3	16	Peloponnesians decide to send fleet to Pharnabazus
8.80.4	4	Afterward, Athenians in Samos keep watch on Hellespont
8.81–8.82	40	Alcibiades invited to Samos, goes to win over Tissaphernes
8.83–8.85.4a	57	Demoralization in Peloponnesian camp
8.85.4b–8.86	49	Alcibiades at Samos, prevents move on Athens
8.87	37	Tissaphernes claims he is fetching Phoenician fleet
8.88	11	Alcibiades goes to meet Tissaphernes
8.89–8.98	275	End of oligarchy at Athens
8.99–8.107	168	Battle of Cynossema
8.108.1–8.108.2	9	Alcibiades back from Caunus and Tissaphernes
8.108.3	3	Tissaphernes hurries after Peloponnesians
8.108.4–8.108.5	13	Antandrians react to ill treatment of Delians by Arsaces
8.109	13	Tissaphernes hurries to Hellespont
Total: 19 narrative segments (incomplete year)		

Note: These divisions are no longer certain and do not reflect structural arrangements; see chapter 6 for discussion of the issue.

· Introductory Sentences of
Units of Action (ii.1–v.24)

1.1   The introductory sentences considered here are not necessarily the ones created by the punctuation of a printed text. The editors of the Oxford text, for instance, when faced with a single subject followed by two coordinate verbs, sometimes make the whole complex into one unbroken sentence (ii.33, iii.103), sometimes
separate the two verbs by means of a colon (iii.18), and sometimes make them into
two separate sentences (iii.25, iv.7). The same variety of punctuation is found when
two short grammatical units, each with its own subject and verb, occur. These may
also be made into one sentence (iv.1, ii.7, iv.133.1) or be divided by a colon (ii.79;
very common for description of military command: ii.90, iv.58) or be separated into
two sentences (ii.31, iii.7).

1.2   The subject in an introductory sentence to a unit may be compound (ii.25);
the verb almost never is. If the same subject is followed by two verbs in a paratactic sequence, generally the second verb may appropriately be considered a new sentence. In 6 of the 119 introductory sentences, the first grammatical unit formed is
actually parenthetic, and the weight of the meaning falls on the second part of the
sentence (ii.25, 69, 71–78, 83–92; iii.89.1, 91). In these cases, Thucydides indicates
by other means that the first sentence actually supplements the second. Either the
first verb obviously looks forward (ii.71, ii.83) or a μέν-δέ or τε-καί construction
warns the reader that the weight comes late in the sentence (ii.25, 69; iii.89, 91). Three
of the latter type concern the Athenian fleet; see pp. 67–68 above.

1.3   Thucydides certainly uses gnomic, political, or impressionistic sentences in other positions in the unit. In the course of establishing table B.1 (fifty arbitrarily selected sentences from ii.1–v.24; see 1.4 below), the following examples occurred: ii.65.9, a gnomic statement ("And what was in name a democracy became . . . ," ἐγίγ-νετό τε λόγῳ μὲν δημοκρατία . . .); ii.8.4, a political generalization ("Public opinion inclined . . . ," ἡ δὲ εὔνοια . . . ἐποίει τῶν ἀνθρώπων); and ii.92.1, an impressionistic statement ("When they saw all this happening, the Athenians were filled with confidence," τοὺς δ' Ἀθηναίους ἰδόντας ταῦτα γιγνόμενα θάρσος . . . ἔλαβε). But the sentences that introduce the units of action are structured to convey limited types of specific information about the new narrative focus that is beginning; interpretation of the above types is relegated to subordinate clauses, when it occurs at all. It never occurs as the first or second element in introductory sentences; see 1.5 below.

1.3.1 The formular nature of Thucydides' introductory sentences could have been better brought out by many translators. Consider Rex Warner's translation of the start of iv.66: "The following events also took place in the same summer. Megarians in the city of Megara were suffering badly from the war with Athens, since the Athenians invaded their country twice every year in full force. They were also hard pressed by their own exiles. . . . They therefore began to talk among themselves." The translation of Steven Lattimore stays much closer to the force of the Greek: "In the same summer, the Megarians in the city, hard pressed in the war by the Athenians, who invaded their land twice every year in full force, and also by their own exiles based at Pagai . . . began suggesting to one another the need to let the exiles return." (I should note that v.20.2, the last unit before the end of the Archidamian narrative, is technically not a unit about the war at all, but a description, at the end of ten years' worth of narrative, of Thucydides' chronological method. As such, it has an introductory sentence quite different from the others as well.)

1.4 The pattern that occurs with impressive regularity in introductory sentences is not found with any frequency within the body of the unit of action. This is demonstrated in table B.1, a summary of the phenomena listed above, as they are found in fifty arbitrarily selected sentences from books ii, iii, and iv of the *History* (for the method of selection, see the note after the table).

1.4.1 Only one of the significant regularities found in well over half of all the sentences that introduce units of action is found in the fifty arbitrarily selected sentences too: verbs are often active, not only at the heads of units of action, but generally in Thucydides. The other elements common in introductory sentences and marking them as formular are rather rarely found in the fifty arbitrarily selected sentences.

TABLE B.1 Elements found in arbitrarily selected sentences, ii.1–v.24

	Sentences 1–25	Sentences 26–50	Total	
Personal subject	8	10	18	(36%)
Active verb	24	23	47	(94%)
Prepositional phrase indicating setting	7	8	15	(30%)
Indication of time	5	11	16	(32%)
Time and subject as first two elements	1	3	4	(8%)

NOTE: The sentence on line 15 of every left-hand page of the Oxford edition of 1942 of the Archidamian narrative was counted, unless it was part of a speech. (Speeches would of course contain a high proportion of sentences unlikely to resemble those that begin units of action; they would unfairly weight the table.) Regarding subjects of sentences: the low proportion of subjects that are personal is partly explained by the exclusion from the table of all unexpressed or pronominal subjects. Seventeen of the fifty sentences counted had subjects that were personal but unexpressed; if these had been added to the chart, 70% of the arbitrarily chosen sentences would have had personal subjects. (The omission of sentences with personal but unexpressed subjects is appropriate because what is being counted is the presence of a formular element in the sentence, and if it is unexpressed, it is not present as part of the formula.) Regarding indications of time: those rare expressions of time found in sentences within the unit are generally different from the time formulae that head units of action. The former are both short and vague, as in iii.50, ὕστερον, or iii.7.3, ἔπειτα. Regarding time and subject as the first two elements of four of the fifty arbitrarily chosen sentences: ii.25.5, iii.81.4, iii.93, and iii.109 are the only examples. These sentences show that within the unit Thucydides could use rough approximations of introductory sentences to suggest a partial articulation, another stage of the action. None of these four sentences, however, displays both a change in the topic under consideration in the unit and an expression of time. See further, pp. 124, 145–48, for ways in which, in the later narrative portions of the *History*, Thucydides makes it more difficult to distinguish first sentences of units from articulations of stages of activity within a single extended narrative unit.

1.4.2   The results of a word search for all uses of θέρος, χειμών, and other related expressions of time often found in introductory sentences in the Archidamian narrative confirm the findings of 1.4. Within the narrative of ii.1–v.24, θέρος occurs only in the introductory sentence of a unit of action or in the formular expressions regularly marking the end of a season. χειμών is found three times within the body of a unit in instances where it does not mean "storm": ii.101.5 and ii.102.2 (twice).

1.5   As we have seen, subject, verb, setting, and time are the four elements that occur regularly in introductory sentences. In the sentences introducing units of action, a large variety of occasional usages and an even larger variety of further possibilities are combined with a solid domination by a few of the most frequent formulae. Thus 69% of the 119 introductory sentences begin with one of the two following combinations: time word and subject (as in iv.1: "In the following spring, around the time the grain was shooting up, ten Syracusan ships set sail . . . with an equal number of Locrian ships," τοῦ δ᾿ ἐπιγιγνομένου θέρους περὶ σίτου ἐκβολὴν Συρακοσίων δέκα νῆες πλεύσασαι καὶ Λοκρίδες ἴσαι) or subject and time word (as in iii.27–28: "Meanwhile, the Mytileneans," οἱ δὲ Μυτιληναῖοι ἐν τούτῳ). Another 12% begin either with verb and subject (as in iii.87.4: "Many earthquakes also occurred," ἐγένοντο δὲ καὶ οἱ πολλοὶ σεισμοί) or with subject and verb (as in iii.70–85: "And this Corcyrean civil war occurred," οἱ γὰρ Κερκυραῖοι ἐστασίαζον). (Note that the γάρ in iii.70 indicates that the previous unit, iii.69, is linked with it. Such connections between units are discussed more extensively in chapter 4. See also above, p. 60.) One of these four orders is used in 81% of the introductory sentences in the narrative of the Archidamian War.

1.5.1   On the other hand, twelve possible combinations of the four main elements of introductory sentences exist, and Thucydides uses eleven of them at least once. In addition three times he uses a combination of elements not covered in table B.2 (see 1.5.3 below). In sum, although Thucydides uses fourteen different patterns for the first two elements of introductory sentences, four of them account for four-fifths of the 119 sentences. Table B.2 sets out the order in which the first two elements of introductory sentences occur, for the units of action in the Archidamian narrative.

1.5.2   The sentences that begin the 119 units of action in the narrative of the Archidamian War begin in a limited number of ways using a limited number of elements. The resulting patterns distinguish introductory sentences rather clearly from sentences occurring at arbitrarily chosen points in the text, as table B.1 above indicates (1.4). Thus the pattern formed in introductory sentences does not anticipate the structural complexity of the rest of the unit but rather emphasizes the bald fact that another unit is beginning. Although Thucydides does not form all first sentences on a monotonously uniform template, in the order of the first two elements in the sentence he provides a strong concentration on a limited number of alternatives within a wide range of possibilities. Introductory sentences, like the patterns formed by the units themselves, provide the reader with new data, but data expressed in familiar patterns; their formal regularity contributes to a sense of narrative continuity.

1.5.3   There are exceptions to the order of the first two elements in introductory sentences for units of action, as set out in table B.2. In ii.29 the first two elements are a time word and a direct object (the direct object in introductory sentences almost always occurs directly before the verb and has been counted as part of the verb unless it stands separately, as here). In iii.33.2 the first two elements are an indirect object and a verb; this is the only introductory sentence in which neither time nor the subject of the sentence is one of the first two elements. In iv.2.2 the subject and direct object again occupy the first two places in the sentence. These

TABLE B.2   Order of first two elements in introductory sentences, ii.1–v.24

	Book ii	Book iii	Book iv	Total	% of total
Time, subject	23	18	25	66	55
Subject, time	4	6	7	17	14
Verb, subject	2	1	2	5	4
Subject, verb	3	3	4	10	8
Subject, setting	1	1	4	6	5
Setting, subject	—	—	—	—	—
Setting, time	—	1	—	1	1
Time, setting	—	2	2	4	3
Verb, time	1	1	2	4	3
Time, verb	—	1	—	1	1
Verb, setting	—	—	1	1	1
Setting, verb	—	—	1	1	1
Other	1	1	1	3	3
Total introductory sentences	35	35	49	119	99

NOTE: The description given here of the order of words found in introductory sentences in the Archidamian narrative of Thucydides generally accords with that in Dover 1960. The "normal" tendency in Greek is for the subject to precede the verb. This is displayed in Thucydides' introductory sentences, as is the choice of a narrow range of preference among a wide number of alternative usages. However, the Greek "resistance to that drift towards syntactical uniformity which has been the fate of other languages" (Dover 1960, 68) is not the most salient feature of Thucydides' deployment of the elements regularly found in introductory sentences to units of action, for the Archidamian narrative at least. Thucydides fashioned his introductory sentences in the Archidamian narrative to appear more formular in nature than not.

three exceptions make all the more impressive the degree of regularity reflected in table B.2.

(One pattern not expressly identified in table B.2 but fairly distinctive is the enclosure of a setting by the article and noun of the subject, in an a-b-a pattern. This occurs in ii.25, 102; iii.88, 99, 103, 115; and iv.6, 24–25, 49. One interesting but rather frigid variation occurs in iv.135, where the subject and verb are interlaced with two halves of the time phrase: "At the end of this winter, Brasidas . . . made an attempt" (ἀπεπείρασε δὲ τοῦ αὐτοῦ χειμῶνος καὶ ὁ Βρασίδας τελευτῶντος).

2.1   Here are listed the subjects of the introductory sentences of Archidamian units of action.

a. Athenians: ii.7, 24, 25, 26, 27, 29, 30, 31, 34, 59, 69, 79, 102; iii.7, 19, 36, 51, 86, 88, 90, 91, 94, 99, 103, 104, 115; iv.2.2, 26, 42, 49, 53; v.b.

b. Peloponnesians: ii.10, 47.2, 55, 66, 71; iii.1, 26, 29, 89, 92; iv.2.1, 6; v.21.

c. Other collective subjects: ii.2, 68, 70, 80; iii.8, 18, 20, 27, 52, 70, 100, 105; iv.8, 24, 51, 52.2, 66, 109, 117, 133.1, 134.1; v.3.5, 13.

d. Of the collective subjects, those identified more narrowly than by nationality: ii.2; iii.8; iv.8, 52.2, 66, 117; v.13. (Note that 5 of the 7 occur in books iv and v; see further the discussion below, p. 39.)

e. Subjects identified by name: ii.13, 33, 58, 67, 93, 95; iii.25; iv.7, 46, 50, 75, 76, 78, 84, 89, 101.5, 102, 109.1, 124, 135; v.2, 3.6, 4, 6, 12. (It is tempting to speculate that in book iii Thucydides consolidates the sense of groups interacting that is initiated in book ii, and therefore only one unit has a personal subject. The emphasis is neither on individual Athenian and Lacedaemonian personalities of the early war nor on the personalities that will emerge from these middle war years, like Brasidas. But such speculations are not capable of proof.)

f. Place (setting) as subject: ii.32; iii.2; iv.120, 123, 133.4.

g. Concrete nouns as subject: ii.1, 18, 28, 47.3, 57, 83; iii.17, 33.2, 69, 87, 87.4, 89.2, 116; iv.1, 52.1, 58, 133.2, 134.1; v.1a, 14, 20.2. (Sentences v.14 and 20.2 are anomalies, since v.14 has an impersonal subject, and the subject of v.20.2 is *tis*.) In these introductory sentences, it is often the concrete noun that is most important to the action. In iii.33.2, heavy emphasis is placed on news; in iv.133.2, it is the temple and not the agency of the priestess that Thucydides wishes to emphasize.

2.2   The previous discussion is summarized, in tabular form, in table B.3.

2.3   The first subject type, οἱ Ἀθηναῖοι, occurs in 32 sentences, or 27% of the total. A typical example is iv.42: "During the same summer, right after these events, the Athenians campaigned against Corinth with eighty ships" (τοῦ δ' αὐτοῦ θέρους μετὰ ταῦτα εὐθὺς Ἀθηναῖοι ἐς τὴν Κορινθίαν ἐστράτευσαν ναυσὶν ὀγδοήκοντα). Especially early in the narrative, the Athenians are found as the subject of the first sentence even where one would expect the unit to begin in another way. For instance, a natural subject for the first sentence of ii.34-47.1 might have been Pericles, the individual who delivered the oration that would take up most of the unit. Instead, the unit begins: "In this winter, following their traditional custom, the Athenians held

TABLE B.3   Distribution of subjects in introductory sentences, ii.1–v.24

(number and percentage of total)

	Book ii	Book iii	Books iv–v.24	Total
Athenians (and allies)	13 (37%)	13 (37%)	6 (12%)	32 (27%)
Peloponnesians (and allies)	5 (14%)	5 (14%)	3 (6%)	13 (11%)
Other collectives	4 (11%)	8 (22%)	11 (22%)	23 (19%)
Personal names	6 (17%)	1 (3%)	18 (37%)	25 (21%)
Concrete nouns	6 (17%)	7 (20%)	8 (16%)	21 (18%)
Place	1 (3%)	1 (3%)	3 (6%)	5 (4%)
Total units	35 (100%)	35 (100%)	49 (100%)	119 (100%)

TABLE B.4   Distribution of verb types in introductory sentences, ii.1–v.24

	Book ii	Book iii	Books iv–v.24	Total
Initiatory	17	17	15	49
Deliberative	7	4	2	13
Summary	11	14	32	57
Total	35	35	49	119

burial rites at public expense for the first to die in this war, in the following manner" (ἐν δὲ τῷ αὐτῷ χειμῶνι Ἀθηναῖοι τῷ πατρίῳ νόμῳ χρώμενοι δημοσίᾳ ταφὰς ἐποιήσαντο τῶν ἐν τῷδε τῷ πολέμῳ πρώτων ἀποθανόντων τρόπῳ τοιῷδε). See 2.1.a above for the list of the 32 introductory sentences with Athenians as subjects.

2.4   Almost a third of the introductory sentences with individual subjects in books iv–v.24 contain Brasidas either alone or in combination with others, but this does not suffice to explain the increase. Simonides in iv.7, Eurymedon and Sophocles in iv.46, Demodocus, Aristides and Lamachus in iv.75, Phaeax in v.4, Ramphias, Autocharidas, and Epicydidas in v.12—these are not men particularly memorable for their own sake, and where before they would have been named in a genitive absolute, a parenthesis, or in the second sentence of the unit, in books iv and v they provide the unit's initial subject. Cf. Westlake (1968, 308), who argues that as the *History* continues Thucydides emphasizes the role of individuals.

3.1   Table B.4 summarizes the various types of verb that appear in the introductory sentences of Archidamian units of action.

3.1.1   As noted above, p. 40, verbs of the initiatory and deliberative type are found less often in book iv, dropping from 69% of the units in book ii to 60% in book iii to 35% in books iv–v.24. Verbs of the summary type rise from 31% to 40% to 65% over the course of the same books.

3.2   These verbs are distributed among the subjects of Archidamian introductory sentences as shown in table B.5.

3.2.1   Lists of verbs of introductory sentences broken down by subject and verb type. These lists give the data from which table B.5 was compiled.

a. Introductory sentences with initiatory verbs include Athenians as subject: ii.26, 31, 69, 79, 102; iii. 7, 19, 51, 86, 88, 91, 103, 115; iv.2.2, 42, 53; Peloponnesians as subject: ii.47.2, 55, 66, 71; iii.1, 26, 89.1; iv.2.1; other collectives: ii.2, 68; iii.8, 18, 105; iv.134.1–2; individuals: ii.58, 67, 95; iii.25; iv.46, 76, 78, 84, 102, 109.1, 124; v.2, 4, 6; concrete nouns: ii.1, 18, 47.3; iii.87.1, 89.2 (total: 49). Only 16 of the 49 sentences listed here are not principally military in focus: ii.1, 2, 47.3, 67, 71; iii.8, 25, 87, 89.2; iv.46 (?), 76 (?), 78 (?), 84 (?), 102 (?), 124 (?); v.4.

b. Introductory sentences with deliberative verbs include Athenians: ii.59; Peloponnesians: ii.10; other collectives: ii.70, 80; iii.20, 27, 52, 100; iv.66; individuals: ii.13, 33, 93; iv.75 (total: 13).

c. Introductory sentences with verbs of the summary type include Athenians: ii.7, 24, 25, 27, 29, 30, 34; iii.36, 90, 94, 99 (s), 104; iv.26, 49 (s); v.1b (s); Peloponnesians: iii.29, 92; iv.6; v.21; other collectives: iii.70; iv.8, 24, 51 (s), 52.2, 109 (s), 117, 133.1 (s); v.3.5 (s), 13; individuals: iv.7 (s), 50, 89, 101.5 (s), 135; v.3.6 (s), 12 (s); place: ii.32 (s); iii.2; iv.120, 123, 133.4 (s); concrete nouns: ii.28 (s), 57, 83; iii.17, 33.2, 69, 87.4 (s), 116 (s); iv.1, 52.1 (s), 58, 133.2, 134.1 (s); v.1a (s), 14, 20.2 (total: 57). The designation (s) after a unit indicates that the unit itself is a simple picture unit.

3.3   Introductory sentences with passive verbs are ii.1 (?), 32, 83; iii.25, 27; iv.133.2, 133.4; v.1.1. Not counted here are deponent verbs (middle or passive forms with active meanings), as in ii.7, iii.92, and iv.123.

4.1   No setting is identified in ii.1, 7, 13, 28, 29, 33, 34, 47.3, 59, 70, 80; iii.17, 20, 26, 27, 52, 70, 87.1; iv.51, 52.1, 101.5, 109.1, 117, 133.1, 134.1; v.1.1, 14, 20.2, 21 (total: 29).

4.2   Setting is expressed in a prepositional phrase in the following sentences: ii.2, 10, 18, 24, 26, 27, 31, 47.2, 55, 58, 66, 67, 68, 71, 79, 102; iii.1, 7, 8, 18, 19, 25, 26, 29,

TABLE B.5   Distribution of verb types in
introductory sentences according to subject, ii.1–v.24

	Initiatory	Deliberative	Summary	Active	Passive
Athenians					
Book ii	5	1	7	13	—
Book iii	8	—	5	13	—
Books iv–v.24	3	—	3	6	—
Peloponnesians					
Book ii	4	1	—	5	—
Book iii	3	—	2	5	—
Books iv–v.24	1	—	2	3	—
Other collectives					
Book ii	2	2	—	4	—
Book iii	3	4	1	7	1
Books iv–v.24	1	1	9	11	—
Personal names					
Book ii	3	3	—	6	—
Book iii	1	—	—	—	1
Books iv–v.24	10	1	7	18	—
Concrete nouns					
Book ii	3	—	3	4	2
Book iii	2	—	5	7	—
Books iv–v.24	—	—	8	6	2
Place					
Book ii	—	—	1	—	1
Book iii	—	—	1	1	—
Books iv–v.24	—	—	3	2	1

TABLE B.6   Distribution of place in introductory sentences, ii.1–v.24

(number and percentage of total)

	Book ii	Book iii	Books iv–v.24	Total units
Prepositional phrase	16 (46%)	20 (57%)	24 (49%)	60 (50%)
No setting	11 (31%)	7 (20%)	11 (22%)	29 (24%)
Object of verb	(1)	2 (6%)	5 (10%)	7 (6%)
Subject of sentence	(1)	1 (3%)	1 (2%)	2 (2%)
Other	1 (3%)	—	(2)	1 (1%)
Combination	7 (20%)	5 (14%)	8 (16%)	20 (17%)
Total units	35	35	49	119

NOTE: Parentheses indicate that the unit is actually counted in the category Combination, which indicates that two or more expressions of place occur in a given introductory sentence. I wanted to indicate the varieties of combinations Thucydides uses, but they are not counted independently into the 119-sentence total.

33.2, 51, 69, 86, 87.4, 89.1, 89.2, 90, 91, 94, 105, 116; iv.2.1, 2.2, 8, 26, 42, 46, 53, 58, 66, 75, 76, 78, 84, 89, 102, 109.1, 124, 133.2, 134.1; v.1, 2, 4, 12, 13 (total: 60).

4.3   Units with more than one identification of setting in the introductory sentence are ii.25, 30, 32, 57, 69, 83, 95; iii.88, 99, 100, 103, 115; iv.6, 24, 49, 50, 120, 123; v.3.6, 6 (total: 20).

4.4   Place is the subject in ii.32; iii.2; iv.120, 123, 133.4. Three of these are also found in 4.3 above, since the place as subject is supplemented by another word or phrase in the same sentence. See the note at the bottom of table B.6. See p. 42 for a brief discussion of those sentences where a place-name is the subject of the sentence. Most of them stand by metonymy for groups of people.

4.5   Place is the object of the verb in ii.30; iii.92, 104; iv.1, 7, 49, 52.2, 135; v.3.5, 3.6; place is a genitive or dative in ii.93, 95; v.3.6, 6. Several of these occur in introductory sentences containing another indication of place as well. See the note at the bottom of table B.6.

4.6   Table B.6 summarizes the lists given in 4.1–4.5 above.

5.1   Introductory sentences introduced by a simple seasonal phrase are ii.27, 28, 29, 33, 34, 58, 66, 69, 70, 71; iii.20, 26, 87.1, 88, 89.1, 90, 91, 100, 103, 104, 105, 115; iv.50, 51, 53, 58, 66, 75, 102, 109.1, 133.1, 133.2, 134.1 (total: 33).

5.2   Introductory sentences whose time is indicated by a neutral prepositional phrase are ii.26; iii.7, 27, 52, 92, 99; iv.7, 24, 46, 78, 123, 124; v.3.5, 4 (total: 14).

TABLE B.7   Distribution of time formulae in introductory sentences, ii.1–v.24

	Number	% of total
Simple season	33	28
Neutral prepositional phrase	14	12
Detailed season	23	19
Precise reference	29	24
Atypical	6	5
None	14	12
Total	119	100

5.3   Introductory sentences whose time includes a more exactly defined season are ii.31, 32, 47.2, 67, 68, 80, 93, 95; iii.1, 25, 86, 116; iv.1, 42, 49, 52.1, 84, 89, 117, 133.4, 135; v.12, 13 (total: 23).

5.3.1   Of these, the sentences including a word limiting the season very exactly are ii.67; iii.86; iv.49, 52.1, 117, 135 (total: 6).

5.4   The introductory sentences referring to a specific speech event in the season are ii.7, 10, 13, 24, 47.3, 55, 57, 59, 79, 83, 102; iii.2, 17, 18, 36, 51, 69, 89.2, 94; iv.2.1, 8, 76, 101.5, 109.1, 120; v.1a, v.1b, 2, 14 (total: 29).

5.5   The introductory sentences with atypical and mostly brief temporal expressions are ii.1, 2; iii.87.4; iv.26; v.6, 21 (total: 6). Sentence ii.2 is exceptionally long and detailed as a temporal formula; see p. 26.

5.6   Introductory sentences with no time formula are ii.18, 25, 30; iii.8, 19, 29, 33.3, 70; iv.2.2, 6, 52.2, 134.1; v.3.6, 20.2 (total: 14). Where time words are lacking and the unit is in effect the continuation of a subject introduced earlier in the same season, descriptive material in the sentence often makes it very clear. For instance, the time formula is not required in iii.29 because other information makes it clear that the narrative time continues from iii.26.

5.7   Table B.7 summarizes the lists given in 5.1–5.6.

· Time Formulae in
Introductory Sentences
(ii.1–viii.109)

TABLE C.1 Distribution of time formulae in introductory sentences, ii.1–viii.109

(number and percentage of total)

	Years 1–10	Years 11–16	Years 17–19[a]	Years 20–21[a]
Simple season[b]	33 (28%)	15 (31%)	3 (5%)	6 (11%)
Neutral prepositional phrase[b]	14 (12%)	7 (14%)	11 (17%)	11 (20%)
Detailed season[b]	23 (19%)	5 (10%)	8 (13%)	8 (15%)
Precise reference[b]	29 (24%)	10 (20%)	19 (30%)	15 (27%)
Atypical[b]	6 (5%)	4 (8%)	10 (16%)	—
None	14 (12%)	8 (16%)	12 (19%)	15 (27%)
Total	119 (100%)	49 (99%)	63 (100%)	55 (100%)

[a] For structural changes that make formulae in these years less important as signs of the *History*'s organization, see chapter 6.

[b] For definitions of types of time formulae, see pp. 43–46.

NOTES

INTRODUCTION

1. Immerwahr 1966. The three volumes of Gomme's *Historical Commentary on Thucydides* (henceforth *HCT*) were published by 1956; Andrewes and Dover published *HCT* IV in 1970, and Andrewes *HCT* V in 1981 (with an appendix contributed by Dover).

2. Rood (1998, 205) begins chapter 9 calling book i "the section of [Thucydides'] *History* most conspicuous for temporal deviations and for overt omissions." For the distinctive structure of its first major section, see Hammond 1952; Connor 1984, 30 n. 29; Ellis 1991; and Marincola 2001, 70 n. 47. For its larger argumentative and rhetorical function, see generally Stahl 1966, 36–64; Connor 1984, 20–51; and for details and relevant bibliography, Hornblower 1991, 3, 56, 59, 65–66, 97–99, 107–8, 133–34, 149, 195, 202–3, 211–12, 226, 231–32. See pp. 160–61, where I suggest some ways in which the structures of book i resemble those of books ii–viii.

3. See Smart 1986 for the summer/winter arrangement as Thucydides' choice to emphasize *physis*, natural articulations of the seasons, rather than *nomos*, conventional or political calendars. For various possibilities concerning its origins, including that it came from the lost genre of the military report, see Hornblower 1987, 39–41. On Thucydides' dating system in general and the problems of positing that it worked by the seasonal year (v.20 vs. v.24.2), see *HCT* I: 1–8; III: 699–715; IV: 18–21; de Ste. Croix 1972, 323–28; Luschnat 1971, 1132–46; and Hornblower 1991, 235 (on ii.1), with bibliography. See Marincola 2001, 65 n. 19, for the unpopularity of this arrangement among later Greek historians and historiographers.

4. See pp. 31–33 for descriptions of the different unit types. Rood (1998, 112–13) uses

year six, as I have done here, to show a particularly stripped-down version of Thucydides' seasonal framework for the narrative.

5. See pp. 120–25 and 130–35.

6. See Connor 1984, 147; Rood 1998, 83. The whole of Rood's chapter 4, "Misreadings: Book V," ably argues that the speed and compression of book v are deliberate.

7. De Romilly (1963, 3–10 and passim), Luschnat (1970, 1183–1229), Dover (1973, 14–20), and Hunter (1977) discuss the relevant issues. *HCT* V: 361–444 lists the most important passages that either figure into the discussion of incompleteness or argue for a particular date of composition. See also Hornblower 1987, 136–54; Rood 1998, 16–17 and 52–54.

8. Both de Ste. Croix (1972, 296) and Rawlings (1981, 250) quote with approval the judgment of de Romilly (1963, 6): "Exhausting by the immense bibliography which it offers, completely negative in its results, the question of the composition of the work can at present be considered as the perfect example of a vain and insoluble problem."

9. In book ii alone, ii.65 and ii.100.2 are clearly late, while ii.23.3 might well be an early passage. See *HCT* V: 405, and more generally 384–444. One of the trends that led to the abandonment of the composition question in the 1970s was what was then called new criticism. It was widely acknowledged as a principle of literary analysis that it was illicit to argue from any text to the biography or the opinions of the individual who wrote it.

10. See further pp. 158–60. Rawlings (1981, 250–54) judiciously assesses the problems raised by the composition question, although his analysis of Thucydides' basic narrative structures is quite different from that advanced here. See Culler 1975 for the problem of reaching a general definition of narrative structure. Toward the end of this introduction I argue that structure/plot is difficult to define in the abstract for a work of narrative history precisely because it is the result of a series of individual and specific choices on the part of the historian about how to arrange the material he or she has deemed relevant, in order to give a coherent and meaningful account to a reading audience endowed with the same commonsense intelligence that the historian has displayed as a writer.

11. Stahl (1966, 88 nn. 20 and 21) cites de Romilly (1956a, 150) for the idea that speeches clarify the issues implicit in an adjacent military narrative; the whole of de Romilly's chapter 2 is worth reading. Stahl (1973, 60–77) develops at length the way the surrounding narrative tacitly judges the quality of the speeches in books vi and vii (see also Westlake 1973, 90–108). Two recent full-length treatments further explore the intellectual connections linking reported speech and third-person narrative: Rood 1998 (narratological in method) and Debnar 2001 (on Spartans as both auditors and speakers). See also Marincola 2001, 69–70.

12. Some full-length studies showing a heightened sensitivity to the interpretive significance of Thucydides' language are Edmunds 1975, Pouncey 1980, Cogan 1981,

Ostwald 1988, Allison 1989 and 1997, Kallet (= Kallet-Marx) 1993 and 2001, Hornblower 1994, Crane 1996, Gribble 1998 and 1999, Rood 1998, and Pelling 2000. See Marincola 2001 for other important recent scholarship, topically organized. Connor's use of the adjective "post-modernist" to describe Thucydides in an important 1977 article was prescient but different from the meaning usually given postmodernism in the next decade; he emphasizes the degree of passionate artistry revealed by some recent studies of Thucydides, in their close attention to the language of the text. Cf. note 29 below.

13. For the beginnings of Greek historiography, see Strasburger 1972, Drews 1973, Pucci 1977, Detienne 1981, Fornara 1983, and Luraghi 2001. For the different notions of historical truth entertained by Herodotus and Thucydides, see Hornblower 1987, 13–33; Marincola 1997, 6–9, 67–69, 117–19, 182–84 and passim; Dewald 1985 and 1999; Gomme 1954, chaps. 4–7, is also still worth consulting. Marincola 2001, 9–39, is an excellent brief survey of the long development in historical thinking that enabled Thucydides to begin to write as he did.

14. I have used the 1998 translation of S. Lattimore throughout this work; because of its close adherence to the wording of the Greek, it is unusually helpful for discussing the formal aspects of Thucydides' style. With the kind permission of Professor Lattimore, I have occasionally slightly changed his wording, ordinarily indicating when I have done so by the use of square brackets. In this passage there are two changes. It is hard to give a comprehensive single-word translation of τὸ μυθῶδες, "the mythic." Lattimore, influenced by Flory 1990, translates it "patriotic storytelling," stressing its possible political implications for Thucydides. Warner (1954) in the Penguin edition translates it as "a romantic element." I have substituted here "a tendency to storytelling and literary polish," as a more general expression that also includes stylistic concerns; see Gomme 1954, 116–17. For Thucydides' awareness of the importance of the technology of writing to his project, see Edmunds 1993 and Marincola 2001, 64 n.16. I have translated τῶν γενομένων τὸ σαφές not as "the plain truth about past events," but rather as a limiting expression, "what is clear about past events."

15. Both Gomme (HCT I) and Hornblower (1991) take the usefulness as a purely intellectual one, for people of the future looking back at events in their past. However, de Ste. Croix (1972, 29–33) makes a good case for the possibility that Thucydides intended the usefulness to be a practical one too, for political decision-making; see also Farrar 1988, 131–37; and pp. 8–9. De Romilly (1956b, 39–66) links the Thucydidean issue to the more basic problem of the role played by generalization in history writing.

16. Thucydides' aspirations to accuracy (i.22.4) have generated a vast bibliography. See Hornblower 1987, 37; Cawkwell 1997, 8–12; and Marincola 1997, 67–69; and, more generally, Marincola 2001, 74 n. 62 and 98–103. See Dover 1973, 25–33; and Rood 1998, 134–58 and index, under "historical approaches, mistakes, alleged" for Thucydidean omissions. For the related problem of accuracy in rendering the speeches included in the History, see HCT V: 393–99; Macleod 1983, 52–53 and 68–70; Hornblower 1987,

45–72; Rood 1998, 46–48; and Marincola 2001, 77–85. In the Peloponnesian War political decisions played an important part in events, and they were often made in Athens as a result of long and intense public debate. Those who impugn Thucydides' good faith in claiming to report what was actually said need to explain what else he could have done than give the relevant "general gist" (ξυμπάση γνώμη, i.22.1) of a selection of the particularly intelligent or influential speeches that were actually delivered; see further Pelling 2000, 112–22. See notes 29 and 46–49 below for the related theoretical issue of narrative's ability ever to represent the past.

17. For differences between the first-person Thucydidean narrator and the narrator in Herodotus's *Histories,* see Dewald 1987 and 1999; Marincola 1987 and 1997, 9–10 and 117–19; Darbo-Peschanski 1987a and 1987b; and Gribble 1998. For the larger question of Thucydides' relationship to and dependence on Herodotus and earlier writers, see Hunter 1982; Hornblower 1987, 13–33; 1991, 58–61; and 1996, annex A and 19–20, 24–38 (which makes some good arguments, despite an oddly combative rhetorical stance toward recent scholarship); see also Rood 1998; 1999, 141–68. For "poetic history," see Boedeker and Sider 2001, on Simonides as the poet of the Persian Wars; and Bowie 2001. For Thucydides' and Herodotus's immediate predecessors and contemporaries, see Luraghi 2001 passim.

18. Cochrane 1929; cf. Hornblower 1987, 110.

19. In the 1800s, at least in the largely Protestant world of the British and American universities, it was midcentury before the fact-based model of the hard sciences was successfully used to disengage the human sciences, both the humanities and the newer social sciences, from religious control, both political and intellectual. The political control was exercised by ecclesiastical structures that still governed many universities and colleges. More diffusely but as strongly, the intellectual control was expressed in various religious assumptions ("biblical inerrancy," for instance, leading to the assertion that the world was created in about 4000 B.C.E.) that had been built into the very reasons for founding institutions of higher education, as a way to study the Bible and thus to provide ministers for the nation's churches. In the English-speaking world, "gradually after the 1850s . . . historians and scientists forged an alliance aided by the new hermeneutics. . . . Together, history and hermeneutics would liberate both themselves and science from clerical influence" (Appleby, Hunt, and Jacob 1994, 47–48; see also 38, 43–51). For additional German and romantic roots of this trend, see Novick 1988, 21–46.

20. See Stone 1979, 4–8, for a variety of recent scientisms in history as a discipline. See Novick 1988, 103–4 and 252–60, for the relativist critique advanced by F. Turner in 1891 ("each age writes the history of the past anew with reference to the conditions uppermost in its own time"), and that of the "pragmatists," like C. Beard and C. Becker after World War I. In classics, Cornford in 1907 had already labeled Thucydides "mythistoricus"; Collingwood (1946, 29) notoriously questioned whether Thucydides' methods were those of bad conscience rather than objectivity. Doubts about the possibility

of historical objectivity certainly occurred before this period. For criticisms raised in the ancient world (in particular, the criticisms of historians commenting on their predecessors' work!), see Marincola 1997, 158–74. Norman (in Fay, Pomper, Vann 1998, 154) mentions the doubts of Descartes; LaCapra (in the same volume, 91) mentions those of Henry Adams, expressed in the first volume of the *American Historical Review*, in 1885.

21. Kuhn (1962) thus deconstructed the model of the valiant Promethean researcher, the Newton or Mendel, boldly exploring new ground and bound alone by an allegiance to what his data turned up. Looking at how science was done in real universities and laboratories, Kuhn proposed that a more accurate model would involve paradigms or widely accepted explanatory systems shaping the assumptions according to which scientific research in normal circumstances was undertaken. If a paradigm broke down under the weight of too much data that did not fit it, the changes that occurred were convulsive and messy, eventually leading to a new paradigm. Kuhn never abandoned his belief, however, in the scientific method; he had himself been a physicist involved in the American war effort in World War II. See Novick 1988, 526; Appleby, Hunt, and Jacob 1994, 65; Danto 1995; Bonnell and Hunt 1999, 27 n. 1.

22. See Novick 1988, chap. 14 ("Every group its own historian"), 469–520; and Appleby, Hunt, and Jacob 1994, chap. 4 ("Competing Histories of America"), 129–59, esp. 146 ff., and 218, 281 (but cf. Smith's expressly feminist dissatisfaction [1995] with the sanguine inclusivist approach of Appleby, Hunt, and Jacob). See also Berkhofer 1995, 156–201, on the recent problems encountered in historical rhetoric by the need for inclusivity in the historian's voice: Who now determines what the Great Story is?

23. Berkhofer 1995, 285 n. 1, cites Rorty 1968 for the formulations "linguistic turn" and "interpretive turn," and Rabinow and Sullivan 1979, 1–21, for "interpretive turn." For a general description, see Bonnell and Hunt 1999, 1–32 and esp. 30 n. 19; see Somers 1999, 124–28. See also F. Jameson 's 1998 collection of previous essays for the cultural turn as an aspect of postmodernism, and more generally Anderson 1998, 47–77, for Jameson's role in articulating a postmodern critique of the relation of language to culture (as a "grandiose finale of Western Marxism," 74). See Munslow 2000, 65 and 151, respectively, for the relation of the Annales school to the cultural turn in history as a discipline and for a brief description of the linguistic turn. For a general response among American and European historians to these trends, see the review articles of Toews (1987) and Maza (1996).

24. For the influence of Geertz's "thick description" and anthropology in general, see Novick 1988, 551–55, and for cultural history more broadly, Appleby, Hunt, and Jacob 1994, 218–23 (Geertz, but also Gramsci, Williams, Althusser, E. P. Thompson, Bourdieu, and the Annalistes). See also Munslow 2000, 64–67, and for a historical critique of the movement, Stone 1979.

25. For ideology, see Novick 1988, 61–63; Berkhofer 1995, 211–14 (including the useful nn. 20–32); Munslow 1997, 2000; and Jenkins's (1997, 1999) discussion of "upper

case" history. Stone (1992, 189–90) caustically observed that the shaping of a historical narrative by the author's implicit assumptions and the constraints of language was not an entirely new idea. Some more recent critics, however, think of it as a problem incapable of solution. The Archimedean fulcrum comes up frequently in discussions of how ideology saturates language: "There is no extra-linguistic platform upon which we can stand in order to exert leverage on reality" (Munslow 2000, 177); cf. Novick 1988, 538; and Jay 1982, 102, on Habermas's hope for a parole [*sic*] from Nietzsche's "prison-house of language."

26. Foucault (1970, 27) uses the example of aconite to illustrate the sixteenth-century theory of resemblances. See O'Brien 1989, 25–46, for Foucault's larger role as a cultural critic and gadfly of the professional historical establishment, and for his career-long interest in power as an organizing principle of culture: "power creates truth and hence its own legitimation" (35). See also Dreyfus and Rabinow 1982 and Rabinow 1999, and for a succinct description of Foucault's role in the articulation of a postmodern historiography, Munslow 2000, 107–11.

27. The four Foucauldian *epistēmai* are the Renaissance, the Classical, the Modern/Anthropological, and the Postmodern. See further White 1978, 230–61 (including Foucault's interest in Vico, 254); 1987, 104–41; and Poster 1982, 137–52. Foucault himself took an ironic stance about the disciplinary (punitive?) constraints of history; O'Brien (1989, 28) cites Megill (*JHI* 48 [1987]: 117) for Foucault's "I'm not a professional historian—but nobody's perfect." For the usefulness of the term *epistēmē*, see Munslow 1997, 132–34; 2000, 86–87; and for difficulties in determining the temporal boundaries of a Foucauldian *epistēmē*, see Berkhofer 1995, 111–15. In the 1970s, Barthes, Foucault, and Derrida had published important work in French but were not yet widely known in the Anglophone world. Foucault's *Mots et choses* was translated into English as *The Order of Things* in 1970, Roland Barthes's important article "Historical Discourse" appeared in 1970, Derrida's *Writing and Difference* appeared in 1978, and *Disseminations* in 1981.

28. In addition to the bibliography cited in note 23, see Jay 1982, 86–110, which traces the philosophical roots of this movement back to Wittgenstein and Austin in Britain and also, in continental philosophy, to Habermas's hermeneutics and his controversy with Gadamer. See also Vann 1995; Kellner 1997, 127–38. Berkhofer 1995, Munslow 1997, Jenkins 1999, and many of the essays in Veeser 1989, Fay, Pomper, and Vann 1998, Bonnell and Hunt 1999, and Burke 2001, as well as others cited in notes 23–27, explore various aspects of the impact of the linguistic turn on the practice of historians. For an appreciative and subtle assessment of the linguistic turn's recent role in shaping history as a discipline, see Spiegel 1990 and 1992 (both reprinted in Jenkins 1997).

29. A classic formulation is that of White 1987, 26–57; see also the volumes of collected essays cited in note 28 above. Postmodernism and poststructuralism are frequently used as equivalent terms (Bonnell and Hunt 1999, 8–9); postmodernism as a more gen-

eral, cultural term came into wider use after Lyotard's 1979/1984 *The Postmodern Condition* (Munslow 1997, 14–15, 29–30; 2000, 11–15 and 188–91; Berkhofer 1995, 220–26 and nn. 60, 73; Appleby, Hunt, and Jacob 1994, 198–237). In the poststructuralist critique of a modernist empiricism, different writers stressed different things: Barthes explored how language—like fashion—is a system, closed and interlocking, one that is generated through discourse; to him it did not make sense to talk of an author consciously in charge of the process. Language itself works its own processes with its own rhythms through texts; the writer is not consciously in charge of many of these processes. Derrida's deconstruction meant a perpetual decentering and recirculation of meaning through the way that words ("signifiers") are linked not to things in the world they represent ("the signified") but only to other words. Thus language does not generate a particular concept that can be concretely applied to something out in the represented world, but rather forms part of an interlocking web of language that works on structuralist principles. For this and other reasons it becomes impossible to point to anything definitively real whose ontology we can get at, break through to, through language (cf. note 25 above).

30. See, for example, Boedeker 1987; Gould 1989; Thomas 2000; Munson 2001; Luraghi 2001.

31. See Gomme's ironic comment (*HCT* I: 152) regarding Thucydides' claim in i.23 to have written an account "so that no one may ever search for the reasons that so great a war broke out among the Hellenes": "This object has not been achieved; the ζήτησις is as lively as ever, if not very fruitful." Thucydides in iii.82 may say that words change their meaning, but he apparently thought that he could account for and evaluate the process. According to poststructuralist thought, however, both he and his text were, like everything else, rather irretrievably part of it.

32. See, for example, Cawkwell 1997; Kallet 1993, 2001. Hornblower (1991 and 1996 passim) discusses important recent historical controversies relevant to a close reading of Thucydides' text; see esp. the discussion of epigraphy (1996, 93–107). Worth noting are the pointed remarks of Rhodes: "The fact that a passage is a topos, that it says what is conventionally said in a particular situation, and perhaps expresses it in a conventional way, does not exclude the possibility that it is an authentic report, or that what is stated is true. Topoi have always been used, in all kinds of writing, but detecting topoi is not enough in deciding whether we should believe what we read" (1994, 157). Cf. Momigliano's classic 1981 review of White's *Metahistory;* see also Hornblower 1994, 133 n. 5.

33. Connor 1977, 289; 1984, 7; 1985, 8–9 (on what is called focalization by Genette [1980, 185–98]), 13–15. See also note 12 above. On Thucydides' reputation for *pathos* in antiquity, see Dion. Hal. *Pomp.* 3; Marincola 2001, 88 and (on tragedy) 73 n. 58; see also Lateiner 1977. For Thucydides' tragic *akribeia*, see Hornblower 1987, 34–35, 113–19, 148, 193; and for his essentially tragic reading of the Periclean vision, Parry 1981, 178–85; 1989, 286–300. For an extreme statement of Thucydides as an author striving for rhetorical effect, see Woodman 1988, esp. 29 and 37. Dionysius characterized Thucydides' style

generally as forceful, using adjectives like *deinon*, "formidable," *pikron*, "harsh," *austeron*, "difficult," and *phoberon*, "fearsome," and thought he was better at depicting emotions than Herodotus was; see also note 38 below.

34. Finley (1942 and 1967) should be mentioned here as an influential forerunner of Parry and Macleod. See Parry 1981 (repr. of his 1957 dissertation) and 1989 (collected articles from 1956–71), and Macleod 1983 (articles from 1970–82). Hunter 1973 is reviewed in Connor 1977; Badian 1993, 125–62, is discussed in Marincola 2001, 102 n. 192. Schneider (1974) also argues that Thucydides is a highly ideological, tendentious author; see, more generally, Loraux 1980 and 1986b.

35. See Zeitlin in Vernant 1991, 3–24, on Vernant's structuralist scholarship, his leadership in founding the Centre Louis Gernet, and the resulting changes in our understanding of ancient Greek myth, literature, society, and culture. See also Vernant's 1996 autobiography.

36. On Thucydidean omissions, see Marincola 2001, 102 n. 190; Hornblower 1992 (on religion); and, more generally, Crane 1996. A small sampling of recent important works exploring the links between Athenian civic life, its performance culture, and its broader social attitudes would include Detienne and Vernant 1991 (originally published in 1974), Vernant 1980 (originally 1974), Vidal-Naquet 1986 (originally 1983), Gentili 1988 (originally 1985), Loraux 1986a (originally 1981), Ober 1989, Winkler and Zeitlin 1990, Edmunds and Wallace 1997, Goldhill and Osborne 1999, and Pelling 2000. Crane (1998) develops the concept of Thucydides' aristocratic "ancient simplicity." (Regarding Thucydidean omissions, it should perhaps be noted that Gomme began the 1945/1956 introduction to *HCT* I with an essay on "what Thucydides takes for granted." He went on to argue that Thucydides was writing a history of the Peloponnesian War per se, not "a political cultural history of Athens from 479–404," 25.)

37. Loraux 1986b and 1980; Darbo-Peschanski 1987b; Edmunds 1993. Thomas (1989 and 2000) points out how extensively the First Sophistic, in whose intellectual experiments Thucydides certainly participated, was the product of a highly oral culture; see also Marincola 2001, 64–65.

38. See note 17 above. Dionysius of Halicarnassus emphasizes the difficulty of Thucydides' prose in *Thuc.* 24, *Pomp.*, and the *Second Letter to Ammaeus* (Usher 1974, 1985; Pritchett 1975). For some of the basic differences in the narrative constructions of Herodotus and Thucydides, see further Dewald 1999.

39. Novick (1988, 565) quotes the somewhat cavalier dismissal of the English scholar E. D. Hirsch: "It is ethically inconsistent to batten on institutions whose very foundations one attacks. It is logically inconsistent to write scholarly books which argue that there is no point in writing scholarly books."

40. After Mink's untimely death, his colleagues brought out an important collected volume of his essays on narrative and history (Mink 1987); White (1978, 1987) developed the implications of many of Mink's questions. For a brief overview of White's

publications and concerns, see Munslow 2000, 225–27. White's important *Metahistory* had been published as early as 1973; his enduring interest in the meaning inherent in figural language is set out in the preface and first essay of *Figural Realism* (1999).

41. Marincola 1997, 12–19; 2001, 5–8; see also notes 33–34 above.

42. In the volumes of La Capra and Kaplan 1982 and Bonnell and Hunt 1999, White articulates his own larger vision. In one respect the argument I advance below is an offshoot of White's. If the current working *epistēmē* (even for postmodernists, in their management of their civic and private lives) does include a continuing belief in the usefulness of verifiable data (facts) in forming judgments, it is also the case that a completely compelling presentist position requires the working historian to give priority in his or her text to the task of respecting the data of the past still available for consideration. See the comment of Rhodes in note 32 above. The current historiographical debate under way on the Holocaust brings this issue out particularly clearly: Jenkins 1997, 384–433.

43. For his use of Northrop Frye and Vico, see White 1973, 7–11 and 31 n. 13. Other groups of four significant to White: the chronicle, story, emplotment, explanation; anarchism, conservatism, radicalism, liberalism; formist, mechanistic, organicist, contextualist; see the introduction to White 1973. See Berkhofer 1995, 95–98 (including nn. 49, 51, 54, 64–68); Kramer 1989, 97–128; Munslow 1997, 11–12; and Jenkins 1999, 120–32 (esp. 126–27), and 218 n. 3.

44. Mink 1987, 199.

45. Munslow 1997. One large category he calls empiricists, subdividing them into reconstructionists and constructionists, and distinguishing them altogether from deconstructionists. Jenkins (1999) divides rather differently, separating "lower case" historians from "upper case" or overtly ideological historians, both of whom are generally empiricists; he also lists five different categories of engagement among historians, depending on the seriousness with which they confront the challenge of deconstruction (1997, 21–25).

46. Munslow (1997, 36–56) discusses both reconstructionists and constructionists critically. The reconstructionist believes in the possibility of empirical data leading to a real knowledge of a real past; the constructionist believes that a theoretical (social-scientific) model is necessary, in order to build a version of the past worth having. Munslow slides from a (deconstructionist) sensitivity about the role of ideology and language in shaping texts to an indictment of empiricists in general, "who view the reconstruction of the past as primarily a skilled engagement with the evidence and who think, therefore, that there is little to dispute about its written form as history" (57). But cf. the "practical realism" of Appleby, Hunt, and Jacob (1994, 247–70) or the "reflexive (con)textualization" of Berkhofer (1995, 243–83) or the comments of Spiegel (1992).

47. Dewald forthcoming.

48. Aristotle's chief concern was the speech made in a judicial or deliberative context, and exploring how to handle arguments from the probable rather than the necessary, using the enthymeme or rhetorical syllogism (1355a6–13). As he saw, the young

had to be taught how to mount a persuasive speech in the assembly or law courts of Athens; the crucial skill to make sure they acquired was precisely that of "making sense" to their audience.

49. In *Rhet.* 1.1, 1355a, Aristotle points out the importance of a *common* sense: *anankē dia tōn koinōn poieisthai tas pisteis kai tous logous*. His concentration on the enthymeme in book 1 and on the psychological and ethical proofs, types of characters, and standard forms of argument in book 2 shows the budding orator what sorts of things make sense to a particular audience and hence carry persuasive force. This observation of Aristotle's is not anachronistic—we use the same standard all the time in our daily lives, to explain our lives both to ourselves and to others. People whose notions of *to prepon* and *to eikos* differ too widely from those of the rest of us are often assigned caretakers to manage their lives for them; even on a more pedestrian level, my neighbor who attributes the health of his lawn to the secret nightly ministrations of elves or spaceships ceases to be someone I consult on lawn care. As Carroll points out (1998, 38; see also Norman 1998, 158) individual historical "events," big and small, have reality by community agreement and thus are from their inception narrativized things: we collectively assign a meaning to terms like "World War II" and "the French Revolution," but also to "Pearl Harbor" and "the St. Bartholomew's Day Massacre," and it is a *communis opinio* that makes any of these, big or small, mean something.

50. Obviously, the budding orator giving an account of past events must not arbitrarily depart too conspicuously from the facts the audience knows or believes to be true, but he is not obliged, either, to include in his presentation true facts that would weaken his overall case (*Rhet.* 3.16, 1417a). Aristotle recommends intelligent omission or obfuscation when necessary (as in the notorious arguments from probability advanced in *Rhet.* 2.24, 1402a, where the weak man tried for assault is to argue that it is improbable because he was weak; the strong man, however, will argue the improbability of his committing assault, precisely because his guilt would be automatically assumed). The chief thing is to depict one's own character as trustworthy (*Rhet.* 1.2, 1356a: "His character may almost be called the most effective means of persuasion he possesses"). For *ethopoiia* as practiced by the ancient historians themselves, see Marincola 1997, 129–30; for *to eikos*, "the probable," see 282–83.

51. Carroll well asks (1998, 41): What is this "past" whose truth White does not think representable in narrative? Strictly speaking, what exists is a series of memories and memorabilia still extant in the present, which we use to point to an otherwise entirely vanished phenomenon. Moreover, why in order to be true does a narrative have to be comprehensive? (See also Carr 1986; 1998, 137–52; Norman 1998, 153–71.)

52. See notes 15 and 16 above.

53. Spiegel 1992, 59–86, repr. in Jenkins 1997, 260–73.

54. See, for example, the famous first chapter of E. H. Carr 1967, 3–35 ("The Historian and His Facts"); Stone 1992; Hexter 1998, 59–68; Berkhofer 1995, 26–27.

55. Halttunen (1999, 166–71) points out that self-reflexivity and alternate representational practices on the part of the historian add to the credibility of contemporary works of history, in the postmodern era. See also Berkhofer 1995, 243–83.

56. Morson and Emerson (1990, 15–36) use the term "prosaics" to cover a number of related terms Bakhtin himself used (including "prosaic wisdom" and "prosaic intelligence"); see also the contrast between dialogue and monologization (49–62).

57. Morson and Emerson 1990, 123–33 and 234–37.

58. Ibid., 125.

59. Ibid., 139–42.

60. Dialogic polyphony is not just a conversational give-and-take but includes the efforts made by one private language to communicate by integrating another's language into itself. In that sense, the author motivated by the sense of the otherness of the languages of the characters systematically practices dialogic polyphony, but the characters inside the account do so only occasionally (Morson and Emerson 1990, 234–41 and 243–46). Bakhtin's study of Dostoevsky (1984) is the central text underlying the discussion of dialogic polyphony; see esp. 32–36, 61–65. At one point, Bakhtin refers to Dostoevsky's abilities in this respect as "something like a sociology of consciousnesses . . . an objective mode for visualizing the life of consciousness and the forms of their living coexistence" (32).

61. I owe thanks to Vasily Rudich for substantial and insightful conversation on Bakhtin's (privately expressed) interest in history and the ancient historians.

62. Rood 1998; Dewald 1999.

63. Jameson 1982, 82 (quoted by Spiegel 1992, 197 n. 9).

64. These ideas owe a great deal to discussion with forbearing friends and colleagues. I would like particularly to thank J. Appleby, D. Boedeker, A. Boegehold, R. Brown, E. Dewald, T. Habinek, S. Hornblower, L. Kallet, J. Kirby, R. Kitzinger, D. Konstan, L. Kurke, D. Lateiner, N. Leonard, J. Marincola, R. Osborne, C. Pelling, D. Schalk, S. Schein, P. Stadter, and W. G. Thalmann.

CHAPTER ONE

1. An almost identical formulation occurs at v.26, although the way the text is constructed thereafter is quite different, as chapters 5 and 6 will explore.

2. For a list of all units and their topics, see appendix A, pp. 165–77.

3. HCT II: 390.

4. One might speculate that Thucydides had recorded many such small annotations "by summers and winters," as events unrolled, that did not make it into the final revised Archidamian narrative. What survived to the final version were annotations that in hindsight helped point to later important themes.

5. See pp. 3, 25–26 for Thucydides' use of the larger "summers and winters" schema to create a chronology. The fact that a brief picture unit resembles a journal entry does

not necessarily mean that it was written earlier than more developed units; it could as easily be the reduction, in Thucydides' final write-up, of an earlier, more extensive set of notes, once it became clear that the event did not merit full description. For the particular chronological issues raised by iii.116 (Thucydides does not mention the explosion of Aetna in 396), see Hornblower 1987, 144, and the surrounding discussion.

6. De Romilly (1956a, 107–79, "Les récits de batailles: analyse et narration") discusses the shifting of focus as a method of analysis in battle narratives. See pp. 53–65, for further discussion of units the length and complexity of iii.92–93.

CHAPTER TWO

1. Such an observation does not mean that any given part of the finished narrative necessarily also formed part of the earliest account; clearly substantial revision occurred. See pp. 4–6, 76–77, 158–60.

2. The introductory sentences considered here are not necessarily the ones created by the punctuation of a printed text. Editorial decisions often follow from principles of euphony and clause length, aspects of Thucydides' prose irrelevant to questions of structure. The first subject, the first verb, and the subordinate elements surrounding these two are the elements of the unit that first strike the reader's ear. For more on the way the first sentences were defined, for the purposes of this study, see appendix B: 1.1, 1.2.

3. See appendix B: 1.3.1.

4. See appendix B: 1.3, 1.4.

5. See appendix B: 1.4 (table B.1).

6. The regularity of the pattern is particularly striking, given Thucydides' predilection for abstraction and his general interest in avoiding parallelism: see Ros 1968. For Herodotean introductory formulas, cf. Immerwahr 1966, 51–66.

7. See appendix B: 1.5, 1.5.1 (table B.2: Order of first two elements in introductory sentences, ii.l–v.24).

8. See further appendix B: 2.1 for a complete listing of all subjects in introductory sentences, by category.

9. For a list of concrete nouns as subjects in introductory sentences, see appendix B: 2.1.g.

10. See appendix B: 2.2 (table B.3: D distribution of subjects in introductory sentences, ii.1–v.24), setting out these figures. See also sections 2.3 and 2.4 for details.

11. See pp. 63, 76–77, 83.

12. See appendix B: 3.1 (table B.4: Distribution of verb types in introductory sentences, ii.1–v.24). See appendix B: 3.2.1.a for a list of specific introductory sentences containing initiatory verbs. See pp. 56–60 for a discussion of military formular language.

13. Introductory sentences with deliberative verbs include ii.59 (Athenians); ii.10 (Peloponnesians); ii.70, 80, iii.20, 27, 52, 100, iv.66 (other collectives); ii.13, 33, 93, iv.75 (individuals). See also appendix B: 3.2 and 3.2.1.b.

14. See appendix B: 3.2.1.c. A "major action" is of course difficult to define exactly. But its general nature can be gauged by the fact that 19 of the 57 units with summary type verbs are units a single sentence long; in these simple picture units, the verb in the introductory sentence is also the verb that conveys the essential information in the unit. See appendix B: 3.1 and table B.4.

15. This change is not an independent one but reflects a development discussed on p. 83: the increasing use of simple picture units late in the narrative of the Archidamian War. Of the 24 simple picture units that occur in the course of ii.1–v.24, 19 have summary type verbs; 14 of these occur in books iv–v.24.33. Thus the change in introductory verbs seen in appendix B: 3.1 (table B.4) indicates one of the ways in which Thucydides conveys a sense of discriminating spareness and boldness in the simple picture units of books iv and v; at this point in his narrative he sharply discriminates between what needs thorough analysis and what can be briefly noted before moving on.

16. In four units altogether in books ii and iii, individually named subjects are coupled with initiatory verbs: ii.58, 67, 95, and iii.25; ii.67 and iii.25 are not directly military. In books iv and v, however, ten individual subjects have initiatory verbs; all but possibly iv.76.2 are military (iv.76 is military only in the sense that iii.25 is, although Demosthenes arrives with forty ships in Naupactus, while Salaethus is smuggled alone into Mytilene). The ten are iv.46, 76.2, 78, 84, 102, 109.1, 124; v.2, 4, 6. To complete the picture of how verbs are matched with personal subjects: there are no individual subjects with summary type verbs in books ii and iii; seven occur in books iv and v, and three of these are directly military (iv.7, 135; v.3.6; the other four are iv.50, 89, 101.5, and v.12). Three units have individual subjects and deliberative verbs in book ii (ii.13, 33, 93), as well as one in book iv (iv.75). Three of the four lead to military results. For a complete list of verbs in introductory sentences in the Archidamian narrative, see appendix B: 3.2.1.

17. ii.59 (Athenians), 10 (Peloponnesians); see also ii.13, 93; iv.75 (individual Athenians and Peloponnesians). The one other example of an individual subject with a deliberative verb: ii.33 (Euarchus the Acarnanian).

18. Presumably some form of book i was already in place, where Athenian and Peloponnesian motives, characters, and arguments at the beginning of the war had been elaborately introduced. See appendix B: 3.3 for the 8 introductory sentences out of 119 that have passive verbs. The two passive verbs found in introductory sentences with personal subjects (iii.25 and 27) both concern Mytilene. This supports an observation made in chapters 3 and 4, pp. 95 and 208n.12, that the revolt of Mytilene is narrated with an unusual emphasis on chance, while less attention than usual is given to human planning.

19. See appendix B: 1.5.3 (table B.2: Order of first two elements in introductory sentences, ii.1–v.24). See appendix B: 4.1 for a list of the 29 units lacking place identification.

20. In many introductory sentences not mentioning setting it is easily deduced from the combination of the subject and the main verb; e.g., "After the second Peloponnesian

invasion, the Athenians . . . had undergone a change in their attitude" (μετὰ δὲ τὴν δευτέραν ἐσβολὴν τῶν Πελοποννησίων οἱ Ἀθηναῖοι . . . ἠλλοίωντο τὰς γνώμας, ii.59).

21. See appendix B: 4.2 for a list of introductory sentences in which the setting is identified by a prepositional phrase, and 4.3 for a setting identified in more than one way in the first sentence.

22. See appendix B: 4.4 for a list of units where place is the subject in the introductory sentence.

23. See appendix B: 4.5 for a list of units where place occurs as the object of the verb or as a dependent genitive or dative.

24. See appendix B: 4.1 for the introductory sentences lacking identification of place. The 16 sentences in which the action is civic, so to speak, are ii.7, 13, 34, 47.3, 59, 70; iii.20, 27, 36, 52, 70, 87.1; iv.51, 109.1, 133.1; and v.21. In iii.47.3, 87.1, and iv.133.1 the collective that effectively identifies the scene is not the subject of the sentence; in all the other sentences it is. The fact that the action is here called civic does not imply that it is political; the city may be suffering some event outside its own control, like the plague. In a sense, the metonymy here is the opposite of that discussed above, notes 21 and 22. Here by metonymy groups of people stand for the setting of the unit.

25. The 11 units are ii.1, 29, 33, 80; iii.17; iv.101.5, 117, 134.1; v.1a, 14, and 20.2. Of these, most clearly involve relations between states; Sitalces' death in iv.101.5 has implications related more to the international balance of power than to the spot where the death occurred. Only iii.17 (a problem for other reasons; see p. 209 n.18) and v.20.2 (see pp. 55–56) are not diplomatically oriented.

26. See appendix B: 4.6, for table B.6: Distribution of setting in introductory sentences, ii.1–v.24.

27. Expressions of time occur in less than a third of the random sentences drawn from the *History* described in appendix B: 1.4 (table B.1); they do not usually hold either the first or the second place in the sentence.

28. E.g., i.97.2, v.20.2. See also the bibliography cited above, p. 193 n.3.

29. See appendix B: 5.1.

30. ii.26; iii.7, 27, 52, 92, 99; iv.7, 24, 46, 78, 123, 124; v.3.5, 4 (total: 14). See appendix B: 5.2.

31. The introductory sentences whose time includes a more exactly defined season are ii.31, 32, 47.2, 67, 68, 80, 93, 95; iii.1, 25, 86, 116; iv.1, 42, 49, 52.1, 84, 89, 117, 133.4, 135; v.12, 13 (total: 23). Of these, the sentences including a word limiting the season more exactly are ii.67; iii.86; iv.49, 52.1, 117, and 135. See appendix B: 5.3, 5.3.1.

32. ii.7, 10, 13, 24, 47.3, 55, 57, 59, 79, 83, 102; iii.2, 17, 18, 36, 51, 69, 89.2, 94; iv.2.1, 8, 76, 101.5, 109.1, 120; v.1, 1.1, 2, 14 (total: 29). These are also listed in appendix B: 5.4.

33. ii.1, 2; iii.87.4; iv.26; v.6, v.21 (total: 6). These are also listed in appendix B: 5.5.

34. ii.18, 25, 30; iii.8, 19, 29, 33.3, 70; iv.2.2, 6, 52.2, 134.1; v.3.6, 20.2 (total: 14). These are also listed in appendix B: 5.6.

35. iv.6 (from iv.2.1).

36. iv.2.2; iv.52.2, 134.1; and v.3.6. The exceptionally short units I call simple picture units; see pp. 31, 50–53. They show changes in the way Thucydides uses units of action late in the Archidamian War, pp. 83–85.

37. Unit iv.120 is perhaps a more subtle example; the time became an important element in the resulting Athenian actions over Scione. See *HCT* III: 607–8; Hornblower 1996, 375–76.

38. Luschnat (1971, 1109–10) discusses the variations in seasonal temporal formulae.

CHAPTER THREE

1. The *a-b-a* pattern of the complex unit does not suggest the dominance of the ring pattern as a compositional principle in the text of Thucydides. Attempts made by Hammond (1952), Katičič (1957), McNeal (1970), and others to find this a governing principle are interesting but not generally convincing (and they concentrate on book i). Much more important is Thucydides' habit of bending all structural patterns to achieve particular interpretive ends.

2. Units iii.20–24 and iv.46–48 are exceptionally lengthy picture units. See pp. 62–63, 98, 103.

3. Picture units twenty-six to fifty lines long: ii.93–94, iii.92–93, iv.76–77; list units: ii.25 and v.4–5; extended narrative units: ii.67, iii.33.2–35, 100–102, v.2–3.4; complex units: ii.29, 68, 102–103, iii.104.

4. The specific formula for the military invasion is described on pp. 56–60.

5. The full list of these two-stage simple units is ii.1, 28, 47.2, 66, iii.89.1, 99, 116, iv.2.1, 7, 49, 101.5, 109.1, 133.4, and v.12.

6. The different particles are listed here, since they will occur as well in all the types of unit that remain to be discussed. Four simple units are introduced by καί (iv.49, 133.4, v.3.6, 12), sixteen by a δέ that does not correspond to a directly previous μέν, two by a δέ corresponding to a previous μέν (ii.47.2, 66), and one by τε . . . καί (iv.109.1). Three contain, in addition to an introductory particle, a μέν in the body of the unit corresponding to a δέ in the following unit (iv.134.1, v.1a, 3.6). Little use, however, can be made of this aspect of Thucydides' narrative style, since such particles are one of the most vulnerable aspects of the text in its transmission; copying errors and even later "improvements" on Thucydides' original choice of particles have almost certainly occurred. See Luschnat 1971, 1311–15.

7. ii.1, 32, 47.2, iii.87.4, 89.1, 116, iv.2.1, 49, 51, 52.1, 101.5, 109.1, 133.4, 134.1, v.1a, 1b, 12 (total: 17). All but 1 of the 6 that fall at the change of season in the middle of the year come from books iv and v: ii.32, iv.49, 101.5, 133.4, 134.1a, v.12.

8. These 3 units represent interests of Thucydides that are well-known. Unit iii.89.2–6 probably reflects the same line of thought as iii.87.4, which *HCT* II: 389 characterizes as follows: "This winter was known for the number of its earthquakes." Units

iv.133.2–3 and v.20 both reflect an interest in chronology, and the discussion of the temple at Argos may have indirectly been related to the war, as an attempt to date the events of year nine with reference to the temple's destruction. I do not find attempts by Jacoby and others (Luschnat 1971, 1136) to date the composition of iv.133 after the publication of Hellanicus's work very convincing. The event must have attracted a great deal of attention at the time; Thucydides did not need to wait for Hellanicus to tell him about it. See further, however, Hornblower 1996, 411–15.

9. See p. 55 See also p. 74 for the same topics presented in extended narrative units (ii.7–9, 47.3–54) that resemble these more static picture units. Units iii.87.1–3 and ii.24 frequently figure in other discussions; iii.87.1–3 is used by Ullrich (1846, 90–92) to argue for a date of composition prior to the Sicilian expedition; *HCT* II: 388 correctly doubts the strength of such arguments. Unit ii.24 is used by Schwartz (1929, 30 n. 1) as one example of a document ("das attische Psephisma von 431") put into Thucydides' own style early in the *History*. Meyer (1955, 12) protests that whatever the status of such an "indirect document," its status in the *History* is very different from that of "eines zwischenstaatlichen Vertrages."

10. They are ii.27, 70, iii.20–24, 25, 27–28, 92–93, iv.1, 46–48, 50, 76–77, 123.

11. Similar subjects can elicit similar treatment. The simple picture unit v.16 and the developed picture unit ii.27, both of which concern people expelled by the Athenians, are organized in much the same way. So also are ii.70 and iii.27–28, the accounts of the surrender of Potidaea and Mytilene.

12. Detailed discussion of the interpretive force of all such arrangements is not possible here. It is intriguing, however, that the beginning of iii.25, with its focus on Salaethus, fits into a pattern established in other units on Mytilene. It conveys some of the elements of chanciness that, for instance, the arrival of Gylippus in Sicily will have later in the *History*—except, of course, the outcome is very different. Chance plays a large role in other units about Mytilene. In iii.3, the unusually quick voyage of a private individual prevents the Athenians from surprising the Mytileneans with their fleet's arrival; in iii.49, the complete destruction of Mytilene after the unsuccessful revolt is averted only by the merest hair. See pp. 95 and 205 n.18.

13. The units involved are ii.31, 58, 79, 93–94, iii.1, 18, 26, 51, 86, 88, iv.134.1–2, 135, v.13.

14. ii.47.2, 66, iii.89.1, 99, iv. 2.1, 7, 49. See p. 51.

15. The single-sentence picture units do not as frequently contain element 4 of the outline; presumably the event is so briefly narrated that such units do not need a formal, independently constructed conclusion.

16. As we shall notice below in the discussion of the 5 picture units that are more than twenty-five lines long, such pictures—narrated with an attention to several stages of the action—become almost linear in form. They lack, however, the clear change in setting that identifies the list units (section 3.3, below), and the alliance of change in place

and shift in focus that is the hallmark of the extended narrative units (section 3.4). They remain clear examples of the picture unit structure, though in a very developed form.

17. Invasion: ii.47.2 (also ii.55–56); the naval expedition: ii.55–56; the plague: ii.47.3–54.

18. *HCT* II: 272–77 sets out very clearly the difficulties of this passage where it stands. If Adcock's suggestion (ad loc.) is correct, iii.17 would not be an independent unit, but part of ii.57, so that the number of units devoted to coordinating the interrelationships among other units would drop to three. Hornblower (1991, 400–401) agrees with Gomme that iii.17 should be kept where it is.

19. See chapter 6 below.

20. See pp. 65–68 and 73–76, for further discussion of military deliberation.

21. See pp. 102–4.

22. See pp. 56–60.

23. See pp. 57–58.

24. Those with a formal indication of termination are ii.30, 33, iii.7, 91, 103, 115, v.4–5.

25. Units ii.26, 30, and 33 and iii.19 and 103 are the units of this simplest type.

26. ii.25, iii.90, and iv.52.2–5.

27. ii.69, iii.7, 91, 115, iv.75, v.4–5.

28. The treatment of Lamachus in iv.75, and the mutual references linking Demosthenes' fleet and Nicias's in iii.91 and 94 (discussed above as part of year six, pp. 29–30), suggest that Thucydides thought of the Athenian fleet as a single entity; thus two parts of it might be discussed in the same unit, either in a structurally connected (iv.75) or unconnected (ii.69) fashion.

29. See p. 55.

30. For the picture units that are over twenty-five lines long, see pp. 61–63.

31. See p. 57.

32. Military action introduced abruptly: iii.33.2–35, 94–98, iv.24–25, 26–41. As in the case of the list units of this type discussed above, the abruptness of the introduction represents the continuation of a previous narrative thread. Unit iii.33.2 takes up the activity of Paches' fleet from iii.28; iii.94 has been anticipated in iii.91; iv.24 continues from iv.1; and iv.26 is the continuation of the investment at Pylos last discussed in iv.23. The reader is expected to be familiar with the setting of the unit and is therefore immediately engaged in the action. (For iv.24, see *HCT* III: 463; the intervening material as well preserves the chronological coherence.) In ii.80–82, iii.100–102, and iv.66–74, there is deliberation. First the military activity is resolved upon, and only then does the action take place. Most extended narrative units with a military focus (ii.2–6, 18–23, 55–56, iii.105–114, iv.2.2, 42–45, 53–57, 78–83, 102–108, 109.1–116, v.2–3.4) contain a general verb of military activity: ἐσῆλθον, ἐστράτευσαν, and so on.

33. See pp. 70–73.

34. See chapter 4 for the impact of the shorter units as parts of ongoing chains of development that last over several years.

35. ii.2–6, 80–82, iii.2–6, 70–85, 100–102, 105–114, iv.26–41, 102–108. De Romilly (1967) discusses iii.105–114 (pp. 128–29) and ii.80–82 (pp. 124–28), although she concentrates on the analysis of battles rather than the structural similarities in the narratives per se.

36. Of ii.2–6, iii.2–6, 70–85, iv.26–41, 102–108, only the last two, concerning Pylos and Amphipolis, represent the climax of the ongoing story, however. The rest narrate preliminary activities that set the stage for more dramatic extended or complex narratives to come (iii.36–50, 52–68, 70–85).

37. For the puzzle of Thucydides' relatively reserved but detailed treatment of Demosthenes, one of the most innovative of the Athenian generals, see Hornblower 1987, 158; and Cawkwell 1997, 17–19, 50–55, 70–74.

38. ii.18–23, 55–56, 67, iii.33.2–35, 94–98, iv.2.2–5, 24–25, 42–45, 53–57, 66–74, 78–83, 109.1–116, 120–122, v.2–3.4

39. See Pritchett 1975, xxx and 8–11, for a response to Dionysius of Halicarnassus's criticisms of Thucydides' tendencies to treat events in very different degrees of detail, or out of their apparently more natural order. See the introduction, pp. 7, 12, and 194 n.12 for the degree to which Thucydidean historiography now accepts that such narrative habits reflect deliberate, interpretive choices on Thucydides' part.

40. I do not mean to imply that the list aspect of the extended narrative unit is always undeveloped. Thucydides uses both list and picture structures internally, in constructing extended narrative units, and either type of structure can be developed in greater detail.

41. A similar juxtaposition unit-to-unit is discussed on pp. 87–101.

42. See discussions on pp. 158–60.

43. Picture: ii.10–12, 13–17, 29, 34–47.1, 68, iii.8–16, 36–50, 52–68, 104, iv.84–88, 117–119, v.21–24; extended narrative: ii.59–65, 71–78, 83–92, 95–101, iv.8–23, 58–65, 89–101.4, 124–132, v.6–11, 14–20.1; list: ii.102–103, iii.29–33.1.

44. Speeches occur in 15: ii.10–12, 34–47.1, 59–65, 71–78, 83–92, iii.8–16, 29–33.1, 36–50, 52–68, iv.8–23, 58–65, 84–88, 89–101.4, 124–132, v.6–11; documents occupy the center of the other 3: iv.117–119, v.14–20.1, 21–24.

45. Units with antiquarian or geographic excursus: ii.13–17, 29, 68, 95–101, 102–103, iii.104.

46. A demonstrative ends the unit: ii.13–17, 29, 59–65, 71–78, 95–101, iii.36–50, 52–68, iv.117–119, v.14–20.1, 21–24.

47. Three other complex units are placed at the end of a season, and therefore conclude with a formula of this sort as well as the one properly belonging to the unit: ii.47.1, 103, iv.88.

48. In ii.95–101, the excursus has some of the same impact as the military speeches

in the other 7 "military" units. That is, it heightens our anticipation of the outcome of this gigantic troop movement and points toward the future, which becomes, because of the focus on the buildup, even more anticlimactic; here Thucydides is implicitly critical of Athens. It is not clear that *HCT* II: 241 and 248 are right that Thucydides gives the event too much importance, and that it was at the time essentially comical. (See also *HCT* III: 584.)

49. See de Romilly 1963, 39: "The whole debate is thus concerned with the attitude which Athens should adopt toward her subject peoples."

50. As iv.114 indicates, the importance of the speech at Acanthus not only concerns the decision of that one city but also is a paradigm for other speeches Brasidas will make, and demonstrates his general attitude. Schwartz (1929, 304) points out that Brasidas is boasting in his speech; we know from information Thucydides gives us that he is not telling the truth, here or in iv.108.

51. The Mytilenean debate, iii.37–48, hardly resolves the issue of how to treat subject states. There the vote is close; the later problems Athens has with Melos, Scione, Chios, and other cities (theoretically elaborated in the Melian dialogue and in the comments of Phrynichus in viii.48.5) suggest that Cleon's arguments are not as ill founded as Diodotus thinks they are.

52. Meyer 1955, 20, 35 and 57.

53. As many have pointed out, the funeral oration also ironically looks forward to the forthcoming plague. See chapter 4, subsection 4.1.4.b, pp. 96–97.

54. The strongest relevance to the surrounding frame occurs in ii.68, where the prehistory of the feud in Amphilochia is discussed. This one complex unit also lacks its own concluding demonstrative (see p. 78); possibly Thucydides thought of it as background material, like v.4–5 and the discussion of the enmity of Leontini and Syracuse, rather than as a formal excursus. The discussion goes so much farther into the past, however, that it suggests an interest on Thucydides' part not entirely connected to the war. See Ziegler 1929, 58–67.

55. Pearson 1942, 30–39; see, more generally, Hornblower 1987, 75–96.

56. There is a drop in both the number of complex units and the number of pages they occupy in book iii. See the conclusion of the chapter, pp. 83–84. Even in book iii, however, they still account for 44% of the text.

57. See the introduction, note 3, above, for important studies on the Thucydidean chronological framework.

CHAPTER FOUR

1. This study deals with those aspects of *taxis* or narrative arrangement that organize the narrative sequence of Thucydides' *History*. It does not consider unity of thought and political philosophy as, for instance, they are considered by de Romilly (1963), or the cohesiveness that comes from the continuing interest through the work in certain

themes, like the impact of character (which Westlake [1968] considers), or the development of political goals or deployment of military strategy on the part of various states. Even less does it deal with broad Thucydidean attitudes and assumptions, as do Cornford 1907, Stahl 1966, Edmunds 1975, and Crane 1998. See pp. 12–13 for some discussion of thematic issues and Thucydidean scholarship; see also Marincola 2001 for a succinct overview of Thucydides' place in the context of ancient Greek historiography as a whole, and Hornblower 1991 and 1996 ad loc. for discussions of the thematic relevance of individual passages, with recent bibliography.

2. The differences are significant: the formular introductory sentence in the inserted unit makes a clear narrative break, while the excursus or *b* material in a complex unit is still thematically connected to the surrounding *a* material. Nonetheless, the narrative habit of alternating *a* and *b* material is the same.

3. See 4.1.2.c below (iv.102–108, 109.1, 109.1–116) for a neutral *a-b-a* pattern formed by three successive units; by the omission of iv.109.1, iv.102–108 and 109.1–116 could have easily become a single unit. More pointed juxtapositions occur in 4.1.4.a (iv.134.1–2) or 4.1.4.b (ii.34–47.1, 47.2–54).

4. Thucydides is not afraid to make judgments or hold opinions when he is so minded: Hornblower 1987, 155–90. When propinquity alone suggests judgment, the juxtaposition often asks for our alertness but does not direct it.

5. iv.67. The Athenians kept Nisaea, as v.17 records (though, as Gomme points out, the argument could have applied with greater force to Amphipolis and was obviously applied to placate Athens and Thebes). It is a curious fact that many of the real military gains Athens made late in the Archidamian War are mentioned in an unemphatic presentation. Nisaea forms part of a predominantly "negative" unit about the failure of the Megarian plans of Hippocrates and Demosthenes; *HCT* ad loc. points out that the strategic importance of the taking of Cythera is also minimized in the text.

6. Gomme 1954, 133: "After this defeat, the Peloponnesian commanders, with unwonted resilience (but Brasidas was one of them), decide to make a sudden attack by sea of the Piraeus." In *HCT* II: 240, however, Gomme rightly wonders if the hesitation and caution then shown were as wrong as Thucydides seems to think they were.

7. These two units form part of a larger cluster as well; see below, subsection 4.1.3.d and p. 94.

8. In iv.84, "without delay . . . in the same summer" (ἐν δὲ τῷ αὐτῷ θέρει εὐθύς), is not sufficient to explain the break for purely chronological reasons, as *HCT* III: 702 points out. Luschnat (1971, 1136) comments that ὀλίγον πρὸ τρυγήτου, "a little before the harvest," has both military and political implications. Brasidas has an overwhelming tactical advantage, and the inhabitants give in with as good a grace as they can muster under the circumstances. Patzer (1937, 105) identifies a terminus post quem of 412 for iv.81.2, arguing that it must have been written after the revolt of Chios. Surely "after Sicily" is the most we can safely say; respect for Brasidas does not necessarily entail re-

volt. Hornblower (1996, 255–286) offers an exceptionally careful discussion of the issues surrounding Brasidas's expedition.

9. Gommel (1966, 69) draws a causal connection between iv.120–122 and iv.123. It is expressed in iv.123.2: "as a consequence of seeing the resolute attitude of Brasidas" (τήν τε τοῦ Βρασίδου γνώμην ὁρῶντες ἑτοίμην).

10. Classen and Steup (1912, 5: 32) argue that Thessalian opposition, which almost stopped Brasidas with 1,700 men, was more than sufficient to stop Ramphias with 900. First, however, Brasidas did not overcome opposition with the numbers of his troops but through the force of his personality, as Thucydides makes very clear (iv.78.4); second, the juxtapositions, of v.12 and v.13 here and of v.13 and v.14 in 4.1.3.b below, draw our attention to other elements than Thessalian military strength. The weight of the explanation does not lie with this "zuerst erwähnte Punkt"; the temporal phrase καὶ ἅμα does not solve the issue.

11. See Rood 1998, 69–77, for a careful reading of how perceptions influence the entire Brasidas account.

12. See Thalmann 1984, 8–24, for hexameter poetry; and Immerwahr 1966 for Herodotus.

13. See p. 183.

14. See p. 64.

15. Unit ii.55–56 is itself something of an *a-b-a* arrangement, although less formally structured. The extended narrative unit begins and ends with a mention of the Peloponnesian invasion; an Athenian naval expedition to the Peloponnese in response to the invasion takes up the long middle of the unit.

16. Later in the narrative Thucydides does not often rely on the rather mechanical separation provided by the *a-b-a* pattern whose *b* element is nonessential; the three loose narrative connections in years eight, nine, and ten (sections 4.1.1.c, d, and e above) are rather bold and apparently arbitrary breaks in what would otherwise be a single undivided story. See, however, the example from year eight in 4.1.2.c immediately below.

17. For discussion of v.6–11, see de Romilly 1956a, 136–38, in particular for the climactic correspondence between Brasidas's speech and the way subsequent events unfold in the battle.

18. One could, perhaps, extend the cluster to include two more units. Eurymedon and Sophocles in iv.46–48 have been part of the Pylos episode. However, their role there is very limited (iv.2, 3, 8); Corcyra is basically a new focus.

19. Element *c* is also examined in subsection 4.1.3.c as a causal connection within this larger *a-b-a* type cluster.

20. Gomme 1954, 135–37.

21. Cf. *HCT* III: 463, on iv.24: "The narrative continued from c.1, and the Pylos episode interrupted to preserve the chronological coherence." One may, with Dionysius, claim in a general sense that individual narratives were broken up to preserve a rel-

ative chronology; but for the reasons behind any specific break, one must look farther and ask what elements in the narrative demand it.

22. Stahl (1966, 30) is correct to emphasize, contra Wilamowitz, that lack of material did not limit the size of unit iv.24–25. Clearly if the discussion of Sicily were extensive there, the sense of a narrative climax building to iv.41 would have been lost.

23. Thucydides is aware of the dramatic moment in iv.14.3 (cf. vii.71). Gomme's comment ad loc., *HCT* III: 452, is strangely harsh: "I should be glad to believe that Thucydides did not write this." The event in relation to the outcome of the ten-year war is not trivial; detail like this is not merely picturesque. Cf. Hornblower 1996, 166–67, which rightly refers to Macleod 1983, 142.

24. Norden 1958, 1: 97. See p. 60 for a discussion of iii.69 as one of the four picture units whose principal function seems to be harmonizing themes from other units.

25. *HCT* II: 279 is not explicit, but Gomme calls it a special levy.

26. Classen and Steup (1912, 5: 33) remark that ξυνέβη τε, "and it happened," at the start of v.14 is "weiterführend."

27. The information about the Peloponnesian grain supply also influences their decision to go home. Here the argument used by Classen and Steup (1912) about v.14 might hold; Thucydides does seem to give pride of place to the information received about Pylos. But the sense of the passage determines our judgment, not the particles *in vacuo*.

28. See appendix B.1.2 for first sentences in which the first verb does not carry the weight of the unit. Classen and Steup (1914) question the manuscript reading of the time formula beginning ii.83, περὶ τὰς αὐτὰς ἡμέρας. Steup wanted to emend it to περὶ αὐτὰς τὰς ἡμέρας, claiming that as it stands it is too vague an expression. The temporal vagueness, however, points up the predominantly causal meaning of the phrase; what we need to know, and Thucydides tells us, is that the ships were not where they said they would be. But Steup is right in stressing the awkwardness of the following genitive: περὶ τὰς αὐτὰς ἡμέρας τῆς ἐν Στράτῳ μάχης. Thucydides is not concerned with the exact chronology of the two events. Here, as in the narrative about Delium, he perhaps implies that elaborate coordinations of separate military forces cannot be counted on. Stahl (1966, 85) emphasizes a different nuance to the connection between these two units. He seems to think of it as a loose narrative link: "Thukydides legt Wert darauf, dass der Leser sieht, wie die Gesamtunternehmung in Einzelphasen zerbricht."

29. See chapter 1 for a more extensive discussion of year six.

30. The delicacy of the links Thucydides draws is occasionally responsible for our failure to understand the text. There are difficulties with ἐπήρχοντο at the beginning of iv.120; see Classen and Steup 1900, 4: 235; and *HCT* III: 607. The context does not tell us whether it is from ἐπέρχομαι or ἐπάρχομαι. Schwartz (1929, 309) is correct that the effect is very striking: "Kunstvoll wird der Leser in Spannung gehalten, bis er am Schluss erfährt. . . . " Only at the end of iv.120–122 do we understand that the time formula in the introductory sentence of the second unit gives the information necessary to solve the problem.

31. See also subsection 4.1.4.f, p. 98 and the discussion of years four and five, pp. 106–8.

32. See chapter 3, note 12 above for the emphasis on accident in determining the course of Mytilene's revolution.

33. I do not understand *HCT* III: 488–89, and especially the distinction drawn there between "chance" and "accidental coincidence." I agree with de Romilly (1956a, 167): "Thucydide insiste, pour tout l'épisode, sur le fait que le plan de Démosthène n'a pu être exécuté que grâce à un heureux concours de circonstances où jouent la chance et la bonne volonté spontanée des soldats." See, however, Rood 1998, 26–31, and, for a different kind of doubt, Cawkwell 1997, 51–52, 73–74.

34. Some of this may shape the very different treatment of Cleon in the two episodes. In the Pylos episode (4.1.2.e), authorial ill will does not overtly shape the narrative; Thucydides does not try to give all the military credit to Demosthenes in the final campaign itself, and his judgment of the event is a military one. In the Mytilenean debate, Cleon's angry speechifying highlights the chanciness of the whole affair.

35. See above, notes 7, 18, 19 in this chapter. The impression of connection is increased because unit connections of the three different types are often contiguous: see, for example, the larger narrative sequences formed by the passages discussed in subsections 4.1.3.d and 4.1.1.b (year three); 4.1.3.f and 4.1.1.d (year nine); 4.1.2.d and 4.1.3.b (year ten); and 4.1.2.e and 4.1.3.c (year seven) above.

36. Thucydides' claim in i.22 is similarly reticent. He hopes that the exercise of looking at the events of the Peloponnesian War will be useful, because of parallels that can be drawn, but he does not specify what usefulness he has in mind: "Yet if they are judged useful by any who wish to look at [what is clear] about both past events and those that at some future time, in accordance with human nature, will recur in similar or comparable ways, that will suffice" (ὅσοι δὲ βουλήσονται τῶν τε γενομένων τὸ σαφὲς σκοπεῖν καὶ τῶν μελλόντων ποτὲ αὖθις κατὰ τὸ ἀνθρώπινον τοιούτων καὶ παραπλησίων ἔσεσθαι, ὠφέλιμα κρίνειν αὐτά ἀρκούντως ἕξει, i.22.4).

37. *HCT* III: 625: they "take advantage of the truce from the major war (in which they were allies) to have a war on their own." As Classen and Steup (1912, ad loc.) comment, v.65.4 explains this enmity; see also Hornblower 1996, 410, 416.

38. See above, subsection 4.1.2.a, for the emphatic *a-b-a* connection begun in ii.47.2 and continuing through ii.56. Here what is being considered is an additional, looser thematic juxtaposition that contrasts the high ideals of the funeral oration at the end of year one with the cold realities of the invasion and plague that begin year two.

39. Gomme (1954, 123) discusses the effect of the juxtaposition, as does de Romilly (1956a, 76). Many "ironic" contrasts do contain a judgment; see 4.1.4.c immediately below. But often the contrast is merely striking and leads one to reflect on the ephemerality of all mortal things (ii.44.4).

40. Patzer (1937, 107) thinks iv.60.1 was clearly written after the Sicilian expedition; de Romilly (1956a, 28) seems to assume it. Unit iv.65 certainly gives that impression,

and it is chiefly because we know about later events in Sicily that the juxtaposition of the two units seems so very ironic. The two events, however, did happen, and sometimes the irony lies in events themselves: Gomme 1954, 122–23.

41. See subsection 4.1.3.g above for the immediately preceding causal connections that highlight the lucidity of Athenian politics from iii.26 through iii.50. Thucydides, however, is not blindly admiring of Athens; he retails unsavory exploits of Paches (iii. 34), Eurymedon and Sophocles (Gomme 1954, 147–48), and Cleon. Unit iii.51 intervenes between the stories of Mytilene and Plataea but does not diminish the impact of the approximate juxtaposition; see Hornblower 1991, 441–42.

42. *HCT* III: 540 and Gomme 1954, 134–37.

43. See p. 106, and Gomme's remarks in *HCT* III: 577–78: "Athens 'held the allies in hand' very lightly."

44. Elaborate description of events that came to nothing can be very ironic; one is tempted to account for the campaign that ends year three (ii.102–103) in the same fashion. There the geographic and mythological material puts in relief the limited nature of Phormio's accomplishments. Implicitly highlighted is the fact that there were no Athenians on hand to meet Sitalces in the events described in the immediately previous unit, ii.101.

45. The circumstances, of course, are very different. One city is inland; the other on an island, with a harbor. Stahl (1966, 116) confirms the general point: "Daß Thukydides den Plataia-Komplex zum Geschehen im Mytilene (die Schilderungen folgen unmittelbar aufeinander) gesehen wissen will, ist von den Interpreten immer wieder festgestellt worden." See p. 95 (subsection 4.1.3.g), for other factors implicit in the narrative of events that create an impression of less than intelligent engagement by the Mytileneans in thinking through their actions.

46. See *HCT* III: 489.

47. See the introduction, note 3, for the problems entailed in Thucydides' claim in v.20 that the war lasted "ten years and a few days."

48. Chapter ii.9 is set off by clauses similar to those that emphasize the excursus in a complex unit: at its beginning, "These were the Lacedaemonian allies" (Λακεδαιμονίων μὲν οἵδε ξύμμαχοι, ii.9.2); in the middle, "This was the Lacedaemonian alliance; the Athenian allies were . . . " (αὕτη μὲν Λακεδαιμονίων ξυμμαχία· Ἀθηναίων δέ . . . , ii.9.4); at its end, "The two sides had these allies and preparations for the war" (ξυμμαχία μὲν αὕτη ἑκατέρων καὶ παρασκευὴ ἐς τὸν πόλεμον ἦν, ii.9.6), which sums up not only ii.9, but the whole unit.

49. To call this connection thematic is not very precise. Actually, the relation between ii.12 and 13 resembles the shifting focus on the same subject seen often within a single unit (e.g., iii.92–93, pp. 61–62, or many extended narrative units). Here, however, a time formula at the head of the first sentence of ii.13 breaks the narrative into two separate units. Like the multiple uses of *a-b-a* patterning, this again demonstrates Thucydides' ability to apply a limited range of techniques in different ways, for different effects.

50. Stahl (1966, 71–72 n. 6) sees another correspondence between these two clusters, each of which he divides into two stages: "juristisch" and "faktisch."

51. In year three, though the invasion does not actually occur, Thucydides knows we will expect it, since the first sentence of the year begins: "In the following summer, the Peloponnesians and their allies did not invade Attica" (τοῦ δ᾽ ἐπιγιγνομένου θέρους οἱ Πελοποννήσιοι καὶ οἱ ξύμμαχοι ἐς μὲν Ἀττικὴν οὐκ ἐσέβαλον). In three cases the years are sketchily linked together. The thematic connection between years one and two is discussed in subsection 4.1.4.b, above; there is also some connection between years four and five (the last unit of year four and the first sentence of year five refer to Mytilene, p. 98) and between six and seven (where the focus remains on Sicily, though it shifts from Aetna to Messina [for the spelling of the latter, see Hornblower 1991, 498]). But compared with the strong dividing effect achieved by the recurring theme of Peloponnesian invasion, these links are trivial indeed.

52. Only in years two (ii.69) and five (iii.87.1–3) is there no connection between the first unit of winter and at least one summer unit in the year.

53. Finley (1967, 123) discusses other passages as well where Thucydides refers back to a previous passage in the *History*.

54. The units that are connected within their years are ii.25, 30, and 33; iii.90, 103, and 115: and iv.52.2–5 and 75. The others are iii.19 (connected causally to iii.18), ii.69 (refers to an element in ii.68, Phormio), ii.26 (probably, as Gomme says, refers to ii.32), v.4–5 (the continuation of Sicily as a theme), iii.7 (the fleet going round the Peloponnese in the stead of the one diverted to Mytilene, iii.3.2), and iii.91 (connected by first sentence with iii.94; see text to this note).

55. Structurally, these themes have been selected because each contains a long picture unit discussed, pp. 62–63. Here the relation of these vivid and unusually long picture units to larger themes is considered.

56. P. 97.

57. P. 60.

58. P. 79, see note 44 in this chapter as well.

59. P. 56.

60. See above, pp. 54–55, for a discussion of the structure of iii.86. This is the first Athenian military activity toward Sicily recounted in the war; it provides a link with the remaining years of the ten-year narrative.

61. As argued by Hunter (1973, passim).

62. See the introduction, pp. 6–7, 16–17, for a more general discussion of these issues. In the dissertation, I quoted with approval this remark by Gomme: "The 'dramatic' character of Thucycides' *History* is thus fundamentally implicit in the events: they were dramatic, and a true history, that is, a scientific history, if well written, that is, if a work of art, will reveal them so" (1954, 122–23). Cf. notes 39 and 40 above.

63. Pp. 30–31.

64. The observations in iv.12 and iv.14 that Gomme finds "frigid" are meant to emphasize this sense of change. The Athenians are on land, while the Peloponnesians are attacking their own land by ship; cf. note 23 above.

65. See pp. 83–85.

66. Although, as noted just above, the Athenian commanders do foil the plans of the exiles from Mytilene (iv.75).

67. See pp. 89 and 94.

68. See section 4.1.5.

69. Pritchett 1975, 5–6 (chapter 9 of Dionysius's treatise on Thucydides).

70. See, for instance, Pritchett 1975, 5 (chapter 8), but see also 58 n. 1.

CHAPTER FIVE

1. Several possibilities have traditionally been advanced to account for the impression of change in v.25–vi.7: "Books V and VIII do nevertheless present, on the whole, a rather hasty and summary character, which we might almost refer to as provisional, and which would suggest that they could be a first version which has not been very thoroughly revised" (de Romilly 1963, 224); "It is generally assumed that the main part of the fifth book (chs. 25–84) and all the eighth book are particularly incomplete . . . although it seems not impossible that Thucydides may have intended to treat certain years in this unemphatic way" (Finley 1942, 77); "Im Übrigen aber weicht das Buch von der sonstigen Darstellungsweise des Thukydides keineswegs ab; die zahlreichen kurzen Notizen über einzelne Ereignisse auf den verschiedenen Kriegsschauplätzen, die eine ausführliche Darstellung nicht erheischen, finden sich in allen anderen Büchern ganz in derselben Weise, nur daß sie sich hier viel mehr haüfen. Das liegt aber an den Ereignissen, nicht an dem Schriftsteller" (Meyer 1899, 2: 364).

2. Eleven examples have a dative, a γάρ-clause, or a direct object as one of their first two elements: v.25, v.32.1, v.35.1, v.36, v.39.1, v.51, v.52.1, v.53, v.82.1b, v.115.2; vi.7.3. Especially unusual is v.36, with the γάρ-clause coming directly after the time formula. Eight of the 11 retain the time phrase along with the nonformular second element, so that all continuity with the formular aspect of traditional first sentences is not broken.

3. The drop in units whose first subjects are people identified by name falls somewhere between a purely stylistic and a content-related change. Military events are less common in years eleven through sixteen; those that are mentioned usually are presented in simple picture units whose brevity discourages the presentation by commander. It is equally true, however, to say that this change reflects a more basic change of attitude: Thucydides has in v.25–vi.7 become much more interested in political developments on a broad scale that precludes isolated consideration of individuals (compare v.4 from the Archidamian War with v.50.5 or v.32.3).

4. It is possible that Thucydides' position outside Athens is a significant cause for the change. His own perspective may well be less Athenocentric, in his original recording of these years. See further pp. 159–60.

5. The existential verbs come in v.35.2, v.49, v.51, v.53, and v.56.4. Other verbs as well appear less specific; compare iii.115, ἀπόβασιν ἐποιήσαντο, with the εἷλον of v.35.1, v.115.4, or v.116.2. It is difficult, however, to isolate the impact of the verbs from that of the surrounding sentence as a whole. See also note 9 below.

6. The atypical phrases occur in v.32.3, v.36, v.56.4, and v.82.2. All of these convey a more flexible perception of time than occurs in ii.1–v.24. In v.82.2, the τηρήσαντες-phrase indicates time; the γάρ-clause in v.36 is an extension of time to involve the concept of the change of ephors in it. There is no time phrase in v.26, v.32.2, v.81.2, v.82.1, v.84.1b, v.115.2, v.115.4, and vi.7.3.

7. Several individual first sentences will be discussed in section 5.2 below, on unit arrangement. See pp. 124, 128, 134. Also of interest is the rather monotonous series of sentences formed in years twelve and thirteen with their existential verbs. Four units occur in as many pages: see note 5 above.

8. That is, when a fully formed first sentence exists, it is still usually a clue to a radical break in subject matter. As we shall see, however, Thucydides at points comes close to abandoning these structural signposts. In v.83.3, the temporal phrase μετὰ τοῦτο is what establishes the fact of a unit break; v.54.3 stands in the same logical relation to what has preceded it, but the time phrase ἀναχωρησάντων αὐτῶν emphasizes connection rather than separation, so the narrative structure is read as a simple action-reaction unit instead of two separate units.

9. In years one through ten, ii.66 (year two) has more than three finite verbs. One corollary to such a development that remains undiscussed in this chapter is that the distinction in kind between simple picture units (those seven lines long or less) and developed picture units (eight to twenty-five lines long) in v.25–vi.7 has virtually disappeared. The average developed picture unit is now eleven lines long and shows the same emphasis on verbs, action, over description. See p. 129.

10. The simple picture units with an action-reaction structure are v.52.1, v.115.2–3, v.115.4, v.116.1, and vi.7.3. The first 3 in this list are also part of the group with four or five main verbs. These 8 units merely represent in an extreme form qualities found in the other simple units too: consider the two-stage motion of v.56.5 or 81.1.

11. Some of the developed picture units contiguous to simple units are also very short. Unit v.50.5 is followed by v.51; v.35.1 (simple) by v.35.2 (simple); v.56.4 (simple) by v.56.5 (simple); v.81.1 by v.81.2 (both simple); v.83.1–2 (developed) by v.83.3 (simple) and v.83.4 (simple); v.115.1 (simple) by v.115.2–3 and v.115.4 (both simple), v.116.1 (simple), and v.116.2–4 (developed). Finally, vi.7.2 (developed) is followed by vi.7.3–4 (simple).

12. See the introduction, pp. 4–6, for discussion of what Thucydides' changed narrative habits might (or might not) say about the composition question.

13. For definitions of these types, see pp. 56–60.

14. The descriptive material itself is rather unsatisfactory. Is it meant to recall iii.92–93? It does not say so, and it is more superficial in scope. It does not explain why this particular offensive occurred at this point in year twelve.

15. One could also express the change in the following way: in years eleven through sixteen Thucydides is inserting fully formed introductory formulae into the middle of what would in the early war have been single action-reaction picture units. The end result of the two descriptions is identical: sense units are no longer precisely contiguous with the units defined by structural criteria.

16. The difference between the effect of this cluster and that of the causal connection linking v.117–119 and v.120–122 (the treaty and the revolt of Scione) concerns both the surrounding text and the nature of the individual units. In v.25–vi.7, the units are becoming less distinct in focus; the clustering that helped shape Thucydides' artistic patterning of the Archidamian years here instead creates uncertainty about the basic structural divisions in the narrative. The reader is not encouraged to linger over the individual units of the years of the Peace.

17. Those who think of speeches in the *History* in terms of "editorial comments" by the author should consider the implications of Thucydides' development and use of these political picture units. Certainly he did not need to convey such material in invented speeches; he had other vehicles at his narrative disposal.

18. In another respect, the whole of book i, of course, has served the function of introducing ii.1–v.24, making the drama of ii.1's simple announcement possible.

19. Gomme (*HCT* IV: 78) comments: "How much we wish that Thucydides had been in Athens to observe the political forces at work just at this time!"

20. Two developed picture units involve some temporal variation after the first sentence. In the military unit v.53, the background given is quite brief. See section 5.2.2.d below for the long unit v.49–50.4, where there is quite a lengthy background account of why the Lacedaemonians were barred from the Olympic sanctuary by the Eleans in the summer of the twelfth year. Cf. p. 55, where the temporal regressions after the first sentence in iii.27–28 and iii.86 are discussed.

21. With the possible exception of the first sentence (from γέγραφε to χειμῶνας) the unit is entirely organized around the fact of the twenty-seven-year duration of the war. It is difficult to see what in it could have existed prior to 404.

22. See pp. 75–76.

23. See pp. 67, 76 for the phrases in list units that indicate Thucydides' awareness of activities not related in detail.

24. This does not contradict the point made on p. 80, that complex units with speeches tend to point to the future for the resolution of the issues in them. They point to the future, but they do not hurry the reader on toward it. The suspense and tension come precisely from the combination of expectation and pause in the present.

25. See pp. 128–29.

26. Thucydides concedes that Alcibiades was acting from what he considered rational grounds: "He saw advantage in turning to Argos" (ᾧ ἐδόκει μὲν ἄμεινον εἶναι πρὸς τοὺς Ἀργείους μᾶλλον χωρεῖν, v.43.2). But he develops not these, but the personal

grounds that put Alcibiades in a less attractive light. Apparently Thucydides thought these important as the more basic motivations. See now Gribble 1999, 16 and 194–204, for Alcibiades' presentation in v.43–44 as part of a larger, more complex portrait constructed by Thucydides and others, of a crucial player in the politics of the demos.

27. Presumably the oligarchy of Melos could count on enough popular support to make resistance feasible, or they would have feared the kind of disaffection that occurred at Mytilene (iii.27). Possibly they hoped, by refusing to let a popular decision be taken, to limit the onus of responsibility and reprisal in the case of defeat. But the fact remains that Thucydides does not make either of these points, while the Athenian assertion at the head of v.85 is allowed to stand unchallenged by the Melian leaders. The more important point is that all human beings, Melians and Athenians and the other actors of years eleven through sixteen too—Mantineans, Argives, Lacedaemonians, Corinthians, Eleans, and so on—are shown trying to discover and live by the principle expressed in v.111. As the example of Melos shows, the difficulty lies in the correct estimation of who is equal, who is inferior, who is superior. The Argives in the summer of year fourteen clearly have an inflated view of themselves; they come to grief. The Lacedaemonians and Athenians differ in their estimation of the power of the Boeotians in v.39; Sparta thinks of Boeotia as more powerful and therefore as deserving more concessions. The Athenian reaction implies that they consider the rise in Boeotian influence to correspond to a lessening of their own status, and they are consequently very angry. There are other angles from which these events can be interpreted too; but the one presented in v.84.1–114 is very far-reaching in explaining the mainsprings of years eleven through sixteen.

CHAPTER SIX

1. De Romilly devotes much of the first three chapters of her 1956 study *Histoire et raison chez Thucydide* to the narrative patterns of Thucydides' Sicilian account; Finley (1967, 126) remarks that it is a "generally recognized fact that books six and seven, more than any other part of the *History*, comprise a unified and consistent whole." This is not to say that analysts have not found breaks, strata, or difficulties therein; de Romilly (1963, 214–24) discusses some of these.

2. *HCT* V: 358, ad loc.

3. Dionysius of Halicarnassus reports that a contemporary of Thucydides, Cratippus, believed the absence of speeches in book viii to have been deliberate: "for he [Cratippus] says that not only have the speeches been an impediment to the narrative, but they are also annoying to the hearers. At any rate he maintains that Thucydides noticed this and so put no speech in the closing portions of his history, though there were many events in Ionia and many events at Athens that called for the use of dialogues and harangues" (trans. Pritchett 1975, 11). See also Pritchett 1975, 67 nn. 6 and 7, for various scholarly evaluations of the evidence about Cratippus's date (as a contemporary and possible editor of Thucydides?) and his scholarly judgment.

4. Schwartz (1929, 72–91) finds many inconsistencies and even "doublets" in the account, in this following Wilamowitz 1908, 578–618. De Romilly (1963, 224) sums up the general opinion: "Books V and VIII do nevertheless present, on the whole, a rather hasty and summary character, which we might almost refer to as provisional, and which would suggest that they could be a first version which has not been very thoroughly revised." Here, however, I argue that the underlying structural organizations of books v and viii are quite different from one another.

5. De Romilly 1963, 53: "And the book runs on, flat and monotonous, offering no outstanding feature as a starting-point for analysis."

6. See Luschnat 1971, 1117–32, for a review of the scholarship on the stylistic distinctions of the *History*'s five main sections, the last two of which are the Sicilian account and book viii. Two recent works including substantial and thoughtful examination of books vi–viii are Rood 1998 and Kallet 2001.

7. See table C.1 in appendix C, which compares the frequency of different types of time formulae in the first sentences of units of the Archidamian narrative and book v, and those of the narrative sections of the Sicilian account and book viii. But the more important point is that in the later books, time words no longer set passages apart from each other. Over a quarter (26%) of the introductory sentences in scenes of book viii have time formulae of the precisely referential type, which have become just another element tying the scene that is beginning more closely with what has gone before it. The same is true of the Sicilian account. And another quarter of the first sentences in book viii (26%) have no time formula at all. See pp. 145, 154 for the kinds of changes taking place in the scenes of book viii that have deprived introductory sentences and their formular elements of significance.

8. Of course, many time formulae of the precisely referential type in the Archidamian narrative and book v serve the same purpose; ii.79 (the Athenians in the Thraceward region) is a typical example. By itself, this type of time word would not suffice to make two otherwise separate units of action blend into one. But when the time expression has become indistinguishable from other types of causal or thematic links also present, it adds to the merging of the scenes, rather than serving to separate them.

9. Because the numbering of the chapters in books vi, vii, and viii becomes increasingly arbitrary, discussions of passages like the present one must generally number by halves of subsections (as in vii.16.2b). John Hudson, editor of the 1696 Oxford edition, probably experienced some of the same difficulties in determining the structural division in these later books as later readers do. For the winter of year eighteen, de Romilly (1956a, 65–66) argues that the significance of Nicias's letter extends well beyond the immediate season to include issues of basic significance for the war.

10. The elliptical nature of some of the causal connections in the narrative as well as the new flexibility in scene boundaries in book viii has bothered attentive Thucydidean readers. Commentators often have had recourse to "interpolation" as the ex-

planation of many difficulties. See Classen and Steup 1929, 8: 142: "Nach (60.1) können die Eretrier hier unmöglich als im Besitz von Oropos befindlich hingestellt werden"; then the acerbic comment on 143: "der Bericht geht so weiter, als ob vorher nur von den Pelopp. gesprochen worden wäre." Ancient commentators went still farther; see Marcellinus's *Vita* of Thucydides, chapters 43 and 44, in vol.1 of Jones and Powell's 1942 Oxford edition.

11. The passage that ties the whole development together is viii. 43–44, which gives the background of the disputes over payment of the Peloponnesian fleet, and the subsequent Peloponnesian decision to go to Rhodes to be independent of Tissaphernes. Delebecque (1967, 76) comments: "Les Éretriens complices *arrivent* à Rhodes, pour appeler les Péloponnésiens en Eubée; mais ceux-ci, avec l'intention—que l'on sait (55,2)—de secourir Chios, quittent Rhodes (60,2): c'est donc la fin de leur inaction de quatre-vingt jours (cf. VIII, 44,4)."

12. The aspect of Thucydides' earlier narrative style that most anticipates this technique is the interior of the extended narrative unit. In a sense, the whole account of books vi through viii can be read as two long extended narrative units, one lasting over books vi and vii, one over book viii. The four Archidamian picture units with subjects that deliberately harmonize topics treated in surrounding units (discussed on pp. 60–61) hint at the complexities of the narrative organization of books vi–viii. Cf. p. 214 n.24.

13. The sentences that are formular introduce the first, second, fourth, fifth, sixth, and ninth scenes in table 6.1 below. Four of them are of the simple seasonal type, and two are prepositional phrases. Delebecque (1965, 74–75) calls viii.29–43 a "section," which he then divides into two "secteurs," in Athens and Sparta. It is odd that Delebecque should have divided book viii into such small segments; he himself says (1967, 11): "Il n'est pas de section ni de scène qui ne possède ses liens internes et des correspondances calculées avec les voisines. Malgré les coupures constantes, tout se tient, tout se suit, et dans un ordre tel qu'il serait impossible de modifier l'emplacement du moindre paragraphe."

14. Scenes in Sicily, as well as showing the kind of blending discussed here for vii.10–18, often follow each other in an action-reaction relation that is only truly equivalent to the change of focus within an extended narrative unit in the early war. The passage in vii.1–8 is a good example. It is comprised of six scenes: vii.1–2 (the arrival of Gylippus and the Corinthians in Syracuse), vii.3 (the Athenians react to Gylippus), vii. 4.1–3 (the Syracusan attempt to build a wall across Epipolae), vii.4.4–7 (Nicias fortifies Plemmyrium and sends twenty ships), vii.5–6 (Gylippus foils the Athenian investment of the city), and vii.7 (twelve Corinthian ships come, and Gylippus initiates other activity in Syracuse). These topics form the substance of the letter of Nicias discussed on pp. 145–47. The time formulae that introduce these six scenes are of the type described in note 7 above; they serve to tie the series together rather than divide it, by providing one more set of mutual references. Only the final scene is introduced by a formula that divides, and it fol-

lows an equally strong formula that falls in the middle of the previous scene, in vii.6: "After this, when the opportunity came, he led them on again" (καὶ μετὰ ταῦτα, ἐπειδὴ καιρὸς ἦν, αὖθις ἐπῆγεν αὐτούς). (Subject, setting, and action have remained the same. This is not therefore an introductory sentence.) Moreover, this set of scenes is tied strongly to those that come before and after it. Scene vii.10–17 sums up these developments, and the first scene in the series, Gylippus's arrival, ties the whole development directly back to the dramatic account of his approach, which begins in the winter of year seventeen. Thucydides emphasizes the narrowness of the Syracusan escape at the end of vii.1–2: "Syracuse came within this degree of danger" (παρὰ τοσοῦτον μὲν αἱ Συράκουσαι ἦλθον κινδύνου). The placement of this judgment itself reveals the change in narrative technique from the early books. In the Archidamian account, such comments sum up and make final certain great developments: Mytilene in iii.50 (and a comment in 49 preparing the reader for the end of the account), Plataea in iii.68, Pylos in iv.41, and Corcyra in iv.48. But here the judgment in vii.2 allows the reader no sense of finality; he is already in the middle of a new situation, the Athenian response to Gylippus's arrival. Though Thucydides could have separated Gylippus's arrival from the events that happened after, he has chosen instead to make the account into one unbroken fabric. Another passage whose scenes form a chain of continuous activity is vii.20–45. Here, thirteen scenes build up the narrative of Demosthenes' gradual approach to Syracuse, the approach that represents the last chance for Athenian success. Within this series occurs vii.27–30, the extended discussion of the investment of Decelea in Attica and the disaster in Mycalessus. These passages have often been criticized by scholars as detrimental to the ongoing narrative; Schwartz 1929, 199–202, provides an extreme example. But even Dover in the course of a sensible discussion (HCT IV: 404) remarks: "If Thucydides had revised book viii, I do not believe that he would have enlarged on the effects of Dekeleia in vii; he wrote about them when they were on his mind." And yet vii.27.3–28.2, describing the hardships the Athenians suffered in year nineteen and would suffer in the future, is effective precisely because it represents the extreme extent of the results of the Sicilian expedition undertaken so lightheartedly in year seventeen. As vi.93 from the winter of year seventeen has already shown, Decelea is invested largely through Alcibiades' efforts to spur the Spartans on; this narrative can reasonably also indicate the extent to which the result would prove burdensome to Athens. The new flexibility of narrative structure allows Thucydides to communicate a sense of this passage's importance in the Sicilian account as a whole. The whole scene, vii.27–30, as it passes from the Thracians who have come too late to embark for Sicily to Decelea's investment as the reason why Athens couldn't afford to keep the Thracians to Mycalessus is itself another convincing demonstration of a larger thesis Thucydides argues throughout his narrative: the war in Sicily was not external, parenthetical, a single event in a very long war. The bad decisions the Athenians made in year seventeen spelled the beginning of the end, and even while the expedition was going on, Thucydides claims, it affected one of the humblest villages in Boeotia with its savage consequences. Thus the blending of scenes in books vi and vii, and the imposi-tion of a single theme on all of them, are not structural developments irrelevant to the action being analyzed, but central to the view of this stage of the war as Thucydides is trying to present it.

15. The five scenes that do not relate to Sicily are all very brief: vi.95.1 (Argos), v.95.2 (Thespiae), vi.105 (Athens in Argos), vii.9 (Euetion marches against Amphipolis with Perdiccas), and vii.34 (Peloponnesians in Naupactus fight Athenians).

16. See viii.47.2 but also viii.73.

17. The only scene in book viii that does not begin with a focus on the events tak-ing place in the Aegean is viii.60, discussed on pp. 147–48. As the discussion there in-dicates, the action does not always maintain an Aegean focus within the scene. Many questions whose answers would lie entirely outside this sphere are, however, ignored: Why has Hermocrates in viii.85 been exiled? Why does the Lacedaemonian reaction to Astyochus appear only as a fleet is coming to judge him, viii.39, and not as part of a more general description of Lacedaemonian politics? In this respect, books vi, vii, and viii show a continuation in technique from book v, where the same rigorous exclusion of detail irrelevant to the scene at hand is practiced; it seems much more emphatic because of the general spareness of the surrounding narrative.

18. See pp. 147–48.

19. Teos is mentioned only in viii.16, 19, and 20. Events at Samos and Chios are a continuing focus throughout the book. If one compares their treatment with those of the account of Corcyra in years five and seven, or Mytilene in years four and five, the new insistence on the integration of the local event with larger issues is very striking.

20. Thucydides makes the point directly in vii.55.

21. Strasburger (1968, 520–21) calls Euphemus's speech a "Trugrede" and analyzes it as a part in the progressive decline in the role of imperialism as the *History* progresses. Certainly enough information about Athenian aims is given throughout books vi and vii to make the claims, as Euphemus sets them out, appear specious.

22. We might note that vi.75–88.2a is another scene whose setting and actors change greatly over its course. It begins as an account of Syracusan preparations for the win-ter; goes to the sending of representatives of Syracuse to Camarina, then to the speeches there of Hermocrates and Euphemus, and finally to a discussion of Camarinaean opin-ion and their decision.

23. Schadewaldt (1971, 18) makes this point about Alcibiades' role in book v: "So wird Alkibiades dem Thukydides hier Hauptrepräsentant für die Athenische Politik, Repräsentant für den Gesamtzustand des damaligen politischen Bewußtseins"; but he argues partly from the cohesiveness of those concerns with Sicily to a composition after 404 of the events after the first ten years. Westlake (1968, 225–30) emphasizes Alci-biades' importance to the direction events take in Sicily. The speech in vi.88.7–93.3, like the mention of Decelea and Mycalessus (note 14 above), is designed to prove an in-

terpretive judgment as well as continue a new structural interest in subordination in the narrative. The introduction of Alcibiades into the Lacedaemonian assembly shows in action how badly Athenian politicians, absorbed in their private bids for power, had miscalculated on this very point. They had failed to see that the war was a single war, and that their ambitions had released to the Peloponnesians the most potent of allies. This would be an interpretation of ii.65.10–12 that easily fits into the narrative of books vi and vii.

24. See, for instance, vii.48–49, 55, 59, 61–64, 71–72, and the piteous spectacle of defeat that ends the book. De Romilly (1956a, 84) claims that the Sicilian books hold many fewer personal judgments than book viii does; however, that is because she defines quite narrowly what constitutes a personal judgment.

CHAPTER SEVEN

1. Cwiklinski (1877, 23–87) was the first to try to establish the independence of the Sicilian books from the account of the larger twenty-seven-year war; see Schwartz 1929, 8–11, for the intellectual ties connecting Cwiklinski and Kirchhoff. The first nineteen pages of Schwartz's book are extremely interesting as a picture of the development of the analytic position as a series of challenges and responses, largely of German scholars, between 1850 and World War I. Schadewaldt (1971 [reprint of 1929]) effectively refuted Cwiklinski's argument, although I do not agree with his post-404 date for the entirety of the *History*'s composition.

2. Some of these are connected to the major events in the Thraceward regions, like iv.7 (the capture of Eion) and iv.133.4 (the blockade around Scione). Others are to varying degrees correlated, like the Athenian expedition against Anactorium in iv.49, the demolition of the Thespian wall by the Thebans in iv.133.1, and the eclipse of the sun in iv.52.1.

3. See chapter 4, sections 4.1.1.c–e above (iv.78–83, iv.84–88; iv.120–122, iv.123, iv.124–132; v.12, v.13).

4. A concomitant change in books iv–v.24 is that very short units for the first time appear in clusters, as in iv.133.1–135. This supports the idea of the change in narrative arrangement here advanced: while earlier single simple picture units are sometimes used to break up long narratives and make them effectively into *a-b-a* accounts (as in iii.94–98, Aetolia; iii.99, Sicily; iii.100–102, Aetolia), in books iv– v.24 loose narrative connection between two contiguous long units about the same subject more often occurs. The parenthetical simple picture units occur in clusters together rather than as interruptions of these longer accounts.

5. It is worth restating here the point made on p. 33, that Thucydides himself would not have thought in terms of five formulae for narrative units. The somewhat arbitrary definitions of different unit types I have made here are useful because they enable us to measure changes in narrative practice more precisely than we could otherwise have done.

6. See pp. 148–50.

7. The years in these later books are very long, in comparison with all the years of the Peace and most Archidamian years. The extant years of the *History*, in order of length in the text (beginning with the longest), are nineteen, seventeen, eight, five, twenty, twenty-one (a fragment!), seven, one, three, eighteen, six, two, ten, fourteen, four, sixteen, nine, eleven, twelve, thirteen, fifteen. All of the last five years are in the first half of this list. Moreover, the very long Archidamian years are long for different reasons. In all of them, it is the inclusion of important subaccounts within these years that draws them out. Year eight includes 415 lines about Brasidas, year five includes 414 lines about Mytilene, 361 lines in a single unit about Plataea, and 279 lines in a single unit about Corcyra.

8. Stahl (1966, 1–11) discusses the role that beliefs were playing in Athens on the eve of the Sicilian expedition. He points out that vi.53–61 is important in its context in book vi (although it has often been suspected of being a "doublet" that would have disappeared if Thucydides had had time to revise his work), since it shows the beliefs that led the Athenians to the catastrophic decision to recall Alcibiades to Athens. This same interpretation could be applied to the overthrow of democracy in Athens in book viii. It largely occurred, Thucydides says, because the Athenians thought Tissaphernes and their subject states would be better disposed to an oligarchy (viii.48), a view Thucydides does not hold at all (viii. 64) but depicts very clearly as the mainspring of one of the most important events of the war. Beliefs (even historiographical beliefs about long-dead tyrants!) are in these late books as significant as action. Rood's narratological study (1998) emphasizes the extent to which Thucydides' narrative, particularly in the later books, reveals perceptions shaping both judgment and action, on the part of all the war's participants.

9. The ἀρξάμενος εὐθύς of i.1, considered together with the γέγραπται ἑξῆς ὡς ἕκαστα of ii.1, also helps sustain this picture of the *History*'s early composition.

10. See Hornblower 1987, 136–54, and the works cited there for other observations about the order of composition; see also Marincola 2001, 63 n.11, and p. 194 note 7. (In the 1975 dissertation, for "Spätindizen" I cited Patzer 1937, 103–9 (Anhang I), and Luschnat 1971, 1195–1208.)

11. Hornblower 1991, 3–232 (the major rubrics). Cf. the remarkably similar sections into which the text is divided by Gomme in *HCT* I: passim and Classen and Steup 1919, 1: passim. Classen and Steup and Gomme, however, treat i.118.3–145 as a single long passage, and Hornblower's distinct smaller rubrics as subheadings within it. Neither Classen and Steup nor Gomme separates i.127 out as a distinct narrative section, as Hornblower does; Classen and Steup treat it together with chapter 126, while Gomme does not explicitly clarify its connections to other narrative segments. These minor divergences among Thucydides' most careful editors show what a high level of integration Thucydides achieves, in linking his various narrative segments of book i together.

(Gomme does not in *HCT* I always use a single consistent set of rubrics that make clear where he thinks the major divisions of the narrative fall. Nonetheless, his divisions are generally the same as those listed by Hornblower, above.)

12. See the developed picture units ii.57, iii.17, iii.69, and iv.6, discussed on pp. 60–61.

13. See Hornblower 1991, 211–212; Hornblower also comments that "like some of the prominent individuals on both sides in the Peloponnesian War itself, these two commanding personalities fell foul of their fellow citizens" (212).

14. The Corcyraean and Potidaean episodes, which developed at roughly the same time, are treated separately, as analytically and sequentially distinct developments that are nonetheless both causes precipitating the Corinthian call to meeting narrated in i.67.1. See Hornblower 1991, 97–98.

15. See Hornblower 1996, 122–45, esp. 125–29 and 138–41; Gribble (1998), however, rightly emphasizes that Thucydides deploys even apparently Herodotean locutions for very different ends of his own.

16. See Dover's discussion of early and late passages in HCT V: 408–10, which is somewhat overprecise in its conclusions. In terms of late material contained in individual passages, i.97.2, the reference to Hellanicus in the Pentecontaetia, does not seem to me obviously to be the single late insertion in an earlier essay that both Dover and Hornblower (1991, 148) think it to be. See now Kallet 2001, 281–94, for the topicality of many of the themes developed in book i (in particular, the Archaeology's insistence on the importance of sea power) to events that transpired at the very end of the Peloponnesian War.

17. Rood 1998, 159–201 and 251–84. In his first chapter Erbse (1989, 1–82) contests Andrewes's judgment in *HCT* V that Thucydides viii is full of signs of incomplete revision; Erbse also stresses the difficulty of constructing such a complex, interlocking narrative (64–67). See Erbse's judgment on book viii as a whole: "Es ist ein Meisterwerk und, was die Bewußtheit, ja die raffinierte Kunst der Komposition betrifft, den besten Teilen der ersten sieben Bücher gleichwertig, wenn nicht überlegen" (66).

BIBLIOGRAPHY

Adcock, F. 1963. *Thucydides and His History*. Cambridge: Cambridge University Press.

Allison, J. 1989. *Power and Preparedness in Thucydides*. Baltimore: Johns Hopkins University Press.

———. 1997. *Word and Concept in Thucydides*. Atlanta: Scholars Press.

Anderson, P. 1998. *The Origins of Postmodernity*. London and New York: Verso.

Ankersmit, F., and H. Kellner. 1995. *A New Philosophy of History*. Chicago: University of Chicago Press.

Appleby, J., L. Hunt, and M. Jacob. 1994. *Telling the Truth about History*. New York and London: W. W. Norton.

Aristotle. 1954. *Rhetoric and Politics*. Translated by W. Rhys Roberts and I. Bywater. New York: Modern Library.

Atkinson, R. 1978. *Knowledge and Explanation in History*. Ithaca, N.Y.: Cornell University Press.

Badian, E. 1993. *From Plataea to Potidaea: Studies in the History and Historiography of the Pentecontaetia*. Baltimore: Johns Hopkins University Press.

Bakhtin, M. 1984. *Problems of Dostoevsky's Poetics*. Edited and translated by C. Emerson. Minneapolis: University of Minnesota Press.

Bakker, E., I. de Jong, and H. van Wees. 2000. *Brill's Companion to Herodotus*. Leiden: Brill.

Berkhofer, R. 1995. *Beyond the Great Story: History as Text and Discourse*. Cambridge, Mass.: Harvard University Press.

Boedeker, D., ed. 1987. *Herodotus and the Invention of History. Arethusa* 20, nos. 1–2.

Boedeker, D., and D. Sider, eds. 2001. *The New Simonides: Contexts of Praise and Desire.* Oxford: Oxford University Press.

Bonnell, V., and L. Hunt, eds. 1999. *Beyond the Cultural Turn.* Berkeley and Los Angeles: University of California Press.

Bowie, E. 2001. "Ancestors of Historiography in Early Greek Elegiac and Iambic Poetry?" In Luraghi 2001, 45–66.

Brunt, P. A. 1993. *Studies in Greek History and Thought.* Oxford: Clarendon Press.

Bunzl, M. 1995. "Truth, Objectivity, and History: An Exchange." *JHI* 56: 651–59.

Burke, P., ed. 2001. *New Perspectives on Historical Writing.* University Park: Pennsylvania State University Press.

Carr, D. 1986. *Time, Narrative, and History.* Bloomington: Indiana University Press.

———. 1998. "Narrative and the Real World: An Argument for Continuity." In Fay, Pomper, and Vann 1998, 137–52.

Carr, E. H. 1967. *What Is History?* New York: Vintage Books.

Carroll, N. 1998. "Interpretation, History, and Narrative." In Fay, Pomper, and Vann 1998, 34–56.

Cawkwell, G. 1997. *Thucydides and the Peloponnesian War.* New York and London: Routledge.

Christ, M. 1994. "Herodotean Kings and Historical Inquiry." *CA* 13: 167–202.

Classen, J., and J. Steup. 1900–1922. *Thukydides.* 8 vols. Reprint, 1963. Berlin: Weidmann.

Cochrane, C. 1929. *Thucydides and the Science of History.* Oxford: Oxford University Press.

Cogan, M. 1981. *The Human Thing: The Speeches and Principles of Thucydides' History.* Chicago: University of Chicago Press.

Collingwood, R. G. 1946. *The Idea of History.* Oxford: Clarendon Press.

Connor, R. 1977. "A Post-Modernist Thucydides?" *CJ* 72: 289–98.

———. 1984. *Thucydides.* Princeton: Princeton University Press.

———. 1985. "Narrative Discourse in Thucydides." In Jameson 1985.

Cornford, F. 1907. *Thucydides Mythistoricus.* London: E. Arnold.

Crane, G. 1996. *The Blinded Eye: Thucydides and the New Written Word.* Lanham, Md.: Rowman and Littlefield.

———. 1998. *Thucydides and the Ancient Simplicity.* Berkeley and Los Angeles: University of California Press.

Culler, J. 1975. "Defining Narrative Units." In Fowler 1975, 123–42.

Cwiklinski, L. 1877. "Über die Entstehungweise des zweiten Theiles der thukydideischen Geschichte." *Hermes* 12: 23–87.

Danto, A. 1995. "The Decline and Fall of the Analytical Philosophy of History." In Ankersmit and Kellner 1995, 70–85.

Darbo-Peschanski, C. 1987a. *Le discours du particulier: Essai sur l'enquête Hérodotéenne.* Paris: Seuil.

———. 1987b. "Thucydide: Historien, Juge." *Mètis* 2.1: 109–40.

Debnar, P. 2001. *Speaking the Same Language: Speech and Audience in Thucydides' Spartan Debates.* Ann Arbor: University of Michigan Press.

Delebecque, É. 1965. *Thucydide et Alcibiade.* Aix-en-Provence: Éditions Ophrys.

———. 1967. *Thucydide Livre VIII.* Aix-en-Provence: Éditions Ophrys.

de Ste. Croix, G. 1972. *The Origins of the Peloponnesian War.* Ithaca, N.Y.: Cornell University Press.

Detienne, M. 1981. *The Masters of Truth in Archaic Greece.* Translated by J. Lloyd. Reprint, 1999. New York: Zone Books.

Detienne, M., and J.-P. Vernant. 1991. *Cunning Intelligence in Greek Culture and Society.* Translated by J. Lloyd. Chicago: University of Chicago Press.

Dewald, C. 1985. "Practical Knowledge and the Historian's Role in Herodotus and Thucydides." In Jameson 1985, 47–63.

———. 1987. "Narrative Surface and Authorial Voice in Herodotus' *Histories.*" In Boedeker 1987, 147–70.

———. 1999. "The Figured Stage: Focalizing the Initial Narratives of Herodotus and Thucydides." In Felson, Konstan, and Faulkner 1999, 229–61.

———. 2002. "'I Didn't Give My Own Genealogy': Herodotus and the Authorial Persona." In Bakker, de Jong, and van Wees 2002.

———. Forthcoming. "Paying Attention: History as the Development of a Secular Narrative." In *Rethinking Revolutions,* edited by R. Osborne and S. Goldhill. Cambridge: Cambridge University Press.

Dover, K. 1960. *Greek Word Order.* Cambridge: Cambridge University Press.

———. 1968. *Lysias and the Corpus Lysiacum.* Berkeley and Los Angeles: University of California Press.

———. 1973. *Thucydides.* Greece and Rome, New Surveys in the Classics, vol. 7. Oxford: Clarendon Press.

Drews, R. 1973. *The Greek Accounts of Eastern History.* Cambridge, Mass.: Harvard University Press.

Dreyfus, H., and P. Rabinow. 1982. *Michel Foucault: Beyond Structuralism and Hermeneutics.* Chicago: University of Chicago Press.

Edmunds, L. 1975. *Chance and Intelligence in Thucydides*. Cambridge, Mass.: Harvard University Press.

———. 1993. "Thucydides in the Act of Writing." In Pretagostini 1993, 831–52.

Edmunds, L., and R. Wallace. 1997. *Poet, Public, and Performance in Ancient Greece*. Baltimore: Johns Hopkins University Press.

Ellis, J. 1991. "The Structure and Argument of Thucydides' Archaelogy." *CA* 10: 344–75.

Erbse, H. 1953. "Über eine Eigenheit der thukydideischen Geschichtsbetrachtung." *RhM* 96: 38–62 (reprint, in Herter 1968, 317–43).

———. 1989. *Thukydides-Interpretationen*. Berlin: Walter de Gruyter.

Farrar, C. 1988. *The Origins of Democratic Thinking: The Invention of Politics in Classical Athens*. Cambridge: Cambridge University Press.

Fay, B., P. Pomper, and R. Vann, eds. 1998. *History and Theory: Contemporary Readings*. Oxford: Blackwell.

Felson, N., D. Konstan, and T. Faulkner, eds. 1999. *Contextualizing Classics: Ideology, Performance, Dialogue: Festschrift Peradotto*. Lanham, Md.: Rowman and Littlefield.

Finley, J. 1942. *Thucydides*. Cambridge, Mass.: Harvard University Press.

———. 1967. *Three Essays on Thucydides*. Cambridge, Mass.: Harvard University Press.

Flory, S. 1990. "The Meaning of *to mē muthōdes* (1.22.4) and the Usefulness of Thucydides' *History*." *CJ* 85: 193–208.

Fornara, C. 1983. *The Nature of History in Ancient Greece and Rome*. Berkeley and Los Angeles: University of California Press.

Foucault, M. 1970. *The Order of Things*. New York: Vintage Books.

Fowler, R., ed. 1975. *Style and Structure in Literature: Essays in the New Stylistics*. Ithaca, N.Y.: Cornell University Press.

Fritz, K. von. 1967. *Die griechische Geschichtsschreibung*. Berlin: de Gruyter.

Gehrke, H.-J. 2001. "Myth, History, and Collective Identity: Uses of the Past in Ancient Greece and Beyond." In Luraghi 2001, 286–313.

Genette, G. 1980. *Narrative Discourse. An Essay in Method*. Translated by J. Lewin. Ithaca, N.Y.: Cornell University Press.

Gentili, B. 1988. *Poetry and Its Public in Ancient Greece*. Translated by A. Cole. Baltimore: Johns Hopkins University Press.

Goldhill, S., and R. Osborne, eds. 1999. *Performance Culture and Athenian Democracy*. Cambridge: Cambridge University Press.

Gomme, A. W. 1954. *The Greek Attitude to Poetry and History*. Berkeley and Los Angeles: University of California Press.

———. 1962. *More Essays in Greek History and Literature*. Oxford: Oxford University Press.

Gomme, A., A. Andrewes, and K. Dover, eds. 1945–1981. *A Historical Commentary on Thucydides*. 5 vols. Oxford: Clarendon Press. (= *HCT*)

Gommel, J. 1966. *Rhetorisches Argumentieren bei Thukydides*. Hildesheim: Georg Olms.

Gould, J. 1989. *Herodotus*. New York: St. Martin's Press.

Gribble, D. 1998. "Narrator Interventions in Thucydides." *JHS* 118: 41–67.

———. 1999. *Alcibiades and Athens: A Study in Literary Presentation*. Oxford: Oxford University Press.

Halttunen, K. 1999. "Cultural History and the Challenge of Narrativity." In Bonnell and Hunt 1999, 165–81.

Hammond, N. 1952. "The Arrangement of Thought in the Proem and in the other Parts of Thucydides I." *CQ* 46: 127–41.

Haskell, T. 1998. "Objectivity Is Not Neutrality: Rhetoric versus Practice in Peter Novick's *That Noble Dream*." In Fay, Pomper, and Vann 1998, 299–319.

HCT = Gomme, A., A. Andrewes, and K. Dover. 1945–1981. *A Historical Commentary on Thucydides*. 5 vols. Oxford: Oxford University Press.

Herter, H., ed. 1968. *Thukydides*. Wege der Forschung, Bd. xcviii. Darmstadt: Wissenschaftliche Buchgesellschaft.

Hexter, R. 1998. "The Rhetoric of History: On the 'Reality Rule.'" In Fay, Pomper, and Vann 1998, 59–68.

Hornblower, S. 1987. *Thucydides*. Baltimore: Johns Hopkins University Press.

———. 1991. *A Commentary on Thucydides*. Vol. 1. Oxford: Clarendon Press.

———. 1992. "The Religious Dimension of the Peloponnesian War." *HSCP* 94: 169–97.

———. 1994. *Greek Historiography*. Oxford: Clarendon Press.

———. 1996. *A Commentary on Thucydides*. Vol. 2. Oxford: Clarendon Press.

Huart, P. 1968. *Le vocabulaire de l'analyse psychologique dans l'oeuvre de Thucydides*. Études et Commentaires, vol. 69. Paris: Librairie C. Klincksieck.

Hudson, J., ed. 1696. *Thoukydidou peri tou Peloponnesiakou Polemou biblia okto*. Oxford and London: Sheldonian Theatre.

Hunt, L., ed. 1989. *The New Cultural History*. Berkeley and Los Angeles: University of California Press.

Hunter, V. 1973. *Thucydides the Artful Reporter*. Toronto: Hakkert.

———. 1977. "The Composition of Thucydides' *History:* A New Answer to the Problem." *Historia* 26: 269–94.

———. 1982. *Past and Present in Herodotus and Thucydides*. Princeton: Princeton University Press.

Immerwahr, H. 1966. *Form and Thought in Herodotus*. Cleveland: Western Reserve University Press.

Jameson, F. 1982. *The Political Unconscious*. Ithaca, N.Y.: Cornell University Press.

———. 1998. *The Cultural Turn: Selected Writings on the Postmodern, 1989–1998*. London and New York: Verso.

Jameson, M., ed. 1985. *The Greek Historians: Literature and History, Papers Presented to A. E. Raubitschek*. Stanford: Stanford University Press (Saratoga, Calif.: Anma Libri).

Jay, M. 1982. "Should Intellectual History Take a Linguistic Turn?" In La Capra and Kaplan 1982, 86–110.

Jenkins, K., ed. 1997. *The Postmodern History Reader*. London: Routledge.

———. 1999. *Why History?* London: Routledge.

Jones, H., ed. 1942. *Thucydidis Historiae*. App. crit. corr. et aux. J. E. Powell. Oxford: Oxford University Press.

Kallet, L. 2001. *Money and the Corrosion of Power in Thucydides: The Sicilian Expedition and Its Aftermath*. Berkeley and Los Angeles: University of California Press.

Kallet-Marx, L. 1993. *Money, Expense, and Naval Power in Thucydides' History, 1–5.24*. Berkeley and Los Angeles: University of California Press.

Katičič, R. 1957. "Die Ringkomposition im ersten Buche des thukydidische Geschichts-werkes." *WS* 70: 179–96.

Kellner, H. 1997. "Language and Historical Representation." In Jenkins 1997, 127–38.

Kirchhoff, A. 1895. *Thukydides und sein Urkundenmaterial*. Berlin: W. Hertz.

Kramer, L. 1989. "Literature, Criticism, and Historical Imagination: The Literary Challenge of Hayden White and Dominick La Capra." In Hunt 1989, 97–128.

Kraus, C., ed. 1999. *The Limits of Historiography: Genre and Narrator in Ancient Historical Texts*. Leiden: Brill.

Kuhn, T. 1962. *The Structure of Scientific Revolutions*. Chicago: University of Chicago Press.

La Capra, D. 1998. "History, Language, and Reading: Waiting for Crillon." In Fay, Pomper, and Vann 1998, 90–118.

La Capra, D., and S. Kaplan, eds. 1982. *Modern European Intellectual History*. Ithaca, N.Y.: Cornell University Press.

Laqueur, R. 1937. "Forschungen zu Thukydides." *RhM* 86: 316–57.

Lateiner, D. 1977. "Pathos in Thucydides." *Antichthon* 11: 42–51.

Lattimore, S., trans. 1998. *Thucydides, The Peloponnesian War*. Indianapolis and Cambridge: Hackett.

Lendle, O. 1960. "Zu Thukydides V 20,2." *Hermes* 88: 33–40.

Loraux, N. 1980. "Thucydide n'est pas un collègue." *QS* 12: 55–81.

————. 1986a. *The Invention of Athens: The Funeral Oration in the Classical City.* Translated by A. Sheridan. Cambridge, Mass.: Harvard University Press.

————. 1986b. "Thucydide a écrit la guerre du Péloponnèse." *Mètis* 1: 139–61.

Luraghi, N., ed. 2001. *The Historian's Craft in the Age of Herodotus.* Oxford: Oxford University Press.

Luschnat, O. 1971. *Thukydides der Historiker.* Sonderausgaben der Paulyschen Realencyclopädie der classischen Altertumswissenschaft. Stuttgart: A. Druckenmüller.

MacIntyre, A. 1966. "Epistemological Crises, Dramatic Narrative, and the Philosophy of Science." In *Knowledge and Postmodernism in Historical Perspective*, edited by J. Appleby et al., 457–67. New York and London: Routledge.

Macleod, C. 1983. *Collected Essays.* Oxford: Clarendon Press.

Marincola, J. 1987. "Herodotean Narrative and the Narrator's Presence." In Boedeker 1987, 121–38.

————. 1997. *Authority and Tradition in Ancient Historiography.* Cambridge: Cambridge University Press.

————. 1999. "Genre, Convention, and Innovation in Greco-Roman Historiography." In Kraus 1999, 281–324.

————. 2001. *Greek Historians.* Greece and Rome, New Surveys in the Classics, vol. 31. Oxford: Clarendon Press.

Maza, S. 1996. "Stories in History: Cultural Narratives in Recent Works in European History." *AHR* 101: 1493–1515.

McNeal, R. 1970. "Historical Methods and Thucydides 1.103.1." *Historia* 19: 306–25.

Meyer, C. 1955. *Die Urkunden im Geschichtswerk des Thukydides.* Zetemata: Monographien zur klassischen Altertumswissenschaft, Heft 10. Munich: Beck.

Meyer, E. 1899. *Forschungen zur alten Geschichte.* Vol. 2. Halle a.S.: M. Niemeyer.

Mink, L. 1978. "Narrative Form as a Cognitive Instrument." In *The Writing of History: Literary Form and Historical Understanding*, edited by R. Canary and H. Kozicki, 124–49. Madison: University of Wisconsin Press.

————. 1987. *Historical Understanding.* Edited by B. Fay, E. Golob, and R. Vann. Ithaca, N.Y., and London: Cornell University Press.

Momigliano, A. 1981. "The Rhetoric of History and the History of Rhetoric: On Hayden White's Tropes." *CompCrit* 3: 259–68. Edited by E. Shaffer.

Montgomery, H. 1965. *Gedanke und Tat.* Lund: C. W. K. Gleerup.

Morson, G., and C. Emerson. 1990. *Mikhail Bakhtin: Creation of a Poetics.* Stanford: Stanford University Press.

Moxon, I., J. Smart, and A. Woodman, eds. 1986. *Past Perspectives: Studies in Greek and Roman Historical Writing.* Cambridge: Cambridge University Press.

Müller-Strübing, H. 1881. *Thukydideische Forschungen*. Vienna: C. Konegen.

Munslow, A. 1997. *Deconstructing History*. London and New York: Routledge.

————. 2000. *The Routledge Companion to Classical Studies*. London and New York: Routledge.

Munson, R. 2001. *Telling Wonders: Ethnographic and Political Discourses in the World of Herodotus*. Ann Arbor: University of Michigan Press.

Norden, E. 1958. *Die antike Kunstprosa vom vi Jahrhundert v. Chr. Bis in die Zeit der Renaissance*. 2 vols. Darmstadt: Wissenschaftliche Buchgesellschaft.

Norman, A. 1998. "Telling It Like It Was: Historical Narratives on Their Own Terms." In Fay, Pomper, and Vann 1998, 153–71. Originally published in *History and Theory* 30 (1991): 119–35.

Novick, P. 1988. *That Noble Dream: The "Objectivity Question" and the American Historical Profession*. Cambridge: Cambridge University Press.

Ober, J. 1989. *Mass and Elite in Democratic Athens: Rhetoric, Ideology, and the Power of the People*. Princeton: Princeton University Press.

O'Brien, P. 1989. "Michel Foucault's History of Culture." In Hunt 1989, 25–46.

Ostwald, M. 1988. *Anagkē in Thucydides*. Atlanta: Scholars Press.

Parry, A. 1981. *Logos and Ergon in Thucydides*. New York: Arno.

————. 1989. *The Language of Achilles and Other Papers*. Oxford: Clarendon Press.

Patzer, H. 1937. *Das Problem der Geschichtsschreibung des Thukydides und die thukydideische Frage*. Berlin: Junker und Dünnhaupt.

Pearson, L. 1942. *The Local Historians of Attica*. Reprint, 1972. Philadelphia: American Philological Association.

Pelling, C. 1991. "Thucydides' Archidamus and Herodotus' Artabanus." In *Georgica: Greek Studies in Honour of George Cawkwell*, edited by M. Flower and M. Toher, 120–42. BICS Suppl. 58. London: University of London, Institute of Classical Studies.

————. 2000. *Literary Texts and the Greek Historians*. London and New York: Routledge.

Pohlenz, M. 1936. "Die thukydideische Frage im Lichte der neueren Forschung." *Göttingsche Gelehrte Anzeigen* 198, 281–300 (= *Kleine Schriften* [Hildesheim, 1965] 2: 210–80).

Poster, M. 1982. "The Future According to Foucault: *The Archaeology of Knowledge* and Intellectual History." In La Capra and Kaplan 1982, 137–52.

Pouncey, P. 1980. *The Necessities of War: A Study of Thucydides' Pessimism*. New York: Columbia University Press.

Pretagostini, R., ed. 1993. *Tradizione e innovazione nella cultura greca*. Rome: Gruppo Editoriale Internazionale.

Pritchett, W. K. 1975. *Dionysius of Halicarnassus: On Thucydides*. Berkeley and Los Angeles: University of California Press.

Pucci, P. 1977. *Hesiod and the Language of Poetry*. Baltimore: Johns Hopkins University Press.

Rabinow, P. 1999. *Ethics, Subjectivity, and Truth: The Essential Works of Michel Foucault, 1954–84*. London and New York: Penguin.

Rabinow, P., and W. Sullivan. 1979. *Interpretive Social Science: A Reader*. Berkeley and Los Angeles: University of California Press.

Rawlings, H. 1981. *The Structure of Thucydides' History*. Princeton: Princeton University Press.

Rhodes, P. 1994. "In Defense of the Greek Historians." *G&R* 41: 156–71.

Roberts, C. 1996. *The Logic of Historical Explanation*. University Park: Pennsylvania State University Press.

Romilly, J. de. 1956a. *Histoire et raison chez Thucydide*. Paris: Les Belles Lettres.

———. 1956b. "L'utilité de l'histoire selon Thucydide." In *Histoire et historiens dans l'antiquité*, 4: 41–66. Vandoeuvres-Genève: Entretiens sur l'Antiquité Classique.

———. 1963. *Thucydides and Athenian Imperialism*. Translated by P. Thody. Oxford: Blackwell.

Rood, T. 1998. *Thucydides: Narrative and Explanation*. Oxford: Clarendon Press.

———. 1999. "Thucydides' Persian Wars." In Kraus 1999, 141–68.

Rorty, R. 1968. *The Linguistic Turn: Recent Essays in Philosophical Method*. Chicago: University of Chicago Press.

Ros, J. 1968. *Die Metabole (Variatio) als Stilprinzip des Thukydides*. Amsterdam: Hakkert.

Schadewaldt, W. 1971. *Die Geschichtsschreibung des Thukydides*. 2d ed. (reprint of 1929 edition, with an afterword). Dublin and Zurich: Weidmann.

Schneider, C. 1974. *Information und Absicht bei Thukydides*. Göttingen: Vandenhoeck und Ruprecht.

Schwartz, E. 1929. *Das Geschichtswerk des Thukydides*. Reprint, 1969. Hildesheim: Georg Olms.

Smart, J. 1986. "Thucydides and Hellanicus." In Moxon, Smart, and Woodman 1986, 19–35.

Smith, B. 1995. "Whose Truth, Whose History?" *JHS* 56: 194–208.

Somers, M. 1999. "The Privatization of Citizenship: How to Unthink a Knowledge Culture." In Bonnell and Hunt 1999, 121–61.

Spiegel, G. 1990. "History, Historicism, and the Social Logic of the Text in the Middle Ages." *Speculum* 65: 59–86.

———. 1992. "History and Post-Modernism IV." *P&P* 135: 194–208.

Stadter, P., ed. 1973. *The Speeches in Thucydides: A Collection of Original Studies with a Bibliography*. Chapel Hill: University of North Carolina Press.

Stahl, H.-P. 1966. *Thukydides: Die Stellung des Menschen im geschichtlichen Prozess*. Zetemata: Monographien zur klassischen Altertumswissenschaft, Heft 40. Munich: Beck.

―――. 1973. "Speeches and Course of Events in Books Six and Seven of Thucydides." In Stadter 1973, 60–77.

Stone, L. 1979. "The Revival of Narrative: Reflections on a New Old History." *P&P* 85: 3–24.

―――. 1991. "History and Post-Modernism." *P&P* 131: 217–18.

―――. 1992. "History and Post-Modernism III." *P&P* 135: 189–94.

Strasburger, H. 1954. "Die Entdeckung der politischen Geschichte durch Thukydides." *Saeculum* 5: 395–428.

―――. 1968. "Thukydides und die politische Selbstdarstellung der Athener." In Herter 1968, 498–530.

―――. 1972. *Homer und die Geschichtsschreibung*. Sitzungsberichte der Heidelberger Akademie der Wissenschaften, Jahrgang 1972/3. Heidelberg: Carl Winter.

Stroud, R. 1994. "Thucydides and Corinth." *Chiron* 24: 267–302.

Thalmann, W. G. 1984. *Conventions of Form and Thought in Early Greek Epic Poetry*. Baltimore and London: Johns Hopkins University Press.

Thomas, R. 1989. *Oral Traditions and Written Records in Classical Athens*. Cambridge: Cambridge University Press.

―――. 2000. *Herodotus in Context: Ethnography, Science, and the Art of Persuasion*. Cambridge: Cambridge University Press.

Toews, J. 1987. "Intellectual History after the Linguistic Turn." *AHR* 92: 879–907.

Ullrich, F. 1846. *Beiträge zur Erklärung des Thukydides*. Gesamtausgabe. Hamburg: Perthes-Besser und Mauke.

Usher, S. 1974. *Dionysius of Halicarnassus, Critical Essays*. Vol. 1. Cambridge, Mass.: Harvard University Press.

―――. 1985. *Dionysius of Halicarnassus, Critical Essays*. Vol. 2. Cambridge, Mass.: Harvard University Press.

Vann, R. 1995. "Turning Linguistic: History and Theory and *History and Theory*, 1960–1975." In Ankersmit and Kellner 1995, 40–69.

Veeser, H., ed. 1989. *The New Historicism*. London and New York: Routledge.

Vernant, J.-P. 1980. *Myth and Society in Ancient Greece*. Translated by J. Lloyd. New York: Harvester Press.

————. 1991. *Mortals and Immortals: Collected Essays*. Edited by F. Zeitlin. Princeton: Princeton University Press.

————. 1996. *Entre mythe et politique*. Paris: Éditions du Seuil.

Vidal-Naquet, P. 1986. *The Black Hunter: Forms of Thought and Forms of Society in the Greek World*. Translated by A. Szegedy-Maszak. Baltimore: Johns Hopkins University Press.

Warner, R., trans. 1954. *Thucydides: History of the Peloponnesian War*. Introduction and notes by M. I. Finley. London and New York: Penguin.

Westlake, H. 1968. *Individuals in Thucydides*. Cambridge: Cambridge University Press.

————. 1973. "The Settings of Thucydidean Speeches." In Stadter 1973, 90–108.

White, H. 1973. *Metahistory: The Historical Imagination in Nineteenth-Century Europe*. Baltimore: Johns Hopkins University Press.

————. 1978. *Tropics of Discourse: Essays in Cultural Criticism*. Baltimore: Johns Hopkins University Press.

————. 1987. *The Content of the Form: Narrative Discourse and Historical Representation*. Baltimore: Johns Hopkins University Press.

————. 1999. *Figural Realism: Studies in the Mimesis Effect*. Baltimore: Johns Hopkins University Press.

Wilamowitz-Möllendorf, U. von. 1877. "Die Thukydideslegend." *Hermes* 12: 326–61.

————. 1908. "Thukydides VIII." *Hermes* 43: 578–618.

Winkler, J., and F. Zeitlin. 1990. *Nothing to Do with Dionysos? Athenian Drama in Its Social Context*. Princeton: Princeton University Press.

Woodhead, A. 1970. *Thucydides on the Nature of Power*. Martin Classical Lectures, vol. 24. Cambridge, Mass.: Harvard University Press.

Woodman, A. 1988. *Rhetoric in Classical Historiography: Four Studies*. London and Sydney: Croom and Helm.

Ziegler, K. 1929. "Der Ursprung der Exkurse in Thukydides." *RhM* 78: 58–67.

GENERAL INDEX

Acanthus, 80, 89, 211n50

Acarnania, 27, 30, 39, 67, 68, 75, 94, 108

Adams, H., 197n20

Adcock, F., 209n18

Aegean War narrative (viii.7–109), xii, 3, 4, 115, 144–45, 147–48, 149–52, 153–54, 159, 175–77, 221n3, 225n17, 225n19; scenes, interdependent, 149, 150–51; similar to Sicilian narrative, 144–63. *See also* Archidamian units of action; Sicilian narrative; units of action (general); years of the Peace, units of action

Aetna, 30, 108, 203n5, 217n51

Aetolia, 29, 40, 75, 91, 226n4

Alcibiades, 21, 127, 128, 130, 135, 140, 141, 142, 151–53, 163, 220n26, 224n14, 225n23, 227n8

Allison, J., 195n12

Althusser, L., 197n24

Ambracia, 29, 40, 42, 78, 105

Amphilochia, 75, 78, 91, 211n54

Amphilochian Argos, 29, 78

Amphipolis, 17, 41–42, 52, 75, 77, 91, 109, 110, 210n36, 212n5, 225n15

Amphilocia, 75, 78, 91, 211n54

Anderson, P., 197n23

Andrewes, A., 2, 127, 193n1, 228n17

Annales school, 197n23, 197n24

Appleby, J., 14, 196n19, 197n21, 197n22, 197n24, 199n29, 201n46, 203n64

Archidamian units of action, 3, 25–34, 35, 48–85, 110–11, 165–70; changes in, 83–85; connections within years, 104–11; initial and concluding clusters, 98–100; lull in narrative, 108; pervasiveness of *a-b-a* patterns, 90; sequences of, 86–111; supporting material (descriptive, causal, motivational), 52–53; unit conclusions, 62; unit types, 31–33, 48–50, 82–85. *See also* Aegean War narrative; Sicilian narrative; units of action (general); years of the Peace, units of action

Archidamian War (ii.1–v.24), xi, 3, 5, 25, 104–10, 124, 155, 156, 158, 160, 219n6, 220n18

Argos, 26, 55–56, 71, 78, 116, 120, 123, 124, 126, 127, 129, 131–35, 138, 139, 140–41, 142–43, 208n8, 220n26, 221n27, 225n15

Drews, R., 195n13
Dreyfus, H., 198n26
Dewald, E., 203n64

Edmunds, L., 13, 194n12, 195n14, 200n36,
    200n37, 212n1
Elis, 67, 79, 127–29, 133, 135, 140, 143,
    220n20, 221n27
Emerson, C., 18–19, 203n56, 203n57,
    203n60
Epidaurus, 76, 116, 120, 128, 131, 140
epistēmē, Foucauldian, 11, 13–15, 18,
    198n26, 198n27, 201n42
Erbse, H., 228n17
Euarchus, 39, 66, 205n17
Euboea, 26, 28, 52, 105
Eurymedon, 62, 68, 146, 213n18, 216n41

Farrar, C., 195n15
Fay, B., 197n20, 198n28
Finley, J., 200n34, 217n53, 218n1, 221n1
Flory, S., 195n14
Foucault, M., 10, 11, 13–15, 198n26,
    198n27
Frye, N., 14, 201n43
Funeral oration, 78, 80, 104–5, 210n44,
    212n3. *See also History,* content
    (speeches)

Gadamer, H.-G., 198n28
Geertz, C., 197n24
Genette, G., 199n33
Gentili, B., 200n36
Goldhill, S., 200n36
Gomme, A. W., 2, 30, 92, 98, 193n1,
    195n13, 195n14, 195n15, 199n31,
    200n36, 209n18, 212n5, 212n6, 213n20,
    214n23, 214n25, 215n37, 215n39,
    216n40, 216n41, 216n 42, 216n43,
    217n54, 217n62, 218n64, 220n19,
    227n11
Gommel, J., 213n9
Gould, J., 199n30

Gramsci, A., 197n24
Gribble, D., 195n12, 196n17, 221n26,
    228n15
Gylippus, 153, 208n12, 223n14

Habermas, J., 198n25, 198n28
Habinek, T., 203n64
Halttunen, K., 203n55
Hammond, N., 193n2, 207n1
Hellanicus, 208n8, 228n16
Heraclea, 28, 30–32, 40, 61, 102, 108,
    122, 125, 140
Hermocrates, 80, 152, 153, 225n17,
    225n22
Herodotus and Herodotean style, 3, 11,
    13, 19, 87, 96, 161, 195n13l, 196n17,
    200n33, 200n38, 204n6, 213n12,
    228n15
Hexter, J., 202n54
Hirsch, E., 200n39
historiography, topics in: accuracy, 7,
    15, 162; Bakhtin, 15, 18–20, 203n61;
    changes, 2–14; common sense, 16;
    credibility, 15, 202n49, 202n50;
    depicting rational behavior, 15–16,
    18; ethics, 18; Foucauldian epistēmēe,
    10–11, 14–15, 198n26, 198n27, 201n42;
    ideology, 10–13, 18, 19, 20–22, 197n25;
    literary criticism, 2, 13–15, 161, 194n9,
    198n29, 199n33; Marxist history, 19,
    197n23; meaning, 15, 21–22; narratol-
    ogy, 2, 7, 162, 227n8; objectivity, 9, 10,
    196n20; poststructuralism and post-
    modernism, 10–11, 20–22, 194n12,
    198n29, 199n31, 201n42; probability
    and appropriateness *(to prepon* and
    to eikos), 16; rhetoric, 14, 197n22;
    "scientific" history, 9, 217n62; struc-
    ture, 194n10; "turns" in historiog-
    raphy, 3, 10–11, 13, 161, 197n23,
    198n28; *wie es eigentlich gewesen*
    (L. von Ranke; see Novick, 28), 7,
    15, 18, 162

History, content: documents, 56, 78, 80–81, 99–100, 206n24, 210n44; military narrative, 30, 32, 49, 51, 55–60, 61, 63, 65–69, 75, 76, 79, 88–110, 104, 105, 106, 125–28, 139, 208n9, 210n37, 210n48, 212n5, 214n28, 215n33, 215n34, 218n3; natural phenomena, 30–31, 38, 42, 45, 51, 108, 204n5, 217n51, 226n2; politics and diplomacy, 1, 13, 42–43, 56, 70–72, 73, 76, 79–80, 88–89, 106–8, 110, 111–18, 120, 124, 125, 127–28, 139, 142–43, 211n49, 211n50, 211n51, 218n3; speeches, 17, 78–80, 133, 144, 194n11, 196n16, 210n44, 211n50, 220n17, 220n24, 221n3, deliberative, 79–80, epideictic, 80–81, funeral oration, 6, 78, 80–81, 104–5, 210n44 . *See also* Thucydides, values and attitudes (military planning)

History, formal narrative traits: *a-b-a* patterning, 3, 6, 33, 50, 77, 87–101, 88, 90–92, 93, 95, 99, 100, 109, 135–37, 146, 149, 157, 183, 207n1, 212n2, 212n3, 213n12, 213n13; action-reaction patterning, 59–60, 123, 124, 128, 130, 134, 138; causal connections, 6, 52, 84–85, 87–101, 91, 93–96, 100, 102, 130, 142–43, 146, 149–50, 153, 194n11, 220n16; changes in narrative, xii, 3–5, 39, 47, 60–61, 63, 68, 76, 81, 82, 83–85, 109, 121, 122–23, 131, 133, 137, 143, 147, 148, 156, 158; detail, distribution of, 51, 52, 53, 60, 61–63, 64–65, 76, 77, 122–23, 133, 137, 224n14; detail, types of (descriptive, causal, motivational), 51, 52, 53–64; discontinuities, 6, 7, 9, 21, 27, 50, 52–53, 66, 85, 87; emotional intensity (drama and pathos), 12, 92, 95, 103, 109, 129, 137, 139, 144, 199n33, 214n23, 224n14, 226n23, 226n24; excursuses (speeches; antiquarian, geographical, historical material), 30–31, 49, 77–82, 135–37,

161, 210n45, 210n48, 211n55; focalization, 162, 199n33; form/content/meaning, integration of, 6, 11, 14, 18–19, 26, 33, 37, 41, 48, 54–55, 58–59, 60, 61–63, 70–73, 75–76, 79, 81–82, 85, 89, 91, 94, 100, 103, 104, 105, 108, 109, 111, 123, 133, 136, 137–38, 142, 149, 158–59, 162, 199n32, 217n62, 224n14, 225n17; initial and concluding clusters, 98–100; irony, 6, 9, 87, 97, 98, 104, 110, 156, 211n53, 215n39, 215n40, 216n44; land and sea, 162, 214n23, 218n64; loose narrative connections, 87–90, 100, 124, 126, 138, 149, 157; odd and mixed metaphors for, xi, 31–33, 34, 35, 48, 81, 83, 87, 103, 109, 110, 115, 133, 134, 135–37, 138, 139, 140, 142, 148, 153, 156, 158, 161, 162, 163; parataxis and change to hypotaxis, xi–xii (terms defined), 4, 5, 21, 26, 46, 82, 99, 101, 108, 127, 130, 138, 145, 148, 155, 157–59; patterns/regularities/themes, 27, 31, 33–34, 36–37, 43, 60, 72–73, 81, 96–101, 101–4, 115, 137–38, 148, 149, 150, 152, 157, 159; reader-response interpretation, 6–7, 86–87, 91–92, 95–98, 111, 126, 163; significant juxtaposition, 7, 60, 76, 87–101, 108, 161; time and temporal organization, 3, 25–26, 27, 30, 35, 36, 39, 43, 44–46, 53, 83, 92, 101–10, 119–20, 125, 137, 139–42, 146–47, 155, 180–82, 183, 188–89, 191, 193n2, 193n3, 203n4, 203n5, 206n27, 207n38, 210n39, 210n47, 212n8, 213n21, 214n28, 214n30, 216n47, 217n52, 218n2, 222n7, 222n8, 223n14. *See also* Aegean narrative; Archidamian units of action; Herodotus and Herodotean style; introductory sentences; Thucydides, values and attitudes; units of action (general); Sicilian narrative; Thucydides, values and attitudes; years of the Peace, units of action

Homer, 19; Homeric Hymn to Apollo, 32

Hornblower, S., xiii, 6–7, 160, 193n2, 193n3, 194n7, 195n12, 195n13, 195n15, 195n16, 196n17, 196n18, 199n32, 199n33, 200n36, 203n64, 204n5, 207n37, 208n8, 209n18, 210n37, 211n55, 212n1, 212n4, 213n8, 214n23, 215n37, 216n41, 217n51, 227n10, 227n11, 228n13, 228n14, 228n15, 228n16

Hudson, J., 222n9

Hunt, L., 197n21, 197n23, 198n28, 198n29, 201n42. See also Appleby, J.

Hunter, V., 12, 194n7, 196n17, 200n34, 217n61

hypotaxis. See History, formal narrative traits (parataxis and change to hypotaxis)

Immerwahr, H., 2, 193n1, 205n6, 213n12

introductory sentences, 35–47, 116–20, 179–91; Archidamian, 26, 27–30, 33, 35–47, 115, 179–89, changes in, 37–39, 184–85 (subjects); 39–41, 186 (verbs); 41–43 (setting), 45 (time), disappearance of, 145, 147–48; regularity within variety, 46–47; three types (summary, initiatory, deliberative), 39–40. See also History, formal narrative traits (time and temporal organization)

Ionia, 4, 147–49, 151, 153, 221n3. See also Aegean War narrative

Jacob, M. See Appleby, J.

Jacoby, F., 208n8

Jameson, F., 21, 22, 197n23, 203n63

Jay, M., 198n25, 198n28

Jenkins, K., 197n25, 198n28, 201n42, 201n43, 201n45, 202n53

Kallet, L., 195n12, 197n32, 203n64, 222n6, 228n16

Kaplan, S. See LaCapra, D.

Katičič, R., 207n1

Kellner, H., 198n28

Kirby, J., 203n64

Kirchhoff, A., 226n1

Kitzinger, R., 203n64

Konstan, D., 203n64

Kramer, L., 201n43

Kuhn, T., 9, 197n21

Kurke, L., 203n64

LaCapra, D., 197n20, 201n42

langue/parole, 18

Lateiner, D., 199n33, 203n64

Lattimore, S., xii, 127, 180, 195n14

Leonard, N., 203n64

Lesbos, 38, 40, 59, 66, 73, 74, 75, 126, 151. See also Mytilene

linguistic turn, 3, 10, 11, 13, 161, 197n23, 197n25, 198n28. See also historiography, topics in

Locris, 26, 29, 31, 52, 102, 105, 122, 124, 139, 142

Loraux, N., 12, 13, 200n34, 200n36, 200n37

Luraghi, N., 195n13, 196n17, 199n30

Luschnat, O., 193n3, 194n7, 207n38, 207n6, 208n8, 212n8, 222n6, 227n10

Lyotard, J.-F., 199n29

Macedonia, 123, 138, 142, 225n15

MacIntyre, A., 14

Macleod, C., 12, 195n16, 200n34, 214n2

Mantinea, 96, 126, 127, 129, 130–36, 138, 141, 143, 221n27

Marcellinus, 223n10

Marincola, J., 193n2, 193n3, 194n11, 195n12, 195n13, 195n14, 195n16, 196n17, 197n20, 199n33, 200n34, 200n36, 200n37, 201n41, 202n50, 203n64, 212n1, 227n10

Maza, S., 197n23

McNeal, R., 207n1

Megara, 40, 61, 88, 91, 105, 109, 123, 134, 212n5

Megill, A., 197n27

Melos, 6, 28, 30, 31, 33, 102, 128, 136, 137, 138, 141, 142, 143, 211n51, 221n27

Meyer, E., 80, 208n9, 211n52, 218n1

Mink, L., 13, 14, 17–18, 200n40, 201n44

Momigliano, A., 199n32

Morson, G. See Emerson, C.

Munslow, A., 14, 197n23, 197n24, 197n25, 198n25, 198n26, 198n27, 198n28, 199n29, 201n40, 201n43, 201n45, 201n46

Munson, R., 199n30

Mycalessus, 224n14, 226n23

Mytilene, 27, 38, 40, 53, 54, 56, 59, 66, 67, 68, 80, 93, 95–96, 97, 98, 106, 107, 109, 126, 205n16, 205n18, 208n11, 208n12, 209n12, 211n51, 215n32, 215n34, 216n41, 216n45, 217n51, 217n5, 218n66, 221n27, 224n14, 225n19, 227n7

Naupactus, 29, 41, 62, 91, 146

Newton, I., 9, 11, 197n21

Nicias, 17, 21, 28, 32, 68, 97, 98, 102, 135, 137, 140, 143, 146, 209n28, 222n9, 223n14

Norden, E., 92, 214n24

Norman, A., 14, 197n20, 202n49, 202n51

North, H., xii

Novick, P., 13, 196n19, 196n20, 197n21, 197n22, 197n24, 197n25, 200n39

Ober, J., 200n36

O'Brien, P., 198n26, 198n27

Olympia, 80, 107, 128, 129, 142, 220n20

Osborne, R., 200n36, 203n64

Ostwald, M., xii, 1, 195n12

Paches, 54, 55, 95, 209n32, 216n41

Parry, A., 12, 199n33, 200n34

Patzer, H., 212n8, 215n40

Pausanias, 160, 161

Peace, years of the (v.25–vi.7), 3, 4, 45, 115–43, 117–20, 140, 159, 218n3, 220n16, 220n19, 221n27, 227n7. See also years of the Peace, units of action

Pearson, L., 211n55

Pelling, C., 195n12, 196n16, 200n36, 203n64

Pericles, 17, 80, 81, 88, 105, 160, 199n33

Persians, 4, 70, 71, 74, 147, 148, 149, 151, 153, 163, 196n17, 223n11, 227n8

Phormio, 67, 94, 106, 216n44, 217n54

Piraeus, 59, 61, 88, 89, 106, 212n6

plague, 73, 81, 90, 100, 102, 107

Plataea, 26, 27, 38, 40, 44, 62, 63, 73, 75, 79, 80, 97, 99, 100, 103, 106, 107, 108, 216n41, 224n14, 227n7

Pohlenz, M., 5

Pomper, P. See Fay, B.

Poster, M., 198n27

Potidaea, 39, 60, 71, 105, 160, 208n11, 228n14

Pouncey, P., 194n12

Powell, J., 223n10

prepon to. See Thucydides, values and attitudes (probability and appropriateness)

Pritchett, W. K., 1, 200n38, 207n39, 218n69, 218n70, 221n3

Pucci, P., 195n13

Pylos, 27, 60, 75, 91, 92, 93, 95, 98, 108, 109, 123, 127, 134, 138, 142

quiddity. See Thucydides, values and attitudes (importance of specificity)

Rabinow, P., 197n23, 198n26

Ramphias, 89, 93, 100, 213n10

Rawlings, H., 194n8, 194n10

Rhodes, P., 199n32, 201n42, 223n11

Roberts, C., 14

Romilly, J. de, 2, 32, 194n7, 194n8, 194n11, 195n15, 204n6, 210n35,

211n49, 211n1, 213n17, 215n33, 215n39, 215n40, 218n1, 221n1, 222n4, 222n5, 222n9, 226n24

Rood, T., 7, 162, 193n2, 193n4, 194n6, 194n7, 194n11, 195n12, 195n16, 196n17, 203n62, 213n11, 215n33, 222n6, 227n8, 228n17

Rorty, R., 197n23

Ros, J., 204n6

Rudich, V., 19, 203n61

Salaethus, 56, 95, 98, 107, 205n16, 208n12

Schadewaldt, W., 5, 225n23, 226n1

Schalk, D., 203n64

Schein, S., 203n64

Schneider, C., 200n34

Schwartz, E., 5, 208n9, 211n50, 214n30, 222n4, 224n14, 226n1

Scione, 73, 89, 94, 122, 124, 139, 207n37, 211n51, 226n2

Sealey, R., 1

Sicilian expedition (vi.8–viii.6), xii, 4, 6, 17, 28, 29, 30, 31, 33, 54, 56, 57, 68, 91, 97, 99, 107, 108, 109, 115, 126, 136, 137, 138, 142, 143, 144, 145–47, 150, 152–53, 159, 162–63, 194n11, 208n9, 208n12, 211n54, 212n8, 214n22, 215n40, 216n40, 217n51, 217n54, 217n60, 221n1, 222n6, 222n7, 223n12, 223n14, 224n14, 225n15, 225n21, 225n22, 225n23, 226n24, 226n1, 226n4, 227n7, 227n8

Sicilian narrative, 145–47, 152–53, 173–75; different from Aegean War narrative, 144–45; similarities, 144–63

Sider, D. See Boedeker, D.

Simonides, 196n17

Sitalces, 51, 71, 79, 81, 88, 106, 206n25, 216n44

Smart, J., 193n3,

Smith, B., 197n22

Somers, M., 197n23

Spiegel, G., 14, 18, 198n28, 201n46, 202n53, 203n63

Stadter, P., 203n64

Stahl, H.-P., 2, 193n2, 194n11, 212n1, 214n22, 214n28, 216n45, 217n50, 227n8

Ste. Croix, G. de, 193n3; 194n8, 195n15

Steup, J. See Classen, J.

Stone, L., 196n20, 197n24, 198n25, 202n54

Strasburger, H., 195n13, 225n21

Stroud, R., xii, 1

Sullivan, W. See Rabinow, P.

Thalmann, W. G., 203n64, 213n12

Thebans, 26, 27, 52, 79, 97, 99, 103, 212n5, 226n2

Thomas, R., 199n30, 200n37

Thraceward region, 27, 71, 72, 79, 88, 89, 99, 125, 222n8, 224n14, 226n23, 226n2

Thucydides, the composition question, 2–6, 20–21, 76–77, 158–61, 194n7, 194n8, 197n9, 203n5, 207n8, 208n9, 212n8, 215n40, 217n53, 218n1, 222n10, 224n14, 225n21, 225n23, 226n1, 227n8, 227n10, 228n16, 228n17

Thucydides, development as historian, 4–6, 7–15, 20, 35, 64, 76–77, 110, 158–61, 200n37, 218n4

Thucydides, scholarship on, xii–xiii, 1–3, 5–6, 7–15, 193–96nn1–18, 199–200nn30–38, 201n41, 203nn61–64, 203–4nn5–6, 207n1, 207n8, 210n37, 210n39, 211n55, 212n8, 213nn9–11, 213n17, 214n23, 215n33, 215n39, 217n61, 217n62, 218n69, 218n70, 218n1, 218n3, 222nn4–6, 222n9, 227n8, 227n10, 227n11, 228n15, 228n16

Thucydides, values and attitudes, 67, 86–87, 110–11, 128–29; accuracy (akribeia), 7, 8, 9, 10, 15, 16, 18, 22, 85, 108, 158–59, 162, 163, 195n16, 199n32, 199n33, 202n54, 217n61, 207n62; in

Thucydides, values and attitudes
(continued)
Archidamian narrative, 86; authority claimed, 15; as chronicler, 83; common sense, 16; dialogism, 15, 17–21, 161–63; disinterestedness, 21, 111; ideology of, 12–13, 64, 67, 143, 145, 200n36; importance of specificity (quiddity), 15, 33, 85, 108, 111; in last years of war, 153–54; military planning, 17, 79, 89, 95, 97, 98, 106, 205n18, 214n28, 216n41, 216n45; postmodernism and, 7, 10–11; probability and appropriateness *(to prepon* and *to eikos)*, 15–16, 162, 202n49; rhetoric, use of, 15–16, 199n3; and *to muthōdes*, 9, 195n14 ; utility claimed for *History*, 8–9, 11, 15–17, 20, 22; in years of the Peace, 123, 128–29. *See also History*, formal narrative traits; *History*, content

Tissaphernes, 4, 147, 148, 151, 153, 223n11, 227n8

Toews, J., 197n23

Turner, F., 196n20

Ullrich, F., 5, 208n9

units of action, general, xi–xii, 3, 48–85, 179–89; changes in units, 3–4, 137, 143; complex units, 6, 32–33, 50, 77–82, 135–37; connections among units, 86–111, 137–38; developed picture units, 31–32, 49–50, 53–65, 125–29; elements remaining in late books, 158; extended narrative units, 32, 50, 69–77, 130–35; list units, 32, 50, 65–69, 129, 155; simple picture units, 31, 49, 50–53, 122–25, 157. *See* also Aegean War narrative; Archidamian units of action; introductory sentences; Sicilian narrative; years of the Peace, units of action

Usher, S., 200n38

Vann, R. *See* Fay, B.

Veeser, H., 198n28

Vernant, J.-P., 12, 200n35, 200n36

Vico, G., 198n27, 201n43

Vidal-Naquet, P., 200n36

Wallace, R., 200n36

Warner, R., xii, 195n14

Westlake, H., 185, 194n11, 212n1, 225n23

White, H., 13–14, 17, 198n27, 198n29, 199n32, 200n40, 201n42, 201n43

Wilamowitz-Moellendorff, U. von, 214n22, 222n4

Williams, R., 197n24

Winkler, J., 200n36

Wittgenstein, L., 198n28

Woodman, A., 199n33

years of the Peace, units of action, 115–43, 170–72; action-reaction units, 123; changes from Archidamian units, 121; four stages of, 135; narrative pattern, 139–43; processes emphasized, 133; speed, density, brevity of, 129

Zeitlin, F., 200n35, 200n36

Ziegler, K., 211n54

INDEX LOCORUM

ii.57	53–65, 60–61, 105, 209n18, 228n12
ii.58	38, 53–65, 59, 205n16, 208n13
ii.59	42, 44, 204n13, 205n17, 206n20, 206n24
ii.59–65	77–85, 80, 210n43, 210n44, 210n46
ii.65	159, 194n9, 226n23
ii.66	50–53, 51, 57, 58, 123, 207n5, 207n6, 208n14, 219n9
ii.66–70	105
ii.67	38, 69–70, 70, 71, 72, 73, 74, 75, 205n16, 206n31, 207n3, 210n38
ii.68	31, 77–85, 78, 81, 137, 206n31, 207n3, 210n43, 210n45, 211n54, 217n54
ii.69	65–69, 67, 209n27, 209n28, 217n52, 217n54
ii.70	39, 53–65, 137, 204n13, 206n24, 208n10, 208n11
ii.71–78	77–85, 79, 80, 103, 210n43, 210n44, 210n46
ii.71–103	106
ii.79	44, 53–65, 125, 126, 208n13, 222n8
ii.80	36, 42, 204n13, 206n25, 206n31
ii.80–82	69–77, 209n32, 210n35
ii.80–92	94
ii.83	214n28
ii.83–92	17, 41, 77–85, 79, 89, 98, 210n43, 210n44
ii.83–94	88
ii.93	59, 98, 204n13, 205n16, 205n17, 206n31
ii.93–94	53–65, 61, 66, 88, 89, 94, 98, 128, 207n3, 208n13
ii.95	205n16, 206n31
ii.95–101	77–85, 79, 88, 106, 210n43, 210n45, 210n46, 210n48
ii.100	194n9
ii.101	216n44
ii.102	31
ii.102–3	30, 77–85, 78, 81, 207n3, 210n43, 210n45, 216n44
ii.103	46, 210n47
iii.1	44, 53–65, 58, 206n31, 208n13
iii.1–25	106–7
iii.2	40
iii.2–6	69–77, 73, 107, 210n35, 210n36
iii.3	98, 208n12, 217n54
iii.4	98
iii.7	65–69, 67, 206n30, 209n24, 209n27, 217n54
iii.8	40
iii.8–16	77–85, 80, 210n43, 210n44
iii.17	38, 53–65, 60–61, 206n25, 209n18, 228n12
iii.18	53–65, 59, 66, 126, 208n13, 217n54
iii.18–19	93
iii.19	67, 209n25, 217n54
iii.20	204n13, 206n24

vii.55	225n20, 226n24
vii.59	226n24
vii.59–71	162
vii.61–64	226n24
vii.71	162, 214n23
vii.71–72	226n24
vii.86	21
viii.1–109	144, 151–54, 218n1, 221n3
viii.7–109	*See* Aegean War
viii.14–16	150
viii.16	225n19
viii.17	150
viii.19	225n19
viii.19–22	150
viii.20	151, 225n19
viii.21	150, 151
viii.22	150–51
viii.29–43	148–50, 223n13
viii.39	225n17
viii.43–44	223n11
viii.44	223n11
viii.45–54	151
viii.48	21, 211n51, 227n8
viii.55	223n11
viii.56	151
viii.57	147
viii.57–59	148
viii.60	147, 148, 151, 223n10, 223n11, 225n17
viii.63–77	144, 151
viii.64	227n8
viii.78	151
viii.85	225n17

Compositor	Integrated Composition Systems
Text	10.25/14 Fournier
Display	Fournier
Printer and binder	Thomson-Shore, Inc.